The Truth About Christianity

DECEIVED

Revised Edition

D. G. Barker

Ocala, FL

Copyright © 2017, 2018 D. G. Barker

All rights reserved. No part of this publication may be reproduced, distributed, or transmitted in any form or by any means, including photocopying, recording, or other electronic or mechanical methods, without the prior written permission of the publisher, except in the case of brief quotations embodied in critical reviews and certain other noncommercial uses permitted by copyright law. For permission requests, write to the publisher, addressed "Attention: Permissions Coordinator," at the address below.

Zeta Publishing, Inc
3850 SE 58th Ave
Ocala, FL 34480
www.zetapublishing.com

The views expressed in this work are solely those of the author and do not necessarily reflect the views of the publisher, and the publisher hereby disclaims any responsibility for them.

Ordering Information:
Quantity sales. Special discounts are available on quantity purchases by corporations, associations, and others. For details, contact the publisher at the address above.
Orders by U.S. trade bookstores and wholesalers. Please contact Zeta Publishing: Tel: (352) 694-2553; Fax: (352) 694-1791 or visit www.zetapublishing.com

First published by Westbow Press

Rev. Date: March 2018

ISBN: 978-1-947191-86-0 (sc)
ISBN: 978-1-947191-87-7 (e)

Library of Congress: 2018939039
Printed in the United States of America

Chapter Index

Chapter 1	The Worldview Conundrum	1
Chapter 2	Have Atheists Invalidated God?	13
Chapter 3	Is Genesis Scientifically Accurate?	61
Chapter 4	Creation or Evolution?	95
Chapter 5	Did Noah's Flood Actually Occur?	134
Chapter 6	Archaeological Evidence for the Bible?	155
Chapter 7	The Jesus Mythology?	188
Chapter 8	Why is Christianity Necessary?	213
	Bibliography	222

Abbreviations

Gen.	Genesis	Nah.	Nahum
Ex.	Exodus	Hab.	Habakkuk
Lev.	Leviticus	Zep.	Zephaniah
Num.	Numbers	Hag.	Haggai
Deut.	Deuteronomy	Zech.	Zechariah
Josh.	Joshua	Mal.	Malachi
Jdg.	Judges	Mat.	Matthew
1 Sam.	1 Samuel	Rom.	Romans
2 Sam.	2 Samuel	1 Cor.	1 Corinthians
1 Chron.	1 Chronicles	2 Cor.	2 Corinthians
2 Chron.	2 Chronicles	Gal.	Galatians
Ez.	Ezra	Eph.	Ephesians
Neh.	Nehemiah	Phil.	Philippians
Ps.	Psalms	Col.	Colossians
Prov.	Proverbs	1 Thes.	1 Thessalonians
Eccl.	Ecclesiastes	2 Thes.	2 Thessalonians
Is.	Isaiah	1 Tim.	1 Timothy
Jer.	Jeremiah	2 Tim.	2 Timothy
Eze.	Ezekiel	Heb.	Hebrews
Dan.	Daniel	1 Pet.	1 Peter
Hos.	Hosea	2 Pet.	2 Peter
Mi.	Micah	Rev.	Revelation

Prologue

Christianity is the largest and one of the oldest religions in the world. It is estimated to be followed by about one-third of the earth's population. It is based on the life of 'Jesus the Nazarene' and is a monotheistic belief in a triune God, arising from Judaism. Many Christians believe Jesus is the incarnate 'Son of God', born to a virgin in the small town of Bethlehem; although this has changed recently with some sects altering their views.

Over the centuries there have been many criticisms, questioning, and falsehoods told about this worldview. Many people say modern science has made this faith questionable. Believers defend their convictions. Either way the two diametrically opposing views cannot both be correct. The journey, through which view is succinct, provides a fascinating trip through reason, logic and undeniable science. This book will explore the core of the Christian faith as well as use recent discoveries to show whether detractors or adherents are being true to facts or stubbornly refusing to abandon their worldview. All a person has to do is, with an open mind, approach the writings contained here-in to see whether or not they have been deceived.

Chapter 1
The Worldview Conundrum

One of the biggest arguments against Christianity is the existence of God. Many people state Christianity is based upon fairy tales and cannot prove God exists. Atheists state God is not real and has been invented by humans to comfort people as it provides a place to go when they die, since human nature is to fear the unknown. It is widely alleged intelligent people no longer believe in God. Secular science tends to reiterate these same ideas. The Big Bang Theory completely discounts any existence of a Supreme Being. Secular scientists say the belief in God is not based upon any scientific evidence or fact. Evolution says God was not required to bring Homo-sapiens onto the planet. Darwinian ideas seem to suggest there is no need for God, since the earth evolved and was not created. If God does not exist, there is no need for the religion based upon His purported Son.

It has been estimated that in Western Europe only thirty percent of people believe in a personal God. This is not shocking, as in the U.S.A. a significant minority of adults can name the four Gospels of the Bible. The idea that religion has an influence on American life has been decreasing from a high of fifty percent in 2001; immediately after the infamous 9-11, to a low of twenty percent in 2009. In detractor's minds, this shows God no longer has a place in our modern world. As we become more educated, are we abandoning the idea of a Supreme Being that has a place in our technological, sophisticated world? Which worldview is the correct one? Can all of them be partially correct? Let's see what the major views are.

Agnostics claim it is impossible to know, for certain, if God exists. This belief is thought to have first emerged in ancient Greece. Protagoros, Pyrrho and Carneades all thought any certainty about God was impossible. One of the first tenants of modern physics is that since it is not possible to test a theory for every conceivable set of circumstances, a theory can never be absolutely proven. David Hume, a Scottish philosopher, contended anything specific about the universe is doubtful. Thomas Henry Huxley asserted, although he had no reason for believing in the immortality of humankind, he also could not categorically deny or disprove it. Bertrand Russell stated, in 1947, that no-one has ever provided *"conclusive argument by which one can prove that there is a God"*. An agnostic cannot disprove or prove the existence of God.

Many religions are based on the premise of different gods; some, a plethora of gods. These beliefs date back before the Egyptians, having their origins in ancient Mesopotamia. Mesopotamian beliefs were threefold. They believed man was created by the gods to do their bidding. Secondly- the afterlife did not consist of rewards or punishment based upon what the person did in their lifetime. Lastly- the people were polytheistic- i.e. many gods and/or goddesses existed and complimented each other. Anthropomorphic in nature, these deities took human form with their own unique idiosyncrasies. They were also pantheistic: i.e. hundreds of these deities existed in every aspect of the world. These many gods were divided into two distinct categories. The gods were either sky or earth-bound. They interacted with humans and displayed their anger or contentment with lesser mortals. A plentiful harvest showed that Enlil was giving back to humans because of their devotion. These gods, in different forms and under different names, would become commonplace over the next few millennia. The Egyptians, Greeks and Romans would all have their own incarnates of these proclaimed benefactors. When the people prayed to their gods and were not answered, they deduced someone had angered the gods. They thought the same of the Jewish God. Since conquerors had demonstrated their superiority by devastating all the countries they invaded, their god was more powerful than all others.

Even modern religions still hold true to some of these ideas. Although conquering is not a normal event, they still believe in gods and goddesses. Hinduism is the third largest religion in the world behind Christianity and Islam. The belief in god(s) varies from sect to sect. They can be monistic, monotheistic and polytheistic. Some believe there is a god, but this god has many different parts. While they worship one specific god, they do not deny the existence of others gods. Reincarnation allows the person to achieve their *moksha-liberation,* if the person commits to becoming fully aware of the *ātman.* Hindus believe in an eternal soul.

Naturalism states that life is absurd; without meaning. Evolution is true. God is dead. One of the leading contributors to this movement was Emile Zola (1840-1902). Naturalism holds that in one form or another, all the matter of the universe has always existed and there is nothing more than this. As a net result, the universe exists within a closed system; there is nothing outside the universe affecting what happens within. They also hold death as the end of everything; there is no afterlife. Ethics and morality are subjective. Whatever the individual feels is right, is correct.

Nihilism basically denies the possibility of knowing anything of intrinsic value. No statement has any value; everything is meaningless and just exists. From this philosophy, the idea of Existentialism evolved. Nihilists believe that the universe is made solely of matter, but reality can appear to humans in the forms of either subjective or objective values. Both groups believe humans are complex machines that determine their own values and attributes. Jean-Paul Sartre said man "*can never choose evil. We always choose the good*". Strangely enough this is accomplished while their core commitment is to him/her.

Pantheists believe that '*Atman is Brahman*' and that the soul of every human being is the soul of the universe; most, if not all roads, lead to the ultimate One; the cosmos. The cosmos is without fault and is perfect at all times. They do believe in an indestructible soul that lives after physical death. An extension of this is Buddhism. Buddhists hold to the idea of *Brahman* being the final reality.

The next view that has been gaining much acceptance is the New-Age movement. Their main teachings varyingly are:

- Living in the natural universe are countless spiritual beings; the top being a sky god; disinterested in human affairs.
- The universe has a personal dimension, but this is not a creator-god
- The spiritual beings temperament varies from benevolence to malevolent in nature.
- We must entice the good spirits with bribes in order to survive this world
- Witch doctors, sorcerers and shamans are able to control the demonic world by means of their arduous training. They have the ability to cast out unclean spirits.
- Transfiguration is possible since people can change into animals.
- Trees and stones possess souls.

One of the proponents of this movement, Shirley MacLaine, once said that since she created everything she knows she is solely responsible for her own reality. This resembles Naturalism and Nihilism as they feel their values and morality are right for them, regardless of what anyone else says. Most New-Agers believe in an after-life and many say that all roads will lead to the same end, similar to Pantheism. With this many worldviews how do we make sense of them?

This is not as large a problem as most people suppose. It is often said, science and religion do not mix. This is a complete fallacy. Albert Einstein said the following: *"science without religion is lame, religion without science is blind."* In order for Christianity to be a viable belief there has to be some proof there is only one God. He must be the one spoken of in the Torah/Bible. We must have proof that the Old Testament is factual and accurate since it predicts the coming Messiah.

Western civilization is about five thousand years old. This roughly coincides, within a few hundred years of the Biblical timeline. While many people purport that there is no tangible proof of the existence of God, all a person has to do, is look at the evidence.

Since we cannot completely and scientifically prove the existence of God, people must have faith. Many are of the notion the more deeply we see into the untold secrets of the universe, the more God fades from hearts and minds. There are many scientists who not only believe in God, but show complete devotion to their Christian faith. It will also be shown there were quite a few scientists from the past who were believers. First, let's look at some of the arguments presented so far against God's existence.

A skeptical person questions why someone believes in God when they had never seen Him. Carl Sagan once challenged God to prove His existence by providing unequivocal evidence for all to see. What about the statement by the first Russian cosmonaut, Yuri Gagarin, who, while in space, said he looked for God, but could not find Him?

This is a common argument, albeit not very effective. How many people have never seen?
- magnetic flux lines
- gravity- but know they will fall if not supported above the earth
- an oxygen molecule-although they are inhaled numerous times per minute
- wind-although they have experienced it.

Now, this is an overly simplistic analogy, but physicists believe in dark matter, dark energy and multiple universes without anyone ever having provided any substantial proof of their existence. Blaise Pascal said that a skeptic's rejection of God is more of a moral dilemma than an intellectual one. Christians say God has provided all the proof one needs. His presence is revealed to everyone through 'General Revelation'. The Apostle Paul said there is no excuse in not seeing it (Rom.2:1). When challenged by the crowd to prove He was the Messiah, Jesus said that even if He told them, they would not believe (Luke 22:67). He also questioned their willingness to believe:
- about heavenly things (John 3:12)
- about being sent by God (John 5:38)
- even though they had seen Him (John 6:36)

After three years of ministry and a myriad of miracles from healing the sick, to restoring sight to the blind and hearing to the deaf; as well as raising people from the dead, the people still did not believe (John 12:37). It is the epitome of narcissistic arrogance to think a person can challenge God to provide undeniable proof of His existence. People saw Jesus perform miracles and did not believe. I suspect if God did do something unequivocal, deniers would find a way to slough it off.

Albert Einstein said, *"the most incomprehensible fact about the universe is that the universe is comprehensible"*. Basically this means that the universe follows rules and is not chaotic. Modern science is based on this principle. Experiments must be able to be reproduced and provide the same result in order for something to be a viable law or theory. Interestingly many of the founders of modern science were heavily influenced by Christianity.

Many courses in philosophy begin with the questions:
- From where did I come?
- Why am I here?
- What is the purpose to my life?
- Where will I end up?

I would hazard to say everyone in the world has pondered at least one, if not all, of these questions in their lifetime. Naturalists deny their beliefs are a worldview, but are actually science. They believe that the world formed out of nothing and that Darwinian action produced humans; the ultimate being. They say this is based upon scientific principles by adhering to the teachings of the Big Bang Theory. As pointed out, Naturalism is a philosophy; as much a religion as any other. The immutable laws of physics; namely the Laws of Thermodynamics, properly applied, show Naturalism to be the worldview it is. The universe had a beginning and is not eternal. This is proposed by Paul Davies, who said the Big Bang gives credence to the belief in God. The more evidence is presented by science, the more science begins to sound eerily like Genesis 1:3; *"And God said..."*

The world and universe around us is a testament to God. Physicists have calculated that if the laws and constants of physics had been slightly different, the universe would have developed in such a way that life would have been impossible. Life is also so intricate that to say it just happened makes little sense. The laws of physics are complex; it is questionable for anyone to say everything was by accident.

It has taken years to map the human genome. A single human cell contains instructions, within its DNA, that would fill six hundred thousand pages of text. Scientists have just recently discovered a second code within DNA. It appears the genetic code not only describes how proteins are synthesized, but it also mandates the manner of control over the genes. Apparently the delay in this discovery was due to the second language buried beneath a first language.[1] The human body also contains over thirty trillion cells. This means the amount of information within the cells of every human contains more information than the total of all books ever published.

God's creation is so fine-tuned it can be seen through bees; capable of computing the travel distance between flowers to be the most expeditious as possible. They must also traverse back to the hive without expending useful energy. Amazingly, a brain the size of a pinhead accomplishes this in mere seconds, while supercomputers require days to mimic the task.[2] Bee's ability to fly, for many years, defied any scientific explanation.

Fredrick Nietzsche philosophized, people are responsible for morality. It was not pre-determined by a deity. He had the tendency to observe animal instinct as a way to explain commonly accepted values and outlooks. This had a decisive impact on Freudian psychoanalysis. Nietzsche's ideas regarding human morality and his proclamation *"God is dead"* provided little to improve the human condition. He emphasised power is the real motivator for people's actions. Since there was no God,

---

[1] www.washington.edu accessed 2013/13/12
[2] Professor Lars Chittka, University of London

the universe must have existed, eternally, on its own. After humanity ceases to exist, nothing significant will have changed. In his book *"The Gay Science"* (1882), Nietzsche made his famous proclamation about the death of God. The problem is; if there is no God, how can He be dead? He contradicts himself further as he recounts God's murder.

In, *"The Antichrist, Curse on Christianity (Der Antichrist. Fluch auf das Christentum)"* - September 1888- Nietzsche expresses his disgust over the way noble values in Roman Society were corrupted by the rise of Christianity. He discusses specific aspects and personages in Christian culture - the Gospels, Paul, the Martyrs, priests, The Crusades - with a view towards showing that Christianity is a religion for weak and unhealthy people. For some incomprehensible reason, Nietzsche fails to see it is his morality that fails to provide ethics and human decency. If there is no godly morality, then only the strongest should survive and we should not care about the weak. We should only care about ourselves and how we make meaning. Christianity's God and His ethics question Nietzschean morality and everything in it.

Modernism may be at the core of up to fifty percent of adults. Their main concerns of technological progress and materialism are systematic of our world. Two, who made major contributing factors, were Charles Darwin and Karl Marx. Evolution lowered humans to the level of lower animals since we are driven by the same impulses. With evolution to explain the world, God is not needed. Karl Marx seemed to present a political version of the same problem; problems with the economic order were not transient, or the result of specific wrong doers or temporary conditions; but fundamental contradictions within the capitalist system.[3] Defenders and schools of thought espousing this view were decisive in establishing Modernism.

The saddest part to the whole evolution vs. creationism debate is that people have failed to understand by eliminating God they must then abandon Biblical mandated morality.[4] Tracy Latimer, who had Cerebral Palsy, was twelve years old the day her father, Robert, waited until the rest of their family was at church and then carried her out to the garage. He then ran a garden hose from the exhaust pipe into the cab where he left her to die of carbon monoxide poisoning. This is the murder people would like you to believe is 'mercy killing'. On February 6, 2015 the Supreme Court of Canada overturned the national ban on assisted-suicide.

---

[3] http://www.newworldencyclopedia.org/entry/Karl_Marx accessed 2012/9/7
[4] Colson. *How Shall We Live?* p. 119

People are not as concerned with morality and ethics as they once were. It is commonplace for people to cheat on their taxes, their spouses, or even their employers. In a survey in 1998, seventy percent of students stipulated that they had cheated on a test at least once in the past year; with forty-five percent saying they had cheated more than twice.[5] Forty percent of males and thirty percent of females admit to stealing. Seventy-eight percent had lied to a teacher at least once with fifty-eight percent lying more than twice. Additionally, twenty-seven percent said they would lie to get a job.[6]

With all the problems in the world, what do we do? Can science save humanity from itself? Many people have started to look inward for peace. We can find our own inner peace according to Prem Rawat, formerly known as Guru Maharaj Ji. This has caused many well-known people to embrace the New-Age movement. Quite adeptly it has been shown; humans make a mess of everything, if left to their own devices. We cannot do this on our own. When people make up their own religion, it can only lead to chaos. So what do we do?

We must examine the results of the worldviews presented. I ask skeptics, why someone would invent a religion that demands altruism; love for your enemies; turning the other cheek; give all of your possession to the less fortunate; and above all else being honest, fair and merciful? The answer is obvious; an Omnipresent, Omniscience, Omnipotent Christian God would. Christianity provides the solution to the problems stated. Christianity shows Modernists, who say that morality is defined by the individual and be altered as needed[7], this idea is wrong-headed. Morality cannot change. Christianity, if followed, maintains order and liberty.

Let's see how the non-Christian worldviews satisfy stringent testing as to its validity as an acceptable and plausible worldview. Ronald Nash suggests the following 3 tests in respect to any worldview:
 1. The Test of Reason
 2. The Test of Experience
 3. The Test of Practice.

<u>Test of Reason:</u>
Believing there is no God is one thing, but thinking that without God the universe just came to be, stretches the imagination. What is

---
[5] http://teenadvice.about.com/library/weekly/aa012501a.htm accessed 2012/9/7
[6] Colson. *How Shall We Live?*
[7] Ibid p. 376

nothing? Even zero or complete darkness is something. For us to understand nothing is beyond comprehension. Even the idea of a complete vacuum; where nothing exists, completely eludes us.

Quantum physicists like to talk about a quantum vacuum, where quantum particles can come into being without causal effect. The material that appears in a quantum vacuum originates by fluctuating energy in the vacuum; but the kicker is that even here things are not appearing out of nothing. There still exists the fluctuating energy that causes particles into being, hence the first Law of Thermodynamics.

The term thermodynamics comes from two root words: '*thermo*' meaning heat, and '*dynamic*' meaning power. Thus, the Laws of Thermodynamics are the Laws of Heat Power. As far as we can tell, these laws are absolute. Matter can change to energy and vice versa, or simply put, energy cannot be created or destroyed. The only discernment is, at the conclusion you cannot have more or less than at the beginning. Simplified, it means that the amount of matter or energy must remain constant. In scientific terms this is a closed system; free from all external influences.

The next option is that the universe has always exited. Good option, except the Second Law of Thermodynamics, more commonly known as the Law of Increased Entropy, shows this is not possible. Entropy is a measure of unusable energy within a closed system. If energy in the universe is constantly being changed into unusable energy, the universe cannot be eternal. There was a beginning. This is what physicists mean when they say the universe in winding down. Heat death will occur when it ceases.

Test of Experience:

Nash says worldviews must be relevant to what we know about the world.[8] Reincarnation, karma, astrology, crystals, the occult and channellings present some serious challenges here. Due to space constraints I shall focus on reincarnation, a main staple of the New-Agers and Eastern religions. New-Agers believe that we are reincarnated either for eternity or until we reach a higher plain of existence. This is completely a faith based belief, and that is acceptable. But, they talk about it as a proven scientific fact: "*Definitely you are an old soul. There is an open-minded left brain intellectually in you that speaks to the profound humani-*

---

[8] Nash. *Worldviews*.

ty in everybody, and that's an old soul".[9] Death is what allows a person to escape the natural existence to enter into the afterlife.[10] Some New-Agers also misquote the Bible to give validity to their claims. They twist Biblical scripture to suit their own claims even though the Bible clearly states that reincarnation is false (Heb. 9:27).

Reincarnation gives people a chance to undo past deeds. Does this diminish the will to be a good and moral person? That is not certain. There are claims that young children have come into the world with scars and blemishes from a previous life; proof, they claim, of a previous existence where the previous host had been injured. This has always intrigued me, but it is far from proof. A person is reincarnated to, hopefully, live a more enlightened life. Deepak Chopra relates there have been instances where multiple children within a single Native-American village can recall sharing a common parent. A similar report has emerged from Japan where children can recount a previous life during WWII. What is eerie about this is the children recall a single soldier's life, as if he was reborn into multiple people.[11] Is this their proof of reincarnation? To what end? Did Adolf Hitler, Dr. Josef Menegle, and Heinrich Himmler all reincarnate? Since they were collaborators in the most horrendous actions ever perpetrated, does this mean they were all reincarnated in a village close to each other? This should be a terrifying thought to anyone.

Does karma dictate reincarnation? If we were good do we come back as even more well-off people? How many times must we endure the depravity of the world before we graduate? If we were bad do we come back as homeless, disabled; either mentally or physically? If we were really bad; think of those who ran the concentration camps or the Gulags, do we come back as a lower life-form? Maybe we return as an animal or even an insect. Not so, according to Shirley MacLaine who said *"people come back as people but not animals. But animals come back as different animals"*.[12] So then, where is the justice?

Test of Practice:
Universalism has some serious flaws. If everyone who ever lived is going to make it to Heaven, then morality goes out the window. If there is no evil in the world; everyone is the same ethically and we should not have any issues with other people's ideology. Chopra scoffs at the idea, say-

---

[9] MacLaine, Shirley. *Larry King Live.* Sept 17. 1987
[10] Chopra, Deepak. *Life. p.25*
[11] Ibid p. 71
[12] Phil Donahue Show. Sept. 9,1985

ing the shakiest of assumptions have everyone going to either Heaven or Hell.[13] Oprah Winfrey said of her TV show that she will attempt to do things that are enjoyable, but this would not involve skinheads and Klan members. She also refuses to do shows about devil worship or sado-masochism.[14] If everyone is going to eventually get to Heaven, why object to these individuals? I would also ask anyone who lives in S.W. Ontario how they would like to have any of the following persons as their neighbours in Heaven: Terri-Lynne McClintick, Michael Rafferty, Karla Holmoka, or Paul Bernardo. Does anyone have to even think about the responses? If everyone eventually gets to Heaven, so will these people: John Wayne Gacy, Caligula, Genghis Khan, Marc Lepine, Richard Speck, Ted Bundy, Timothy J. McVeigh, Karl Marx and Richard Olson. All of the Nazi's involved in Birkenau, Auschwitz, and Sobibor will also be there. I can imagine very few people who would not be outraged by this.

Shirley McLain once said "*I have my perceptions and my reality, and it's made me a very happy person, and you can take it or leave it*".[15] Reality is defined as "*existence in fact, as contrasted to existence in imagination, illusion or mistaken opinion*".[16] Reality is reality. It cannot change from one person to another. The phrase "*my reality*" is an oxymoron. "*And you can take it or leave it*" is a way to shut down the discussion without having to validate claims. This relates directly to the belief that all is one.

Since we have many views as to what or who God is, how do we know what is right? The Apostle Paul, when talking about how man has perverted the existence of God, said individuals know the truth about God because it has been made obvious (Rom.1:19). For anyone who truly seeks to know if God does actually exist, all they have to do is to observe the universe to know the answer. Sigmund Freud, the 'so-called' father of psychoanalysis, proclaimed that religion was a neurosis. Freud's theories have since been fervently debated. I am certain it would have caused Freud much distress to find that one of his brightest students, Carl Jung, used religion-related concepts to treat disturbed individuals.[17]

---

[13] Chopra, Deepak. *Life. p.25*
[14] Winfrey, Oprah. *Wisdom.* p. 71
[15] Phil Donahue Show. Sept. 9,1985
[16] Winston Dictionary of Canadian English.
[17] Dunne, Clare (2002). *"Prelude". Carl Jung: Wounded Healer of the Soul: An Illustrated Biography.* Continuum International Publishing Group.

This will only serve to reinforce those who believe in God, since this shows the universe as finite with a definite beginning. Unfortunately, many, who try to deny His existence, will be obviously upset and try to deny the evidence. They do not want to listen and refuse to see any evidence that contradicts their hypothesis. Like the old riddle, *"Which came first- the chicken or the egg?"* the text above would seem to suggest a cosmic egg birth of our universe requiring a cosmic chicken.

With all this in mind it will be shown in order for life to exist on earth, conditions had to be exact. The chances of all the right conditions being present are enormous. Everything that must have happen within the cosmos for the current forms of life to appear on the earth must have been orchestrated from the beginning by a Supreme Being.

In summary, what are the traditional proofs for the existence of God?

1. Cosmological argument: refers to the fact that every known thing in the universe has a cause. The cause of this vast complex universe can only be from God
2. Teleological argument: looks at the evidence of harmony, order and design. As the universe appears to have been designed there must be a purposeful God who created it.
3. Ontological argument: the idea of God who is greater than anything that can be imagined. The characteristic of existence must belong to Him since it is greater to exist then not to exist.
4. Moral argument: deals with man's sense of right and wrong. God must be the source of morals since no clear source of morality, is an incongruity.

Chapter 2
Have Atheists Invalidated God?

All scientific arguments regarding evolution and Creation will be discussed in chapter 4. Let's first look at the argument the Bible says the earth is flat. Everyone knows about Christopher Columbus. It was falsely hypothesized he had problems because some Europeans thought the earth was flat. This is a fallacy of history perpetrated by individuals trying to discredit the Christian faith. Washington Irving wrote, around 1830, Columbus had to convince a skeptical church the earth was round and not flat. The Christian faith has never taught the earth was flat. The earth was known to be spherical since approximately 600 B.C., over two thousand years before Columbus. The Bible clearly says the world is round (Is. 40:21, 22; Prov. 8:27, Eccl. 1:6; Job 26:10) and hangs on nothing (Job 26:7). Aristotle postulated the earth must be spherical. Eratosthenes calculated the circumference of the earth to forty thousand kilometres, whereas the actual is approximately forty thousand seventy-four kilometres. Even before Aristotle, Pythagoras observed that the earth was a sphere. By the time of Ptolemy in the first century B.C., all knowledgeable Greeks and Romans had learned this fact. Now there were some deniers, but they were without doubt in the minority.

Antoine-Jean Letronne was an academic who held to strong anti-religious prejudices and spread this lie in his writing *"On the Cosmographical Ideas of the Church Fathers"* (1834). He, along with Irving, who is well known for his revisionist history, spread this balderdash. Unfortunately these false accounts became entrenched into society. It began to appear in school textbooks similar to the Ernst Haeckel skulduggery still proliferating textbooks today. It only makes sense that these untruths became ingrained due to the so-called war between 'good' science and 'bad' religion. This is so profound; the falsity is still present in Daniel Boorstin's, *'The Discoverers'*. It is just another argument against the 'uneducated' and 'uniformed' Christians. The argument was simple and powerful. Basically hypothesized; Christians are stupid. They hinder scientific knowledge and discovery. By denying 'science', they are akin to people who denied the world was round.[18]

The Ecclesiastes 1:6 reference can be taken two ways. It can refer to a round earth where the air currents go north and come back around through the South; as is theorised would be necessary for life to exist on a spherical planet, or it can refer to our air currents. Either way it directly speaks to advanced scientific knowledge. The Isaiah 40 reference says the earth is a circle and a circle can be flat[19] if viewed two-dimensionally. Intriguingly the Milky Way Galaxy is said to be a flat spiral-shaped disc that is one hundred thousand light years across and has a depth of ten thousand light years.[20] I am a bit confused. How is a spiral disc with depth, flat? But, accepting the premise if a galaxy can be flat and 3-D so can a circle. By definition a 3-D circle is a sphere.

It seems to be pedantic to say the earth is flat since it is called a circle, especially when the original Hebrew word was *chuwg*. Although translated as circle in many versions, it can also be translated as sphere. A modern reading has the Hebrew for circle; and the translation into English is *"to surround, to revolve"*. It is quite difficult to reference either of these to a 2-D circle. The rest of the verse should also be taken into consideration. Isaiah tells us that God sits above the *"circle of the earth"* with humans appearing like grasshoppers to celestial beings. How does one *"sit above"* a 2-D object?

He also stretches out space like a curtain (Is.40:22). This can be interpreted to mean a bowl-shaped sky surrounding the earth (Job 22:14) or an outer horizon encircling the earth (Job 26:10). When remembered the text was written for the people living in the A.N.E. and not for modern-day hypercritical despondence, it should be obvious they knew the earth was not flat.

Another complaint is the notion of eternal suffering in Hell being clear teaching. This is completely false. While there are verses that may suggest this is true (Luke 16:19-31; Rev. 20:13-15), and others that are often quoted, they do not directly say sinners will be in eternal torment (Mat. 25:30, 41, 46; Mark 9:43, 48). The fire will burn forever, but sinners may not be left to writhe in the flames for all eternity. The ones who will burn forever are Satan and his minions, along with the False Prophet and the Beast. Satan and his angels were with God in Heaven, they should

---

[18] http://www.asa3.org/ASA/topics/history/1997Russell.html accessed 2013/7/9
[19] Stenger, Victor. *Hypothesis* p.189
[20] Ibid. p. 156

know better. The Beast and False Prophet, because they cause billions to reject God and follow Satan, also deserve this fate.

There are many more verses that suggest immediate eternal torment for humans to not be true. People who have died are said to be "*asleep*" (John 11:11; 1 Cor. 15:6, 18, 20). Stephen prayed for God to forgive the transgressions of the mob and then he fell "*asleep*", but was not taken into Heaven (Acts 7:60). Obviously he did not fall asleep, but died. David was said to have fallen "*asleep*" after serving his generation (Acts 13:36). Paul said many of you are weak and sick, with multitudes sleeping. These verses say that the people who have died are "*asleep*" and not in torment. Paul did not say that he will immediately go to be with God, just that it is his earnest desire to be with God after his death. (Phil. 1:20-24).

The Bible says the dead shall be resurrected at the redemption of the body (Rom. 8:23), in the day of the Lord (1 Cor. 5:5), at the last trumpet (1 Cor. 15:15-55), when Christ shall appear (Col. 3:4). He descends with a shout (1 Thes. 4:16), at which time all will be blinded by His coming (2 Thes. 2:1). The faithful dead will hear His voice and come forth (John 5:28). At the time of the Resurrection of the just and unjust (Acts 24:15), some arise to everlasting life and some to everlasting shame (Dan. 12:2). Although they are not suffering right now but still dead in their grave, will they be resurrected to everlasting torment in Hell? Jesus taught to fear God who can demolish a person's body and soul in the lake of fire (Mat. 10:28). The suggestion of destruction seems quite self-evident. Hell was not made for humans but was made for the devil and his angels (Mat. 25:41).

If there is still some confusion let's look at the most well-known verse in the Bible. "*For God so loved the world that he gave His only begotten, that whosoever believes in Him should not perish but have everlasting life*" (John 3:16 KJV). This may mean only those who believe in Jesus will live forever. Burning in Hell is living, forever, in torment. Paul also said that only the redeemed will receive immortality (Rom. 2:7). Everyone who is not a believer could die at one point. This doctrine is termed annihilationism. It states the evil will be sentenced to damnation, but after a period of time, depending upon the life they lived, they will be annihilated; i.e. no longer exist.

The Apostle John revealed the coming times when he talked about the GWTJ (Great White Throne Judgement). He saw a vision where everyone who ever lived stands before Jesus to be judged. The Book of Life is opened. If your name is not found there, you will be cast into the eternal lake of fire (Rev. 20:12, 15). The righteous are rewarded for their faith and the wicked suffer based on what they did (Mat. 10:14-15; 11:22; 16:27, Mark 12:38-40, Luke 12:47-48, Heb. 10:29). Those who did unspeakable evil (think Stalin, Hitler and his cronies, Chairman Mao) will obviously be punished more severely.

Some of the other verses that seem to counter the idea people burn in hell forever immediately after they die are:(Rev. 20:9, 2 Pet. 2:9;3:8,10, John 12:48; 5:28-29, Job 21:30,32 ,James 1:15, Mat. 7:13; 16:27; 10:28, 2 Thes. 2:8, Luke 12:47-48, Jude 7). One particular verse does not suggest it is a slow, persistent, torturous punishment, but the fire will consume all who are enemies of God (Heb. 10:27). The NKJV version says the enemies will be devoured. Devour and consumed both mean that nothing is left afterwards.

Peter also told us that, Jesus suffered and died for a one-time payment (1 Pet.3:18). The covenant of a yearly sacrifice had passed and was to never be repeated.[21] If people are sentenced to Hell for all eternity, it could be suggested Christ died in vain. They are being punished for sin that Christ died to forgive. This is not a certainty and only an idea proposed by some. People, though, must accept His sacrifice for their sins to be completely absolved. Until this happens (Acts 16:31, Rom. 13:11, Titus 2:12-13), people are in the process of being saved (Rom. 8:13, Phil. 2:12). If, when they stand before Jesus at the GWTJ, their names are not written in the Book of Life, they will be cast into the Lake of Fire (Rev. 20:15). But we are also told that at the GWTJ people will be judged based upon their works (Rev. 20:12b-13).

This is where many people get the idea they can get into Heaven by good works. This is not what the Bible teaches (Eph. 2:9, Rom. 11:6, 2 Tim. 1:9). The Bible teaches that Salvation, through Jesus, is the only way to enter into Heaven and escape eternal damnation (Acts 2:21, 4:12; 15:11,16:31, Mark 16:16,31, Rom. 10:9-10, Eph. 2:8, 1 Pet.1:5, 1 Thess.5:9, John10:9; 14:6, Heb. 9:28). The reward one receives is based upon their works. For unbelievers it will be the severity of their punishment in the Lake of Fire. What believers have to offer Christ will be based upon what they have done while on the earth. Those that have done much will have many things to offer while those that have done little, while granted eternal life in Heaven, will have little to place at the feet of Jesus.

---

[21] MacArthur, John. *Commentary*. p. 1915

There is also a doctrine that says people will be given another chance to repent on Judgment day. This is based upon Scripture that says Satan has confused and blinded many individuals through this world of depravity, indulgence and immorality (2 Cor. 4:4). This is though, not a certainty. Pandering to the illicitness of the world leaves man without God's influence and keeps them in a state of perpetual darkness. People cannot see the message unless they open their hearts to it. People deny God because they do not want to submit to His authority; they do not want to admit they are sinners. They think they control their own destiny or they have listened to the fabrications of which they have been indoctrinated. But as we shall see, God has displayed all the evidence we need. All a person needs to do is look around and it will be quite evident.

Christianity is under constant bombardment from people who criticize a loving God who would condemn anyone to an eternal, conscious torment in Hell; many who had never heard of Jesus. As shown this is not a definitive doctrine of Christianity. Let's look at what Allah says (Why this important will become evident). We will examine it chronologically from the Qur'an.

- Anyone who rejects Allah will be cast into the lake of fire. As often their skins burns off they will received replenished skin only to have it burn off over and over again (Surah 4:56).
- While in Hell the condemned is given boiling putrid water to drink. Unable to consume the water he will be forever tormented (Surah 14:16-17)
- While being tormented forever in fire, any attempt to escape will be met with banishment back into the eternal fire (Surah 32:20)
- As a sadistic punishment the evil-doer will be given boiling water and a dark fluid that is extremely cold, along with punishments not specified (Surah 38:55-58).
- They will be forced to march in unison with a heavy chain attached that measures 70 cubits (Surah 69:30-32; 79:21-25).
- This punishment is eternal (Surah 87:13).

There is no ambiguity in these verses. Non-Muslim infidels will spend eternity in Hell being burned, with relief provided and then to be subjected to the torment again and again for all eternity. Even believing Muslims do not know if they will be condemned to eternal Hell; sounds sadistic to me.

The only verses in the Bible that seem to be a strong indicator of eternal suffering say any person who worships the beast and his image by accepting the mark will be subjected to God's wrath. The torment will be in sight of the angels and Jesus. Smoke from the furnace fire will rise forever, and those in the flames will have no rest from the torment (Rev. 14:9-11).

But this is after the Rapture (1 Cor. 15:51-55, 1 Thess. 4:16-17) when believers are removed from the earth (Rev. 11:12) in full sight of the unbelievers. It follows the Great Tribulation (Dan. 7-12) and the ministry of the Two Witnesses (Rev.11:3); where they will prophesize in Jerusalem for one thousand, two hundred sixty days (Rev. 11:3). Anybody trying to stop or harm them will be consumed by fire (Rev. 11:5). The Two Witnesses are able to prevent rain from falling anywhere on the entire earth for the length of their witness. The Witnesses will proclaim the message of Jesus Christ. They will chastise the world for its idolatry and immorality. They will speak of God's love and the message of Salvation. But, on the whole, the world will reject the message. They will tire of hearing about their sins. The Beast kills them (Rev. 11:7). People will rejoice at their death and celebrate exchanging gifts (Rev. 11:10), maybe like the Munchkins in the Wizard of Oz who sang "*ding-dong the witch is dead*". Their bodies will remain unburied in the streets of Jerusalem for three and a half days. To utter dismay, people will see them resurrected back to life (Rev 11:11). This must absolutely terrify all the earth's inhabitants. God then calls them to ascend with a loud voice from Heaven (Rev. 11:12). Almost immediately a great earthquake will level one-tenth of Jerusalem and seven thousand people are killed (v. 13). When the Rapture and these events occur, it will be evident to everyone left. That many people cannot just disappear from the earth, or rotting corpses resurrect without anyone noticing. How anyone can deny God after all this, bewilders me.

This though will not be the only evidence of God's prophecy being fulfilled. The prophet Ezekiel warned about what was to come. He spoke of the hordes of Gog, Magog, Meshech and Tubal. He warned that their attack on Israel would be repelled. He warned that these mighty armies would be decimated by the Israelites. He prophesized it would take seven months to bury the dead. God said His Sovereign power will be displayed for the entire world to see (Eze. 38 & 39). The king of the east will march with an army of two hundred million soldiers (Rev. 9:16). How anyone can know the small country of Israel defeated such a formidable foe and not comprehend something beyond this world is involved, is beyond me. God will be giving more evidence than any reasonable person can deny.

People have predicted the Rapture in the past, only to be proven wrong. They are ridiculed in the press, so the doctrine of the Rapture is not unknown to most people. As it will be evident to everyone, those 'left behind' should know enough to explore a Bible to know what to expect and to understand how to not be deceived. If they choose to ignore these warnings their fate is in their own hands. 666 (Rev. 13:18) is known to be Satanic or anti-Christian. Anyone who lives through all of I have shown above, plus all the physical signs in the sky prophesized in Revelation, and accepts the mark of the Beast (Rev. 13:16-17) has no-one to blame but themselves.

Fulfilling the command of witnessing to a world that is dying (Eze. 47:9) and the Great Commission (Mat. 28:19-20), there are numerous evangelical ministries that preach/broadcast a weekly message into every country of the world. There is no longer any valid reason for a person to claim ignorance about the message of the Gospel. Christianity cannot be criticized, since full warning has been given and the Rapture will show Scripture's veracity.

Another point to ponder is this: let us assume a person gets their reward immediately. They either go to Heaven or Hell. They remain there until Judgment Day. They are resurrected to stand before Jesus and be judged upon what they did in their lives. The wicked will be cast into the Lake of Fire. So to get this straight; God pulls people out of the torment in Hell to judge them, only to send them right back there. Does that make any sense?

What about children, people who are unable to understand the message of Salvation or those who were never given the chance? Will they be sent to burn forever? Jesus said, if a person does not change and become innocent, like a child, they cannot enter into the kingdom (Mat. 18:3). According to Dr. David Jeremiah this means people must humble themselves and become innocent like children to get into Heaven.[22] This must mean there is an age of accountability whereby children will be required to accept Jesus to escape judgment. This could also mean anyone not capable of making this decision due to mental limitations will also be exempt if they do not make this decision.[23] How can they be held accountable if they do not understand the consequences of their actions?

---

[22] Jeremiah, David. *Heaven.* p. 40
[23] Ibid p. 41

Deep down, everyone candidly knows God exists. If a person responds favourably to General Revelation, they will be given the opportunity to hear the Gospel.[24] But there is still some diversity amongst Christians. The Bible does not provide a definitive answer to all these questions. God's ways are above our understanding and He will have His own methods of accomplishing His goal.[25]

Now I am not criticizing anyone who believes eternal damnation in Hell for anyone who does not confess the name of Jesus, but it is not clearly taught in the NT. The NT does not give a clear and concise answer as to the final condition for all unbelievers, just as it is not completely clear what happens during the Great Tribulation. Does the Rapture happen before? Does it happen in the mid-point? Does it happen afterwards? Does it happen after the completion of the Millennium?

There are some scholars who question eternal torment in the Lake of Fire. The Bible seems to suggest there may be such a judgment, but there are some verses that are ambiguous. Too many times, unschooled people try to interpret Scripture, only to make a complete mockery of the process. The best advice I can give anyone is; accept Christ's sacrifice for your sins and the point is moot.

The argument that God and Jesus care not for the entire world is also nonsensical, and to say God is racially prejudiced[26] is laughable. To begin, the idea of different races is a fallacy for any educated person, and will be shown, in scientific terms, why I make this statement, later. Jesus was not concerned with the entire world? Jesus is the light of the world (Mat. 5:14, John 8:12, 9:5, 12:46), who came to take away the sin of the world (John 1:29). God loved the world so much he sent His only Son (John 3:16) so that through Him the world would be saved (John 3:17). The Samaritan woman, whom Jesus amazed at the well, said He was indeed the Christ, the Saviour of the world (John 4:39-42). There are many other references namely:

- The Prophet who has come into the world (John 6:14)
- Came down from Heaven and gives life to the world (John 6:33)
- He did not come to judge the world but to save it (John 12:47)
- He is the prince of the world (John 14:30)
- He is substitution for the sins of the world (1 John 2:2)
- He came to be the Saviour of the world (4:14)
- The kingdom of God (Rev. 11:15)

---

[24] MacArthur, John. *Bible Commentary*. p. 1507
[25] Moo, Douglas J. *Romans*. p. 82
[26] Templeton. *Farewell*. p.33

Quite a few references of God doing everything possible to save the world are above. Seems kind of misnomer to say God or Jesus do not care about the world. Jesus also told His Disciples to preach the Gospel to the entire world (Mat. 28:18-19). This is what is known as The Great Commission. Is it just me? I do not see any restrictions on to whom they can preach the message of Jesus? *"All nations"* (KJV) seems to suggest everyone in the world. Jesus also predicted that in the end times the entire world would be proselytised (Mat. 24:14).

When an individual woman anointed the feet of Jesus and some of the attendants chastised her, Jesus replied her actions would be shown as a memorial to Him when being taught to the whole world (Mark 14:9). Does it seem likely He would command His Disciples to act in a manner diametrically opposed to His actions? I highly doubt any reasonable objective person would suggest such a thing.

So it appears the instructions to preach only to Jews are completely false. From where did this idea originate? Jesus initially instructed His Disciples to preach to the Jews; the lost sheep (Mat. 10:5-6). The initial ministry was to be to the Jewish people, before it would spread to the entire world (Acts 1:8). This was because Jesus came first for the Jew and then for the Gentile (Acts 14:21-28).

These instructions were given when Jesus initially sent the Disciples out, long before His crucifixion and before the beheading of John-the-Baptist sometime around 30 A.D. It was at the very beginning of His ministry not after the Great Commission, given forty days after His resurrection, just before He ascended into Heaven, as suggested by some.[27] How do naysayers get it so wrong? I can only think of two possibilities. I shall assume ignorance, as many people who argue against Christianity claim to be somewhat knowledgeable in Scripture recitation. After careful examination it is easily shown they are no-where near as erudite as they claim.

The criticism of Genesis is also quite rampant in our world today. There are claims in the story of Creation, two different deities are involved.[28] First it is Elohim and then Yahweh. That does sound like a problem; until you spend some time investigating the claim. What are the names for God in the Bible?

---

[27] Ibid. p.33
[28] Ibid. p.38

- Jehovah/Yahweh: to be or I am who I am (meaning only God can define Himself)
- Yahweh Yireh: The Superintendent God
- Elohim: God (plural form i.e. the Trinity)
- Jehovah-jireh: The Lord will provide
- Jehovah-nissi: The Lord is my banner
- Jehovah-shalom: The Lord is peace
- Jehovah-shammah: The Lord is there
- Jehovah-tsebaoth: The Lord of Hosts
- Jehovah Elohe Israel: Lord God of Israel
- El Olam: The everlasting/enduring God
- El Elohe Israel : The God of Israel
- El Shaddai: God Almighty
- Adoni: Lord

So how can one God have so many names? As we can see each one describes Him a little differently. God told Moses, He appeared to Abraham, Isaac and Jacob as El-Shaddai, not as Yahweh (Ex. 6:3). This is not made completely clear to us, but God appears by different names when different aspects of His being are being displayed. Satan is called by twenty-five different names. Most people are called by different names by different people depending upon the relationship.

What other example do skeptics use to try to show inconsistencies of the Creation story? Day four is when the sun and moon first appeared. But wait, how could that be? There have already been three sunrises.[29] Well, first off the three sunrises' statement is completely an incongruity. The Bible does not say that. It does say that the evening and the morning were the first, second and third day. But, again if a person knows what Scripture says they will realize this is a false argument. At the 'Renewed Creation', God will provide the needed light after the sun, moon and stars are destroyed (Rev. 22:5). Is it not completely logical to assume whatever light this is, it was the same light for days one to three of Creation?

Let's look at the comment that God needed to rest after Creation.[30] After taking six days to create the universe God stopped. The Bible must then say God was tired,[31] so He took a break. Does it? No matter how many times I read Gen. 2: 2-3, or how many different translations

---

[29] Ibid. p. 39
[30] Ibid p. 46
[31] Stenger. *Hypothesis*. p. 157

I use, I have never seen the words God needed to take a break.[32] Then why did God rest of the seventh day?

By resting on the seventh day God was giving ordination to look after the world for six days and then rest for one day. Not only is there a six-day work week, God also instituted a six year cultivation of the planet. The seventh year fields would remain bare, to rest (Ex 23:10-11). I doubt a field needs to take a break from producing corn, wheat, oats or any other vegetable or fruit. These practices are meant to mimic God. Work shall be followed by rest. God could have done everything in an instant, but He did not. It ties back to the meaning and purpose of the Sabbath.

The Hebrew word for Sabbath means 'cessation'. This rest is designed to allow His people to reflect and enjoy God's bounties. The Sabbath was a special time for His people to get together to worship and submit completely to Him (Ex. 31:13, Eze. 20:12). This includes the sacramental idea of finding eternal rest (Salvation). The Sabbath is a holy day that is to be honoured (Ex. 20:8), since the Sabbath was made for man, not man for the Sabbath (Mark 2:27). This allowed everyone, even slaves and servants to rest on the Sabbath (Ex. 20:10). It also gave a day off to merchants so they could honour God (Neh. 10:31). This allowed God's Word to be preached on a day where everyone was free from labour (Acts 13:14-15, 44; 17:2; 18:4).

Even though God made the Sabbath for people to rest and allow a blessing, the Pharisees made humans a slave to their plethora of man-made rules and regulations.[33] Jesus was telling them they should not be confined by the Sabbath; it was a gift from God. God made the Sabbath to show us, He deserves our constant worship but He knows we cannot do this, so we are let off with only doing it one day per week.

It has also been said by many unbelievers; Jesus is not even indirectly mentioned in the OT[34] and not at all during Creation. Let's explore these hypotheses. God made human beings in "*our*" image (Gen.1:26 KJV). To whom does the "*our*" refer? It has been proposed that the "*our*" is like the royal 'we'. On the surface that looks like a valid hypothesis. If God is speaking in the royal sense, why does He say to Adam, "*I have given you every herb that yields seed…to you it shall be for food*"? (Gen. 1:29 KJV)?

God uses the word "*I*" in Gen. 2:18; Gen. 8:21; Gen. 9:3-17; and Gen. 18:21 (KJV). In these specific instances He clearly is speaking of

---

[32] Templeton. *Farewell*. p.46
[33] MacArthur, John. *Commentary*. p. 1203
[34] Templeton, *Farewell*. p. 153

Himself as He does in numerous places throughout the Bible. When God uses the term "*I*", He is obviously telling us He alone will do what He is proposing (Gen. 18:27-32). The "*us*" refers to the three members of the Trinity usually acting in unison.

This is a difficult doctrinal concept. When God said let "*us*" make "*man*" in "*our*" image He was saying that "*man*" would be made in the image of God-the-Father, Jesus-the-Son, and the Holy Spirit. This is not physical form but spiritual. Jesus and the Holy Spirit are part of God and share some of the attributes. All three have existed throughout all of eternity. People take on the spiritual aspects of their being and gained the knowledge of good and evil the Trinity espoused. This term "*us*" is only used in a minimal number of places and the word "*I*" is used many more. So the royal 'we' is not a valid argument. If "*us*" does refer to all three members of the Trinity then Jesus is mentioned during Creation. That abrogates the last part of the argument. Remember there is supposedly not even an indirect mention.

There are many predictions about Jesus in the OT. To relay all of the spots where Jesus is indirectly mentioned would be a daunting task so I shall abbreviate and show a few examples. This should suffice as we are led to believe Jesus (Yeshua in Hebrew) was not mentioned. God commanded someone to sit at His right hand, until He made His enemies a footstool (Ps. 110:1). Who is this person told to sit at the right hand of God? Numerous times in Scripture we are told that Jesus sits at the right hand of God. After Jesus ascended into Heaven He was stationed at the right hand of God (Acts 2:33). When Stephen, the first Christian martyr, was dying, he proclaimed to see the Heaven opened and the Son-of-Man standing at the right hand of God (Acts 7:56). When facing the Sanhedrin Jesus said the Son-of-Man will be seated at God's right hand (Luke 22:69). Since the NT references clearly show it is Jesus that sits at the right hand of God; the psalmist references may not be a direct first person reference, but it is more than an indirect reference. Another example, using the original Hebrew, recalls the name Yeshua being used (Hab. 3:13; Is. 12:2-3). These are more than indirect references.[35]

Prov. 30:4 speaks of someone who can control the wind; move Heaven and earth. It also asks the name of His son. There is only one person that can control the wind; move Heaven and earth. That person is God and He has a son. Other references to Jesus in the OT do occur (Ps. 2:7-12; Ps. 16:10; Ps. 104:30; Is. 53:5; and Mic. 5:2). Additionally

---

[35] http://menorah.org/yeshname.html accessed 2013/8/8

Jesus confirmed that Moses spoke of Him (John 5:46, Luke 24:44). Either Jesus was lying or Moses did speak of Him in the OT. The statement that Jesus is not mentioned in the OT is categorically false.

'Scientific' means to validate arguments. 'Hypothesis testing' has been used to dismiss God.[36] Unfortunately for unbelievers the vast majority of the arguments using this method are not scientific but philosophical. It would take a great deal of time to deal with all arguments so I shall concentrate on only a few of the more obvious.

We must first begin with the god called the Judeo-Christian-Islamic God[37] by modern critics. It is completely true that this god does not exist. The god worshipped by Jews, the Christian god and Muslim deity are not the same. It is quite common today, for some Christians and Muslims to say that they worship the same god. This appears to be a prequel to combining the two religions into a newly formed one, termed Chrislam, which is gaining wider acceptance as time goes by. So if the god worshipped by these religions is not the same god, whom do they worship?

Let's first look at the Jewish god. The Christian god is the God of Abraham, Isaac and Jacob. I do agree with Scripture that they are the chosen people and will be rewarded when Christ comes in all His glory, but there will be some drastic changes before that happens. The Jews have rejected Jesus as the Messiah, even though they have not been rejected by the one true God (Rom. 11:1). Jesus reiterated, although they are physical descendants of Abraham, only those who believe in Him (Rom. 2:28-29; 9:6-8) are of God. The Pharisees and Sadducees corrupted things so badly, many were practicing apostasy. When Jesus does return to Jerusalem, to set up His kingdom, He will save all of Israel (Rom. 11:26 NIV).

As for the Islamic god being the same god as the Christians, there are a plethora of arguments against that thought. Islam has many of the same prophets as the Bible, only Muhammad is supposed to be the chosen prophet. Let's explore that a bit. According to the Qur'an, Allah sent Gabriel to speak to Muhammad. How did God speak to the other prophets?

- God spoke directly to Abraham and revealed His plans for the descendants of Abraham (Gen. 12:1)
- God spoke to Moses face-to-face clearly and concisely to Moses as he saw God's form (Num. 12:8)

---

[36] Stenger, V. *Hypothesis*, p.18
[37] Ibid. p.11, 12, 21, 169 and many other places throughout the book.

- Joshua was hand-picked by God to continue the work of Moses (Deut. 34:9; Josh. 1:1,5)
- The first prophet after Joshua remains unnamed (Jdg. 6:7-10) showing that God's exaltation is more important that the messenger[38]
- Iddo had visions granted to him (2 Chron. 9:29; 12:15; 13:22)
- Elijah was granted super-powers (1 Kings 17:17-24; 2 Kings 2:11) as was his student, Elisha (2 Kings 13:21)
- Isaiah was given many visions
- Jeremiah was called before being born (Jer. 1:5) as was John-the-Baptist (Luke 1:13-16)
- God spoke directly to Daniel, Hosea, Amos, Jonah, Micah, Zephaniah, Haggai and Zechariah.
- God used visions to direct Obadiah, Nahum, Habakkuk and Malachi.

I find this quite bewildering. God interacted directly with His Jewish and Christian prophets, but to the chosen prophet Muhammad, He used an intermediary? Something is amiss here.

Muhammad, 'the true prophet of God' (Muslims' title) lived in the late sixth and early seventh century A.D. When he was born, the Arab people were polytheists, worshipping hundreds of different deities: Allah, the moon god, was one of many. Muhammad told his wife Khadija he was hearing voices. She replied the words must be of an angel (Gabriel) and he must be a prophet. Muhammad was told to choose an already existing god, Allah; an invented god. This god was the one true God? Allah was always the moon god to them. This is similar to the Greeks and Romans who had many different gods, all invented within their own minds. The holy Qur'an, the 'word of God' to Islam, outright states that the gods they worshiped were invented (Surah 53:19). Allah was amongst the invented gods, so by logical deductive reasoning he must also be invented.

Muhammad relied on human sources and any claim of pre-Arab origin is erroneous.[39] In reading the Qur'an it can be shown there are foreign words on three hundred pages; disproving the pure Arabic claim of Muhammad.[40] Interestingly, Allah commands Satan, along with the rest of the angels, to worship Adam (Surah 15:28-39). Does this mean Allah is elevating Adam to the same status as himself even though he

---

[38] Lockyer, Hebert Sr. et al. *Dictionary*. p.878
[39] Copleston, F.S. *Christ or Mohammed?* p.383
[40] Ibid

forbids such a suggestion (Surah 18:110; 4:116)? Allah also says that both he (Surah 6:39) and Satan are deceivers (Surah 7:176,185). Jinn and men were created for Hell (Surah 11:119) and to worship him (Surah 51:56). Why would he condemn people created to worship him, to Hell? God forgives sin, while Allah does not forgive sins, but will reveal who will enter into Heaven based on their earthly works. God clearly says that Salvation is based upon acceptance of Christ, not works (Eph. 2:9).

Jesus told His Disciples to love those who hate them (Mat. 5:43-44), while Allah tells Muslims to behead infidels (Surah 47:4). Allah created the universe and then re-created it (Surah 10:4; 27:64; 29:19-20). Allah condemned Noah's wife as unrighteous (Surah 66:10). Noah's son was killed with the unbelieving during the flood (Surah 11:43-47). If Noah's wife was killed because she was unrighteous and his son died, how was the earth repopulated afterwards? As with the God of Abraham, Isaac and Jacob; Allah says he created the heavens and the earth in six days (Surah 7:54). Later he tells Muhammad he created the earth in two days (Surah 41:9) and just one verse later, Allah must have misspoken because tells Muhammad it was actually four days (Surah 41:10). Allah must have Alzheimer's because he then says it was two days (Surah 41:12).

It also appears the all-knowing Allah (Surah 4:176) suffers from dyscalculia. Let's use two simple examples of dividing up an inheritance set out in Surah 4:12. 1) A man is survived by his parents, wife/wives and daughters. 2) A man is survived by his mother, wife/wives and sisters.

66.7%= 2/3 for daughters	16.7% = 1/6 for mother
33.3% = 1/6 for parents X 2	25.0% = 1/4 for wife/wives
12.5%= 1/8 for wife/wives	66.7% = 2/3 for sister(s)
112.5 % = total for case (1)	108.4% = total for case (2)

Well I can tell you one thing with certainty; Allah does not know how to do simple arithmetic. Anyone with an elementary school education can see this adds up to more than one hundred percent, even without my final percentage being provided. I can guarantee, with math skills like this, Allah and Muhammad would both fail basic arithmetic classes at any grade three in the province. God is Omniscience and created the universe and everything within. Allah cannot do simple arithmetic. Sounds like two completely different gods to me.

Muslims will say Allah means god. That is, of course, true. But so did the name of the worshippers of Baal. That does not mean that deity is God, but a god. Let's now look at the stark differences between the words of Allah and the words of God to show they are not the same person. Remember both the Christians and the Muslims say their holy book is the word of God. It would be an oxymoron to say they worship the same God since the words of their inspired holy books are a dichotomy. The intriguing part is that according to the Qur'an, Jesus taught no false worship (Surah 5:116-118), yet He allowed His followers and others to worship Him as God and went as far as to say He was God (John 10:30).

The inspired Qur'an is also filled with historical inaccuracies. Now, some have challenged the historicity of the Bible, saying some of the events have not happened, but critics do not point to flat out falsehoods. Surah 20:85-95 talks about Moses and Samaria; the problem is Samaria did not exist until after Moses died. Surah 21:60-69 tells of Abraham being thrown into fire by Nimrod. Nimrod was dead long before Abraham was even born. The side-by-side comparison shown below only exacerbates the problem showing there are many stark differences between the two texts. They cannot both be the inspired teachings of an Omnipotent, Omniscient God. This is a simple truth that cannot be rationally denied by anyone who reads the holy books as written.

Allah also allows outright lies to advance Islam. *Taqiyya* (also spelled *taqiya* or *taqiyyah*) is using prevarications to advance Islam and/or prevent harm to Muslims (*taqiyya* literally means 'prevention').[41] How can we believe anything in the inspired Qur'an, when its author admits to being a liar, especially if necessary to advance his religion? The Muslim is to swear by Allah, but he can toss that oath if he finds something better. Believers are allowed to be deceitful in order to prevent persecution, whereas God:
- Hates lying lips (Prov. 12:22).
- Rewards those who are persecuted (Mat. 5:10).
- States outright those who love godly lives will be persecuted (2 Tim. 3:12)
- Tells believers to be glad with suffering (Rom. 5:3)
- Does not lie (Titus 1:2)

Obviously these are not the same person. The stark differences are so apparent it would take willful neglect to not recognise the disparity.

---

[41] http://www.billionbibles.org/sharia/taqiyya.html accessed 2014/28/02

Bible	Qur'an
Man created on the earth (Gen. 1:26-27)	Man created in paradise and cast to earth (Surah 2:36)
Man was originally vegetarian (Gen. 1:29)	Man was originally carnivore (Surah 6:142, 40:79)
Jesus is eternal (many verses)	Jesus was created from the dust (Surah 3:59)
Man was to toil after the Fall (Gen. 3:17)	Man was always to toil (Surah 90:4)
Jesus was crucified (many verses)	Jesus not crucified (Surah 4:157)
Jesus was the Son of God (91 times in NT).	Not the Son of God (Surah 9:30)
Jesus taught the people to worship Him (Mark 14:62; Mat. 26:64; Gal. 1:15-16 and many other places)	Taught no false worship (Surah 5:116-118)
Jesus was the Saviour of the world (Acts 13:38; Titus 1:4)	Just a messenger (Surah 4:171; 5:75; 43:59, 63-64
Jesus is God in the flesh (Already mentioned with Trinity)	Jesus was not God (Surah 5:17,72)

What about science? Does the Qur'an say anything that is unequivocally unscientific? According to the Qur'an the earth is flat (Surah 88:20; 2:22) whereas the Bible says it is round (already shown). Allah says that he dropped the mountains onto the earth (Surah 16:15). Geologists tell us that the mountains arose from the earth due to tectonic movement, as confirmed in the Bible (Am. 4:13; Is. 2:14). Allah also made the earth stationary (Surah 40:64); the sun revolves around the earth (Surah 36:38). The Bible states that the earth is not stationary as proposed by those I have mentioned.

When Allah made the universe, he put the stars closer to the earth than the moon (Surah 37:6). How did he allow for man to procreate? Sperm, that originates between the backbone and the ribs (Surah 86:6-7), unites with the egg and when the fetus is growing, the bones form before the flesh (Surah 23:14).[42] I do not claim to be very studious on how the human body works, but even I know how preposterous all of this is. Yet, the all-knowing person who created the universe gave this revelation to his chosen prophet?

Muhammad's wife informed him he was being given divine revelations. Given the role of women Islam provides, this sounds highly

---

[42] All interpretations are not mine but made by Ibn Ishaq who lived and died with a few decades of Muhammad. He is considered to be a proficient scholar. Unlike critics of the Bible, I am not qualified to interpret the Qur'an just because I have read it.

suspicious to me. The problem with this idea is that not all angels are from God. Satan disguises himself as an angel (2 Cor. 11:14). Reportedly, the illiterate, Muhammad recorded what this so-called angel instructed him; his first revelation in 610 A.D. It was 622 A.D. that he sojourned to Medina. It was here that the message of the Qur'an changed and his violent tendencies appeared. One of his voluminous violent edicts is found in Surah 4:24. He conquered Mecca with a surprise ambush in 630 A.D.

There are also opposing teachings in the Qur'an. Muhammad was zealous to be accepted as a prophet in his native Mecca. Originally he acknowledged that Allah approved of Al-Lat, Al-Uzza and Al-Manat, his three daughters, due to the fondness felt for them by the Mecca Arabs. Unable to attribute these three to his new monotheism, he was forced to retract his statements saying he had used Satan's words as those of Allah.[43,44] Biblical prophets proclaimed only God's words and not their own (Num. 11:29; 24:4). The Bible predicts such a deceiver (Deut. 18:18-22). Since Satan influenced the words of Muhammad, how can anything in the Qur'an be trusted? Now, I am not being hateful to Muslims. Many of them are God-seeking, reverent people. They have just been misled and deceived. They believe the ranting's of one lone man, whereas the Bible has forty authors giving the same message over a fifteen hundred year period. Opposed to what many people are trying to promote, they do not worship the same god.

Finally, we have already discussed what Jesus said about those who reject him. They do not worship the one true God. Since Jesus is also God, they are an anti-Christ (2 John 1:7). The Judeo-Christian-Islamic god does not exist. But this does not mean the Christian god is non-existent. Many have fallen into this trap.

Next on my list; most atheists agree the existence of God cannot be disproven[45], Professor Dawkins included. This is somewhat puzzling given the thesis of Mr. Stenger's book is 'science has proven God does not exist'. This is not a scientific statement, but is a worldview. Lodewijik Woltjer, Columbia University astronomer capitulates that scientists are no closer to understanding the origin of the universe than the author of Genesis.[46]

---

[43] Al Tabari, *The History of Al-Tabari*, vol. 6, p.111
[44] Ibn Ishaq, Sirat Rasul, *Allah*, pp.165-166
[45] Stenger, *Hypothesis*. p. 27, 37, 241, 264
[46] Garraty and Gay, Columbia University. *History of the World*. p. 3

We have already discussed good and evil. Personally, I have never met anyone that does not believe good and evil exist. I would ask such a person, if there is not evil in the world please explain: Sept. 11, 2001 or the Holocaust or Al Qaida, or the Taliban or ISIS. What about the atrocities in our own country? If life is meaningless why try to make the world a better place by helping the unfortunate and disadvantaged. It should be dog-eat-dog and only the strongest survive. I seriously doubt few would subscribe to this mentality.

Petitionary prayer is another hot-button issue. It has been said God does not answer prayer[47,48] so there is no sense in asking Him for anything. One example used is that of two Christians from opposing teams asking God to let their team win.[49] The strange thing is this is not a particularly strong argument. Ex-hockey player, coach and national icon Don Cherry said, during an interview on 'Context with Lorna Dueck', hockey players do not pray for victory, but, as a general rule, pray for a good game free of injury. This attitude is exemplified in the movie "*Facing the Giants*" where football coach Grant Taylor tells his team they will "*praise God when we win and praise Him when we lose*". Baseball great Orel Hershiser expressed the same sentiment when asked about his faith. He never prayed for a win, only an injury-free game. These examples show non-believers speaking about something they have no direct knowledge.

Studies from Columbia and Duke Universities have also been used. The statistical results show small differences in the prayed for and not prayed for group. The theory was that if a group receives petitionary prayer they should fare better than those that did not.[50]

The STEP project also provided questionable results. I have had some of my requests honoured and some not. This does not prove much. To say God does not answer prayer is making a humungous assumption. The assumption is either 'yes' and the requests happen; or if the prayer request is not honoured, then God does not answer prayer. But there are two other possible answers to prayer. The reply could be either 'no' or 'not now, wait awhile'. Are these people trying to tell us that everything their children asked for they received? I highly doubt that. To expect your result and only your result is beyond arrogant and not very scientific.

---

[47] Templeton. *Farewell*. p. 145, 230
[48] Stenger. Hypothesis. p. 102
[49] Templeton. *Farewell*. p.230
[50] Stenger. *Hypothesis*. p. 95, Templeton, *Farewell*. p.230

Is it possible that God did give an affirmative response to the ones that showed a positive response and a negative to the ones that did not? The fact the ones not receiving prayer achieved a similar result is an uncertainty; it is not absolute proof. A possible reason is that they were also given healing.

Bob Dutko, radio personality for WMUZ in Detroit Mi., tells the story of how his irregular heartbeat was cured. He was twenty-three years old and had always had an arrhythmia. One night while watching a movie with his then girlfriend, she laid her head on his upper torso. Within a few seconds Mr. Dutko noticed a definite change. His heartbeat was regular. Totally mystified, he mentioned the change to her. She responded that she had prayed for God to heal him. Is it possible that his heart suddenly began to beat normally at this exact moment? Yes it is. People have been known to suddenly have their arrhythmia cease, but this is highly suspect. His heart chose that exact moment? This was possible, but not very plausible.

I shall relay a medical condition I know better than anyone as it happened to me. I was born with a congenital pseudo-arthrodesis of the right ankle with a partial absence of the right fibula. I had my first orthopaedic surgery when I was about fifteen months old. I had further surgeries in grade one, four, seven and at the end of grade eleven. The entire time I was growing there was always a length discrepancy of approximately two inches between my legs. This necessitated, at seventeen, my left leg to be shortened by removing a section of femur bone and joining the two sections together to allow fusion. The prognosis was for a two month recovery time for complete fusion to take place. It took over four months.

All went well until I was thirty-eight years old. My right ankle had severe osteo-arthritis and the only solution to the persistent pain was to perform an arthrodesis. Reluctantly I agreed, seeing no other option, and being told the recovery time was about twelve weeks. This surgery was performed in May 1995. Fourteen months later, July 1996, the ankle had not yet fused.

A revision surgery was scheduled for Oct. 31, 1996. This time a rod was inserted inside my tibia to make fusion more certain. An iliac crest harvest was performed both surgeries because the iliac crest provides ideal cells for bone grafting. I again anticipated a twelve week recovery. The fusion was not completed until May 1998, a time period of nineteen months not twelve weeks. One might assume from these three instances that my bones do not knit very well. That is a reasonable hypothesis.

In 2011 further complications set in. On Oct. 16, 2012 a sub-talar arthrodesis was performed. I shall say here that there are a few differences. I was now fifty-six years old, not seventeen, thirty-nine or forty years old. Secondly I was attending a Baptist Church in London, Ontario, Canada. When I went in for my surgery, a church of two hundred people plus three very close friends were praying for a quick recovery. I was not completely optimistic given my past, but I did hold out some hope. Low-and-behold on my eighth week post-surgery visit the joint had almost fused and by week twelve it was completely fused. I highly doubt my advancing years were the contributing factor for my speedy recovery. An iliac crest was also not performed this surgery. Is it for certain that the prayers were answered and I was healed quickly? Of course this is not proof, but it is decidedly suggestive.

There are also numerous cases world-wide where medical recoveries defy logical or medical explanation. Tumours on x-rays, CT scans, or MRI's disappear from one test to the next. Physicians are at a complete loss to explain 'miraculous' recoveries. The idea that *"well just because science cannot explain it right now, does not mean someday it will not be able to do so"* is an untenable argument. The cases I have presented are not concrete proof of answered prayer. I will concede to that. But I challenge any non-believer to provide a single logical explanation other than "*I do not know*". The suggestion that God does not answer prayer does not seem to hold much validity. True the Bible says ask to receive (Luke 11:9), but the prerequisite to receiving is faith (Mat.17:20; Luke 17:6). Everyone has doubts, even devout Christians. To ask them to pray with absolute certainty the prayer request will be fulfilled is unreasonable. But most importantly, thinking we can manipulate God into doing our bidding is practicing pure paganism.[51] Naysayers, answer one question. Why do studies show a significant decrease in depression for those that pray regularly?[52] Why do 64.4% of medical schools in the US teach the benefits of prayer for healing?[53] Next we turn to even more falsehoods.

Prophecy and prognosticating can be a difficult thing. Many people have tried to predict the future with poor results. Even the psychics and mediums of today do not have an accuracy record that even comes

---

[51] Walton, John. *Genesis*. p. 383
[52] http://www.ncbi.nlm.nih.gov/pubmed/22641932 accessed 2014/10/07
[53] https://www.ncbi.nlm.nih.gov/pubmed/12228082 accessed 2014/10/07

close to matching that of the Bible. A recent study showed that of the top twenty-five world renowned psychics, the best average accuracy was only eight percent. Simple arithmetic tells us that they are wrong ninety-two percent of the time. The famed seer, Nostradamus was somewhat accurate, probably due to the fact that many of his prophetic utterances could be termed vague, but was wrong some of the time. True, some of his predictions were eerily precise and although he does have many followers and believers the world over, his accuracy is pale compared to the Bible. This is even more astonishing when it is remembered that there were many prophets in the Bible and not just one. The fact that several people were completely accurate in their predictions is mind-boggling. Biblical scholars have determined that there are approximately eighteen hundred predictions or twenty-seven percent of the Bible. This includes the numerous prophesies in the book of Revelation. There are hundreds that have been fulfilled to date.

There are three hundred and twenty-two prophesies in the OT about Jesus. If we calculate the odds of all these prophesies being fulfilled by one person during the same period of time, the probabilities all predictions would be fulfilled accurately and completely as written, is in excess of 1 in 84×10^{100} chances.

Bible prophecies have predicted the rise and failure of ancient nations among other things. The prophet Ezekiel talked about the great city of Tyre about 585 B.C. (Eze. 26:2-14). This once mighty city has been attacked and destroyed numerous times over the centuries. Nebuchadnezzar began the assault in 585 B.C. The Persians in 530 B.C. and Alexander the Great in 332 B.C. fulfilled this prophecy. The Romans added Tyre to their empire. In 638 A.D. Muslims invaders would dominate this besieged city. Assaults took place in 1124 A.D. when Crusaders captured Tyre, to be used for their military conquests. The city was then finished off as having any significance in 1291 A.D. when it was again taken over by Muslims. Although still in existence, Tyre has become the fishing village that was predicted. (Eze.26:5).

Some of the greatest prophesies were revealed by Daniel. Most people remember Daniel from their childhood. He and his three friends; Shadrach, Meshach and Abednego were captives in Babylon. Considering the statistical probabilities of his prophecies coming true; Daniel is truly amazing. Jesus unequivocally stated that Daniel was indeed the author of this book of prophecies (Mat. 24:15). This is important because some have claimed that this book was written in the second century, many years after then events actually unfolded. The question that could also be asked, if the book of Daniel was written centuries later, how was Ezekiel able to mention him (Eze. 14:20)? Remember Ezekiel prophesized in the sixth century B.C. Obviously since Jesus and Ezekiel both talked about Daniel, these statements are flawed.

When Daniel was summoned to interpret Nebuchadnezzar's dreams, God showed him the future until the end. Nebuchadnezzar had a dream that terrified him and confounded his magicians, soothsayers and astrologers (Dan. 2:1-10). Only Daniel, through God's direction, was able to soothe Nebuchadnezzar's fears. The beast in the dream consisted of four different parts. There was a head of gold; a chest and arms of silver; the belly and thighs were made of bronze; the legs of iron and the feet of an iron/clay mixture. These parts were symbolic of the five kingdoms that would rule the world.[54] The head of gold was Babylon. The chest and arms of silver represent the Medes and Persians. The belly and thighs of bronze would represent the empire of Alexander the Great. The Greco-Macedonians were famous for their use of bronze for head dress, armour and protective shields.[55] The legs of iron were to represent the Roman Empire. It has been said that the Romans ruled with a 'fist of iron'. Taking all of these things alone the prediction accuracy would be quite amazing. Take them together and it becomes quite astounding.

The only remaining empire is the feet of iron and clay. Bible scholars say this represents the coming revived Roman Empire. This is a prediction that has not yet been fulfilled although there have been many attempts to bring back this empire.

The Damascus prophecy of being a heap of ruins is another excellent example (Is. 17:1). It is still standing to this day. With the events taking place in Syria right now, only the future can tell when this will come to be. Whenever I watch the news, Damascus is beginning to look like a city of rubble.

Daniel foretold the fall of King Belshazzar. King Belshazzar threw a great feast in his honour (Dan. 5:1). He was unconcerned with the Medo-Persian army laying siege to his city. He felt the city was impenetrable. During the feast the image of a human hand appeared and began to write a cryptic message on the wall (v.5). As before, only Daniel was able to interpret the message. Belshazzar was told that like his predecessor, Nebuchadnezzar, he too would be punished for all of his wrong-

---

[54] Jeremiah, David Dr. *Modern Europe. What in the World is Going On?* Turning Point. Vision TV Sunday April 25, 2010

[55] Ibid.

doing (v.17-29). That night he was killed by Darius the Mede (v.30-31). This can be verified.

Found in 1929, the "*Verse Account of Nabonidus*" indicates that Nabonidus entrusted the kingdom to Belshazzar while he was at Tema in Arabia for an undisclosed period of time. A Babylonian text called "*The Nabonidus Chronicle*" shows that Nabonidus returned to Babylon to secure its defenses. The city was overthrown on 16 Tishri in the seventeenth year of his reign. It can be shown that this happened on Oct. 12, 539 B.C. The book of Daniel accurately relayed it was Belshazzar who was in charge that night and not Nabonidus. So we can know that Daniel was present and he was able to predict the events of later that evening.

The prophet Jeremiah predicted that Babylon would be attacked and deserted, but it would not be destroyed, seventy years before it happened. He said the city would be a desolate heap of ruins (Jer. 50:26, 39-40; 51:26, 29, 37). Babylon was a great city approximately 556 hectares in size. Xerxes broke down the walls and temples in 482 B.C. It is noteworthy to mention then when Jeremiah made his prophecies Babylon was at the pinnacle of its power. By the end of the first century A.D. Babylon was completely desolate and uninhabited. To this very day Babylon remains uninhabited.

Saddam Hussein started to rebuild the city with the intent on moving his capital city. During Desert Storm in 1991, after he invaded Kuwait, he was forced to abandon the construction to concentrate on the U.S. counter-attack. Then, when he was nearing completion he was forced to stop again to shore up his defenses during the Iraq invasion of 2003. The city remains abandoned. The Arabs who were working on the city refuse to inhabit it. They think it is either cursed or haunted. Twenty-five hundred years after Jeremiah made a very bold prediction, it remains fulfilled prophecy. Since Babylon was at the pinnacle of power I would consider this a very risky prognostication.

But let's look at the criticism not one risky prediction can be shown to have been fulfilled.[56] The prophet Isaiah speaks of a future leader named Cyrus. Cyrus would allow the Israelites to return to their homeland (2 Chron. 36:22-23; Eze.1:1-4). Isaiah made this prediction during the second half of the eighth century B.C. Cyrus did not come into the picture until approximately 560 B.C. almost two hundred years after Isaiah spoke of him. This was a fairly amazing feat.

---

[56] Stenger, Victor. *Hypothesis*. p. 176

The prophet Nahum predicted the fall of Nineveh when he prophesized between 655-650 B.C. Nineveh was destroyed in 612 B.C. some forty years after his prediction (Nah. 1:8; 2:1; 3:7). These two seem like fairly risky predictions to me.

Next was the prophecy of Alexander the Great. Daniel predicted the coming Macedonian Empire (Dan. 8:2-8). When he died at thirty-three, his kingdom was divided amongst his generals, as he did not specify a replacement. This division can be shown by the symbols of four horns that arose after the central horn was broken off the goat (Dan. 8:8, 22). We know this because historically it was shown that the horn was Alexander. To verify it as a prediction and not history after the fact, Josephus indicates that this prophecy was known before the fourth century B.C., well before critics claim that it was written in the second century.

While on his way to Egypt, Alexander detoured to Jerusalem. While there, he was shown the prophecy about himself. Content with what was said about him he granted the priests a sabbatical from tax payments. Josephus recounts the event:

> *"And when the book of Daniel was showed him, wherein*
> *Daniel declared that one of the Greeks should destroy the*
> *Empire of the Persians, he supposed that himself was the*
> *person intended; and he was then glad...whereupon the high*
> *priest desired that they might enjoy the laws of their forefathers,*
> *and might not pay no tribute on the seventh year. He granted all*
> *they desired"*[57]

The critical dismissal can be countered with references in extra-biblical sources; namely 331 B.C. was a sabbatical year.

Zephaniah prophesized in Judah (627-626 B.C.) during the reign of Josiah (640-609 B.C.). Zephaniah was mostly concerned with initiating changes due to a warning of God's judgment on wickedness. In 612 B.C. the Medes and Neo-Babylonians attacked the Assyrians at Nineveh. During an extremely violent assault, the Medes were victorious. Nineveh was completely decimated. The headquarters of the Assyrian empire was desolate. The city had reaped its reward. Remarkably this had been prophesized by Zephaniah over a decade before (Zep. 2:12-13).

There were also predictions during the time of Jesus that happened. When Joseph and Mary presented Jesus in the temple, Simeon prophesized about what would happen. He told Mary of the future set out

---

[57] Josephus. *Antiquities of the Jews*. Book 11 chapter 8 paragraphs 337-338

for her son (Luke 2:34-35a). Any person who has ever lost a child will confirm the pain is akin to *"pierce through thy own soul"* (KJV).

Finally there is the prediction by Jesus of the destruction of Jerusalem and the Temple. In 70 A.D. the destruction of the temple happened (Mat. 24:2). Remember Jesus was killed around 33 A.D. The Roman attack began in the fall of 66 A.D. In the spring of 67 A.D. the Romans began a relentless surge that culminated in the destruction of the Temple in 70 A.D. This is quite an audacious prophecy.

How do people explain these things away? They state that the predictions were made after the fact. No empirical evidence is presented, just the statement, as if it is the unmitigated truth. Critics say there are no predictions, but when shown the predictions, they are discounted. Daniel is a prime example. Critics say the book of Daniel was written years after the actual events, so there was no prophecy. But unfortunately for detractors, Ezekiel spoke of Daniel long before he was born. They also try to say this was a different Daniel. Josephus countermands that. Why is Scripture suspect? Could it be that accepting it as fact would cause a major upheaval in their worldview? When evidence is presented, it is totally discounted. Sounds to me like cynics not only want to have their cake and eat it too but they also want a scoop of Rocky-Road ice cream on the side.

The last thing I shall discuss about prophecy is what has been come to be known as the Bible Codes. This is the idea of hidden, in the pages of the Pentateuch and even the New Testament, codes about future events. Scholars have unlocked this code with some amazing results. First I would like to say that critical claims about a code being evident in almost any large body of writing can have some merit. If say 'War and Peace' was analyzed using the needed algorithms; analyzing the text at equidistant intervals, I would be willing to stipulate there would be words, phrases or even short simplistic sentences appear. But here is where their argument falls substantially short. The codes within the Bible are not spread out over large numerical Equidistant Letter Sequence (ELS), but many can be found is a small section of writings, some only a few verses in a chapter. People have tried to duplicate this phenomenon, but these attempts have been met with utter futility. The statistical odds of the codes happening are quite large, as will be shown. It is also known no other Hebrew literature has anything remotely close to the ELS of the Bible. This includes the First Maccabees, Mishneh, Samaritan Pentateuch, Talmud or the Tobit.

The Bible Code has been subjected to many tests devised by skeptical people. Some of the criteria proposed went beyond-the-pale. Even though it appears, deliberate attempts to conjure up an impossible-to-pass test, the Bible has met nearly every requirement. The odds of writing so accurately and fulfill the prophecies within the text is near impossible for any man-made device or clairvoyant. Professor Harold Gans of the National Security Agency has determined that the codes actually do exist and could not be happenstance or human design. The only logical explanation is divine inspiration.

The first five books of the Bible were told to Moses by God in a direct sequence. First, the reader must realize that ancient Hebrew was written as letter-by-letter text. Ancient Hebrew also did not have vowel letters, only twenty-two consonants and is written from right-to-left as opposed to left-to-right. The reader supplies the missing intonations. If the vowel points, which appear either above or below the consonant, are applied this does not change the ELS intervals. The regular form and final form letters are recorded the same, either way. This alleviates the claims that the word being formed can be many different ones and not the one recorded. So it cannot be claimed that there is actually a different word being formed. I have seen this argument made by people who do not completely understand how ancient Hebrew language was written.

The code appears both right-to-left and left-to-right. The people who analyzed the text were not Biblical scholars, per se, but actual physicists, scientists and mathematicians. This would help alleviate the eventual claims of bias. There is a claim that since the ELS varies, the results cannot be trusted. This would be true if the ELS were large, but many of the codes that appear have ELS of less than one hundred. Of course there are a few exceptions, with the majority being less than fifty.

- Genesis 1:1 forward every fiftieth letter, Exodus every fiftieth letter, Numbers every fiftieth letter left-to-right and Deuteronomy every forty-ninth letter left-to-right have the word Torah encoded (Chance odds 1 in 3,000,000)[58]
- The word Eden appears sixteen times within the passage of Genesis 2:4-10. The ESV translation contains two hundred eight words.
- Genesis 2 lists twenty-five different Hebrew tree/plant names. Vine, Grape, Chestnut, Dense forest, Acacia, Bramble, Cedar,

---

[58] Michelson, Dr. Daniel, Associate Professor of Mathematics UCLA. *Codes in the Torah." B"Or Ha"Torah* #6 1987

- Nut, Fig, Willow, Pomegranate, Aloe, Tamarisk, Oak, Poplar, cassia, Almond, Mastic, Thorn bush, Hazel, Olive, Citron, Fir, Wheat. (Chance odds 100,000 to1)[59]
- Genesis 8 states the five names of ancestors of King David in the proper chronological order hundreds of years before their birth. (Chance odds 1 in 800,000)[60]
- Genesis 18 displays the names Anwar, Sadat and Chaled as well as 8, Tishri 5742 (October 6, 1981). The words president, gunfire, shot, murder and parade are all found in this sequence. President Sadat was murdered while reviewing a military parade on October 6, 1981 by Chaled Islambooli.
- Genesis 19:15-17 shows the word AIDS. This passage recounts the destruction of Sodom and Gomorrah. Genesis 5:1-8:10 has the following encoded: AIDS, Virus, In the blood, Death, Immunity, HIV
- Genesis 35:5-44:4 and surrounding has: Oklahoma, Terror, Murrah, Building, Desolated, slaughtered, Death, His name is Timothy, McVeigh, Day nineteen, on the ninth hour, in the morning
- Genesis 45 has codes referring to King Franz Joseph I. As king of Austrian Empire he was quite disposed to treating Jewish people quite favourably. The words encoded are: Franz, Joseph, Hapsburg, King of Austria, Jerusalem, and Auerbach. Ironically this chapter shows how the Pharaoh of Egypt showed kindness to the family of Jacob.
- Genesis 48:13-49:3 relates: Yitzchak, Rabin, Will be murdered, Yigal, Amir, Israel, 5682 (year of Rabin's birth, 1922). First Adar (Day of his birth), 5756 (year of his death, 1995), Heshvan (Month of his death, November) and Oslo.
- Genesis displays the names of sixty-six very prominent Jewish sages and rabbis from 90 A.D. until 1900 A.D. The coding appears in close proximity to the person's birthdate or death. (Chance odds 1 in 2,500,000,000). The chances of the birth city also being correct as encoded in Genesis are 1 in 250,000,000.[61]
- The following words/names are found in the books of Deuteronomy and Numbers: Hitler, Auschwitz, Holocaust, Germany,

---

[59] Ibid
[60] Ibid
[61] Drs. Witztum, Rosenberg and Rips, Hebrew University & Jerusalem College of Technology

Crematorium, Plagues, Eichmann, Poland, Nazis, Genocide, Fuehrer and Mein Kampf. Hitler, Nazis and Holocaust were found in Deuteronomy 10:17-22. In English, 135 words or about one-quarter of a typed page.

- Exodus 18:19- 19:8, a short passage we find: Israel, Arafat, PLO, Treaty, Peace, Yitzchak, Shimon, Peres.
- Exodus 28:10 and surrounding passages have the following: Princess, Diana, Wales, Spencer, Fayed, Death, Paris, France, River, Tunnel, and Av (August), 5757 (1997). Princess of Wales, Diana (Spencer), died in Paris France with Dodi Fayed in the Pont de l'Alma tunnel near the Seine River in August 1997.
- Exodus 28-30 has: Yeshua, Nazarene, Messiah, Shiloh, Passover, Galilee, Mary (three times), Peter, Matthew, John, Andrew, Philip, Thomas, James, Simon, Nathaniel, Judas, Thaddaeus, Matthias, and Let Him be crucified. [62]
- Leviticus 1 encodes the name of Aaron twenty-five times in this one chapter. This chapter gives the priesthood laws whereas Aaron was the chief priest. (Chance odds 1 in 400,000)[63]
- Numbers 33:28-36:5 has: CNN, Peter, and Arnett.
- The name Yeshua appears in almost every single OT prophecy about -the coming Messiah. Genesis 3:20-21, Leviticus 21:10-12, Nehemiah 8:17, Psalm 22 (includes Yeshua, Anoint, King, Branch, Jesse, Messiah, Nazareth, and Salvation), 41:8-9; 72:13-15, Isaiah 53:10; 61:1-2, Jeremiah 11:12, Daniel 9:26 (includes Yeshua, Nazarene, King, Branch, Jesse, Messiah, Nazareth and Salvation), Zechariah 12:10.

Suffering Servant (Isaiah 52:13-53:12)[64]

- Over forty names of people associated with the crucifixion.
- The Nazarene starts in Isaiah 53:6 and found several times through Messianic passage
- Isaiah 52:1-53:12 lists the Disciples: Andrew, James son of Alpheus, James son of Zebedee, John, Matthew, Matthias (the disciple that replaced Judas), Peter, Philip, Simon, Thaddaeus, Thomas.
- Isaiah 52:1-4 lists the Disciples: Andrew, Peter, Thomas.

---

[62] Jeffrey, G. *Mysterious* p. 132-133
[63] Ibid p. 14
[64] Ibid p. 103-128

- Isaiah 52:15-53:4 list high priest Caiaphas and Annas
- Isaiah 52:15 Salome- one of the Mary's at the crucifixion. Also "the Mary's weep bitterly"
- Isaiah 53:2 forward has Joseph
- Isaiah 53:6 forward encodes the man Herod
- Isaiah 53:7 onward finds Galilee
- Isaiah 53:8- Let Him be crucified.
- Isaiah 53:10 lists the three Mary's and John encoded beside Yeshua
- Isaiah 53:2 forward has Joseph
- Isaiah 53:8 Yeshua and Messiah
- Isaiah 53:10 Passover
- Isaiah 53:9 and on shows the evil Roman city
- Isaiah 53:11 encodes wicked Caesar to perish. Interestingly Tiberius Caesar died just five years after Jesus
- Isaiah 53:12 on has the disciples mourn, adjacent to disciples is priest. Also we see: from the Atonement Lamb
- Isaiah 52 and 53 encodes all of the following: Yeshua, Shmi, Nazarene, Messiah, Shiloh, Passover, Galilee, Herod, Caesar, Evil Roman City, Caiaphas, Annas, Mary, Mary (Magdalene), The Disciples, Peter, Matthew, John, Andrew, Philip, Thomas, James, Simon, Thaddaeus, Matthias, Let Him be Crucified, Cross, Pierce, Lamp of the Lord, His signature, The Bread, Wine, Zion, Moriah, Obed, Jesse, Seed, Water, Levites, Pharisee, From the Atonement Lamb and Joseph.[65]

The odds of these coded events happening is in excess of 1 in 6×10^{40}

The New Testament was written in Greek. As of yet there have not been a great number of codes found. The codes found deal mostly with Jesus Himself. There are seven thousand nine hundred fourteen verses in the NT and the following is what has been found so far: Jesus, Nazareth, Lamb, Mercy, Blood, Son, Innocent, Jonah, and Saviour. Obviously as history unfolds and we near His second coming we may find more prophecies fulfilled, especially within the prophetic book of Revelation. This though is pure prognostication on my part. Next we turn to more fallacies about Christianity and its followers.

---

[65] Ibid p.130-131

Christians are not more charitable than non-religious people have been reiterated as empirical fact.[66] The problem is with the definition of charitable. Is it only of monetary giving? My dictionary defines charity as: *1) "love of fellow man; kindness; benevolence. 2. A gift or aid given to the poor, ailing or needy".*[67] So being charitable entails more than giving financially. Do Christians do this?

There are many Christian charities that help the less well-off throughout the world, just as there are many non-Christian charities. They all do good work and should be commended. But let's look at the statement Christian charities are no more giving than the secular. A magnitude 7.6 earthquake on Oct. 8, 2005, killed about eighty thousand people in Northwestern Pakistan and Kashmir and left more than three million homeless. It is fact; Christian charities were amongst the first to respond to the need. True, secular charities were also there, but there is a stark difference. Pakistan does not have a history of terrorizing secular people working for these charities. Many in Pakistan are defiantly anti-Christian and systematically target Christians for discrimination, even murder at times and burning of their churches, in accordance with Qur'an verses (2:190,216; 5:51; 8:12,36,65; 9:5,12,14,26,29,37,73,123; 47:4; 48:13,16,29).

As I am finishing this chapter the third anniversary of the Syrian Civil War is approaching. This was a result of the Arab Spring that began in 2011. The killing is monstrous. Over one hundred seventy thousand people have been killed and millions have been left homeless as refugees. Other countries are urging leader Bashar al-Assad to step aside, to no avail. The rebels continue to fight, although it appears they may be losing ground as the guard loyal to Assad have been making gains. Numerous countries have donated large amounts of money to help the Syrians. But as is the norm in situations like this, the money is not making it to the people in need. The only bright spot appears to be the Christian agencies doing their best to alleviate the suffering. Even though the Christian population is only about fifteen percent, they are putting themselves in harm's way to improve the dire situation. Instead of just throwing money at the problem they are actually in the trenches trying to make a difference.

How many people would willingly go into a country, where hate is common against them and some want to kill them, to give aid? I wonder

---

[66] Stenger, *Hypothesis*. p. 249

[67] *The Winston Dictionary of Canadian English*. Intermediate Edition. Holt Rinehart and Winston Canada. Toronto On. 1970

how many non-religious people, their friends, relatives and associates would do so. Christians put themselves in harm's way to help someone they do not even know, without any financial gain. They love their enemies as they have been commanded. The Pakistan earthquake is not the only example. This is standard operating procedure for Christians.

- In 2011, the majority of charitable dollars went to religion (thirty-two percent), education (thirteen percent), human services (twelve percent), and grant making foundations (nine percent).[68]
- In 2011, there were approximately 1,080,130 charitable organizations in the United States, a sixteen percent decrease from 2010.[69]
- There are an estimated 322,485 congregations in the United States in June 2013.[70]
- The top four volunteer areas are for religious (thirty-four percent), educational (twenty-seven percent), social service (fourteen percent), and health (eight percent) organizations[71]

It appears from these numbers, religious giving to be quite a high percentage. With over one million charities and over three hundred thousand congregations, thirty-two percent of the charitable dollars went for religious reasons. It has been estimated that about twenty percent of people attend church on a regular basis.[72] But that does not mean twenty percent of people are practicing Christians. Many people in the churches are just 'pew warmers', going to church for various reasons. Surveys also have shown that only about fourteen percent of people who claim to be Christians actually exhibit Christ-like qualities.[73]

It would appear that the religious give more than the non-religious, when it comes to actually showing compassion or charity. The comment against Christians does not appear to merit consideration. Anyone can throw money at a situation for the tax write-off and so they can feel good about themselves. It takes a special person to put their lives and personal well-being on the line to be charitable. Below is a list of the best known of numerous recognized Christian charities that help those in need at the

---

[68] Giving USA 2012
[69] Ibid
[70] The Urban Institute, National Center for Charitable Statistics, from the Internal Revenue Service, Exempt Organizations Business Master File (2010, Jan)
[71] The Corporation for National and Community Service
[72] Ontario Consultants On Religious Tolerance
[73] http://www.christianmessenger.in/are-christians-more-like-jesus-or-more-like-the-pharisees accessed 2013/30/12

most devastating times in their lives or strive to help, feed, clothe and educate the most down-trodden in our world (there are numerous more):
- World Vision
- Samaritan's Purse
- Compassion International
- Covenant House
- Christian Children's Fund
- Habitat for Humanity
- Salvation Army
- The Plan
- Leprosy Mission Canada

I have never heard of: Atheists' World View, Agnostics' Compassion Council, Heathens for Humanity or Pagan Parents' Plan (obviously fictitious names, but that is the point).

But the most telling aspect is what the Bible says about charity. These verses also speak of benevolence (2 Sam. 9:1-13; Job 29:16; Prov.3:27; 11:25; 18:16; 19:17; 21:13; 22:9, 25:14,21; 28:27; 29:7; Is. 58:10; Mark 14:3-8; Luke 3:11;6:38; 10:30-42; 14:12-14; Acts 4:36-42; 11:27-30; 20:35; Rom. 12:13; 15:26-27; 2 Cor. 8:1-5; Eph. 4:28).

Elvis Presley displayed incredible acts of charity for thousands of child victims affected by poverty. He said *"If I have faith and not charity, I am nothing"*.[74] The evidence clearly shows Christians are more compassionate when giving than the general population. Christians were in the centre of the recent initial Ebola outbreak in western Africa, before it became an epidemic, putting their lives on the line to help. Atheist Brian Palmer recently suggested people should just stand aside and let the missionaries and God do their jobs.[75]

Next we will deal with quoting of Scripture. Most critics have a habit of quoting Scripture to make their arguments. This is a serious mistake many people make if they do not properly understand Scripture. If you cherry-pick verses, taken out of context, to make a point, most often the person sets themselves up to be shown to be in error or foolish. So, what you may ask gives me the right to challenge these people? What special qualifications do I have? I am a graduate of Heritage Bible College in Cambridge Ontario. I believe this gives me the required credentials

---

[74] Movie World Magazine Sept. 1961. p.34
[75] Palmer, B., *In Medicine We Trust: Should we worry that so many of the doctors treating Ebola in Africa are missionaries?*, slate.com, 2 October 2014

Let's begin in Genesis where the coming Messiah was predicted (Gen 3:15). Here God is speaking to the serpent and it does not necessarily mean a snake. Satan is referred to as the serpent in the Bible (Ps. 91:13; Rev. 9:12; 12:15; 20:2). What the scripture is saying is that a future descendent of Eve, God in human form, will be the person to defeat Satan, not just be born of a woman.[76] Biblically, children are known by the father and not the mother (1 Chron. 1-9). At this time the people would also be unfamiliar with the science of conception. For them the man planted his seed inside a woman.[77] This verse seems to hint at the virginal conception of Jesus. The bruising of the head is more serious than the bruising of the heel. So the redeemers' suffering will be temporary, whereas Satan's will be more permanent. This verse refers to the coming Messiah and not specifically to whom Jesus would be born. Another example of what happens when unschooled people in Hermeneutics try to interpret the Bible.

In Matthew 16:28 Jesus tells His Disciples that some who are witnessing Him at that time will not die before the Kingdom of God is established. This is also repeated in Mark 9:2-10 and Luke 9:28-36. It appears from the placing of this event it refers to the transfiguration since this event happens in chapter Matthew 17 verses 1-9. The same event is also recorded immediately after Mark 9 and Luke 9. During the transfiguration Jesus takes Peter, James and John with Him up the mountain. They were able to see how Jesus will appear when He comes in the power of the eternal kingdom. This is also supported in 2 Peter 1:16-18 when Peter likens Jesus' glory with His transfiguration.

As Jesus did not know when He would return; only the Father knows the day and the hour (Mark 13:32), He could not reassure His Disciples that He would return before they died.

Mark 13:3-37, and Matthew 24:3-51 foretells the coming of the 'End of the Age' or as many people falsely claim the end of the word, even though Scripture clearly states that the earth is a world without end (Eccl. 1:4, Eph. 3:21, Is. 45:17). Jesus was warning all believers what was to come at the time of the end. There will be deceivers claiming to be Jesus (Mat. 24:5, 23, 24, 26), wars and rumours of wars (v.6) as nations rise up against other nations. There will be famines and earthquakes in various places (v.7). Believers will be persecuted and killed because they are hated by all nations (v.9). The Gospel will be preached

---

[76] Stenger, *Hypothesis*. p. 177
[77] Walton, *Genesis*. p. 225

throughout the entire world (v.14) even though many will defect from the faith (v.10) due to the enticement of false prophets (v.11). They were warned to be ready when the prophecies of Daniel start coming to fruition (v.15). He also warns that this will be like a time of no other (v.21). He then provides the celestial clues where the sun will become dark and the moon will not give light (v. 29). After all this happens He will appear in the sky for all to see and come in His glory to set up His eternal kingdom. It is the generation that sees all this that will not pass away, not the one present at the time Jesus spoke.

Jesus also spoke of the Kingdom of God when He chastised the Pharisees about His casting out of demons (Mat.12:28, Luke 11:20). They were trying to say that Jesus was able to do this through the power of Beelzebub. He also rebuked the Pharisees when He said the coming of the Kingdom of God will not be displayed with visual signs, but has arrived (Luke 17:20b). The Greek word used here is *'parateresis'* and is used nowhere else in the Bible. This seems to say the coming kingdom is through Him and is already here, although not yet completely realised. Remember, the transfiguration had already happened at this time. Also the Greek word *'semeion'*, which means miracle, is not used in this verse. Obviously Jesus' return could be put under the category of a miracle.

We have already discussed Luke's handling of the transfiguration in chapter 9 of his Gospel. This would strongly suggest this is to what the 'Kingdom of God' refers. Saying the Kingdom of God has come near, it is obvious he was not speaking of a future event. Luke also quotes Jesus as saying the Kingdom of God is within (Luke 17:21). In his gospel, Thomas quotes Jesus as saying:

> *"The kingdom will not come by watching for it. It will not be said, "Look here! or look there!". Rather, the kingdom of the Father is spread out upon the earth and people do not see it".*[78] *The kingdom is within you and is outside you".*[79]

When challenged at the temple by the elders and chief priests Jesus told them those whom the Pharisees condemned would see the kingdom before them (Mat. 21:31b-32). To say Jesus said He would return to set up His kingdom in one generation[80] is categorically erroneous. The Kingdom of God, as a metaphor, arrived with the ministry of Jesus (Mat. 12:28;

---

[78] Gospel of Thomas 113
[79] Ibid. 3
[80] Stenger. *Hypothesis.* p. 179, 236

Mark 1:15; Luke 4:21; 10:18), but it will not be fully consummated until He does return[81] to set up His eternal kingdom on the earth (Mat. 6:10; 13:36-43; Luke 13:28,29; 19:11).

Let's now turn our attention to the topic of women's rights. Naysayers say the Bible gives women absolutely no rights. Islam sets limitations on a woman's rights, but the NT testament does not do this. The scripture found in Ephesians 5:22-24 is often used to keep women subservient, and many use these words to justify their ignorance in saying Christian men are misogynists. These three verses are used in an attempt to validate improper treatment of women. Reading on a little further, Paul commands the husband to give himself up for his wife in a self-sacrificial manner (Eph. 5:25-29). It is obvious that this means the husband will lay down his life for his wife in direct opposition to any tyrannical rule over her. In this chapter Paul uses only three verses to explain the wife's duty while he expands significantly and takes nine verses to command husbands how to behave. Husbands are to love their wives and not be harsh with them (Col. 3:19). Read the sections for yourself and honestly tell me how anyone can interpret the Bible to give women no rights. It is not a legitimate argument.

The first marriage was Adam and Eve (Gen. 2:18). The word used to describe Eve in Hebrew is *'ezer'*. The proper use of this word does not indicate a subordinate, but in actuality it is meant to be fulfilled as a purpose. The term is also used to describe when God aids man (Ps. 33:20; 121:1-2). Eve was to complement Adam. Eve was formed from Adam's rib (Gen 2:21-22). That is to say she was to be beside him not under him.

Additionally Jesus did not treat women as the leaders of the time did. Many people think that Jesus wandered around the land with only twelve Disciples. This is completely false. There were actually up to eighty-two Disciples (Luke 10:1). The remaining eleven after the crucifixion, were Apostles. Jesus also travelled with women. Some of them were wealthy; namely Joana the wife of Chuza, Herod's business manager; and Susanna who was married to a high-powered civil leader. It was their family wealth that was used to help pay the expenses of the travelling crew (Luke 8:1-3). In the Bible woman had value (Ruth 4:9-12) and they decided the name of sons born (Luke 1:59-66). They were not to be completely subservient as suggested by detractors.

---

[81] Pate, C. Marvin. *End of Age*. p.167

Jesus lovingly spoke to the Samaritan woman at the well who was living in an adulterous relationship and had been married five times (John 4:7-26). Jews did not associate with Samaritans, yet Jesus interacted with a Samaritan woman? No Jewish man would do such a thing at this time. Jesus forgave and did not condemn the woman taken in adultery (John 8:3-11). Jesus showed the example of how He expected everyone to be treated. Jesus and His teachings cannot be blamed for people who twist things to fit their perverted faith. If a person is going to criticize Christianity they must criticize what Jesus said and did, not on what people who purport to follow Him say or do.

Another argument against Christianity is the OT practice of slavery. The image of the slavery practiced in the USA for a few hundred years is horrific. People were stolen from Africa and brought to America. Whole families separated, some to never see each other again. They were at the mercy of their masters. Some plantation owners could make the term sadistic look benevolent. Violence, abuse, maiming and/or killing were all in a day's work for some of these owners. Slavery in the Bible is nowhere near this description and there are verses inhibiting slavery. First off what does inhibit mean? My dictionary says: *"to restrain; hold in check; to suppress"*.[82] So any verse that tries to prevent, constrain, hinder, impede, obstruct, deter, reduce, stall, hamper, slow or stop[83] the practice would be considered inhibiting. What does the Bible say about slavery?

Slavery had been practiced for millennia (Gen. 9:25). Jewish law, though, had strict regulations regarding slavery. Moses forbade the practice whereby someone could be kidnapped and sold to another. This exemplifies the slave trade practiced in the USA from about 1619 until 1865 when President Abraham Lincoln signed the Emancipation Proclamation. But if Biblical law had been followed, the entire slave trade in the US would have never occurred. The penalty to forcibly take another person from their home and sell them into slavery was death (Ex. 21:16). This certainly sounds like inhibiting to me. Look at the synonyms for inhibit above. In his letter to Timothy the apostle Paul reiterates that kidnapping is partaking in lawlessness. So he is confirming the written Law of Moses.

In the OT people were able to pay their debts by becoming a slave (Ex. 21:2-6; Neh. 5:1-5). If they were unable to pay off their debts

---

[82] The Winston Dictionary of Canadian English. Intermediate Edition.
[83] Canadian Thesaurus.

they must have some option open to them. If they received some sort of payment this would not be slavery, in the general sense of the word. The payment may not have been substantial but there was still some sort of remuneration. A thief who could not repay what he had stolen could become a slave to work off the debt. If a person prospered they could buy their freedom (Lev. 25:48a). A family member could buy him/her out of servitude (Lev 25:48b-49). The word slave is not appropriate in this case- the Hebrew word *'ebed'* can also be translated servant, or attendant.

There was also regulation regarding treatment. The masters were not to rule harshly (Lev. 25:39; Deut.15:14). If a master beat or harmed a slave, the slave would be set free (Ex. 21:26-27). Hebrew law also prohibited life-long servitude. After six years of service a slave was to be freed (Ex. 21:2; Deut. 15:12). During the celebration of the Year of Jubilee all slaves were released regardless of the length of time they served (Lev. 25:37-43). The prophet Amos called disaster upon Tyre and Gaza because of their practice of slave trading (Am. 1:6-9). God talks about His punishment of slave owners in Gen 15:13-14. God punished the Egyptians for making slaves of the Jews and mistreating them through ten plagues, the last being the death of the first born in every household. That seems to be quite a severe punishment for enslaving them.

God gave a slave the right to redemption after he has sold himself (Lev. 25:48). If he prospered he could buy his freedom. A blood relative could redeem him. Then either at Jubilee if any of these conditions were met, or it was the Year of Jubilee both he and his family were to be freed. *(Lev. 25:54).* If these laws were not obeyed God promised those who did not follow these commands would face harsh punishment (Lev. 26:14-17).

During the Babylonian siege the Lord did have His prophet Jeremiah instruct King Zedekiah to proclaim freedom for all the slaves. All of the people were to free their Hebrew slave (Jer. 34:9). All of the inhabitants of Jerusalem agreed (v.10). But being the "stiff-necked" people they were they reneged on their covenantal agreement (v.11). Moses also gave the Israelites specific instructions just before they entered into the Promised Land about slavery (Deut. 15:12-18). Speaking about marrying captive women Moses disavowed any idea of servitude (Deut. 21:14). Moses also told the Israelites in his farewell message:

- Give protection to slaves if they seek asylum (Deut. 23:15-16)
- Capital punishment must be used for anyone kidnapping someone for the purpose of selling them into slavery (Deut. 24:7)

Hmm, not one single verse? I take the above verses and especially those in Jeremiah, as a severe punishment for not freeing their slaves, and the instructions from Moses quite blunt. Can this be anything but God trying to inhibit slavery?

What does the NT say about slavery? Did Paul endorse the practice, and Jesus never does anything to disavow slavery? First let's explore the Greek word *'doulos'*. It can be translated as slave but it can also mean servant[84], so it would be up to the translator which word he/she chose. Paul did advise slaves to obey their masters (Eph. 6:5; Col. 3:22; Titus. 2:9), but he also advised slaves how to free themselves (1 Cor. 7:21). If Paul affirmed the practice, why would he help slaves become free men? Although the Bible does not attempt to completely abolish slavery, since it was ubiquitous in the culture, the teaching of Jesus to 'love thy neighbour' is in unadulterated opposition to the practice. You cannot love someone and subject them to servitude. Titus 2:9 telling slaves *"to be obedient"* has been often quoted for rebuttal. But children are also to obey their parents. If your employer or boss tells you do to something does your job not require you to obey? The OPSEU collective agreement for college professors/instructors has the words *"lawful order"* within the text. The writers of the NT knew this and thereby enacted strict guidelines. After making this statement Paul gets even more specific in the next book of the Bible. I wonder why they do not read a few pages more after this quote from Titus.

Paul writes to Philemon, who personally knew Paul, and he appeared to be a wealthy person. A slave of his, named Onesimus, runs away to Rome, probably to blend in with the large population and escape detection. While in Rome he found Paul and was led to a believing faith is Jesus (v.10). It seems that Onesimus decided to return to his master and attempt reconciliation. Paul writes a letter to Philemon on his behalf asking for mercy. In his letter Paul acts as if he expects Philemon to grant freedom upon Onesimus' return (v.21). An inscription discovered at Laodicea near Colossae is dedicated to Marcus Sestius Philemon by a freed slave. Although not conclusive, it is highly suggestive that this could be the same Philemon in the story. The crux of the story is that since Philemon was a believer and Onesimus was now a brother-in-the-body-of-Christ, he should no longer be considered a slave.

---

[84] Moo, Douglas J. *Romans*. p. 35

Slaves also had rights afforded to them. They were members of the covenant (Gen. 17:12-13); allowed to rest on the Sabbath (Ex. 20:10; Deut. 5:12-15); could expect equal justice (Job 31:13) and could even inherit land or goods (Gen. 15:2-3). Paul also compared slave traders to murders, adulterers, morally deficient, liars and other malcontents. He also ordered slave masters to treat salves the same way they wanted to be treated (Eph. 6:9). Paul affirmed a slave and his/her master were equal to each other in Christ (1 Cor.12:13; Gal. 3:28; Col.3:11; Philemon 15-16). Diametrically opposed to this, pagans such as Aristotle stated some people were natural slaves.[85] Bishop Anselm (1033-1109 A.D.) was adamant in his condemnation of slavery. Thomas Aquinas (1225-1274 A.D.) prohibited slavery. Pope Paul III (1468-1549 A.D.) forbade the practice. John Chrysostom, an early church preacher, enticed believing Christians to purchase slaves so they could free them from bondage.

Just how prevalent was slavery in the first century A.D.? Although not completely clear, records insinuate that twenty percent of Roman residents were slaves.[86] But this is speculation since Seneca recalls a defeated proposed law by the Roman senate for slave to wear distinctive clothing. The fear was that the actual number of slaves would become transparently obvious.[87] So Paul, calling on the teachings of Jesus, did acknowledge that slavery was widespread and any attempt to eliminate would have been futile. He did the best he could to try to attempt people to reduce it as much as possible.

Ex- president Jimmy Carter recently said 200-300 young girls are sold into sexual slavery in Georgia, his home state, every month and most people are oblivious to it.[88]

As for Jesus, He did say things that could be construed as avowing slavery. All are called upon to spread the His Gospel to everyone, since everyone is one in Him (Col. 3:1-11). With Jesus, social status was irrelevant. Everyone is a brother or sister in Him (Gal. 3:28; Col. 3:11) and according to Paul an heir to the throne of God (Gal. 4:7). What about the following messages from Jesus?

- The Golden Rule (Mat.7:12)
- Be merciful as God is merciful (Luke 6:36)
- A form of Karma (Luke 6:38)

---

[85] Wieland, C. *Family*. p. 117
[86] Ferguson, Everett. *Backgrounds of Early Christianity*. Eerdmans. Grand Rapids MI. 1987 p. 46
[87] Seneca. De Clementia 1.24.1
[88] https://ca.finance.yahoo.com/news/jimmy-carter-slavery-worse-now-1700s-053114778.html accessed 2014/29/09

- Love everyone as yourself (Mat. 22:39)
- Love one another. (John 13:34)
- Love one another as I love you (John 15: 12)
- Everyone is a slave to sin (John 8:34)

Jesus did not specifically disavow slavery, but His teachings can only be taken as opposition to it. You cannot do any of the words of Jesus and support slavery. Jesus knew that any words from Him abolishing slavery would be met with extreme, rebellious violence. He indirectly spoke against it, but focused on His mission, which was to free all men from the slavery of sin. As already mentioned slavery was made illegal by Abraham Lincoln, a devout Christian. It is so unfortunate people have to make things up, because, in their zeal to destroy Christianity, they cannot find anything Jesus said/did that is unloving. Maybe they should use some of that energy to follow His commands.

Pastor Mark Hughes of The Church of the Rock in Winnipeg, Manitoba, Canada suggests; *"anyone who says the Bible does not condemn slavery did not do a very good job of reading the book"*[89], especially since experts now estimate there are currently thirty to thirty-six million humans in bondage world-wide.[90,91] Condemning the Bible because it acknowledges the existence of slavery, while ignoring the state of our present world, is ignorance to the facts.

Does the Bible have much to say about laws governing peoples' action? Most people know of the Ten Commandments. Mr. Stenger implies that the Bible only gives ten rudimentary commands or laws that govern actions of people, whereas the Code of Hammurabi would be a suitable replacement since it has 282 detailed laws.[92]

Solon (638 BC – 558 BC) was an Athenian statesman, lawmaker, and poet. He is remembered particularly for his efforts to legislate against political, economic, and moral decline in archaic Athens. His reforms failed in the short term, yet he is often credited with having laid the foundations for Athenian democracy.[93] What do scholars of antiquities have to say about him? Ancient authors also say that Solon regulated

---

[89] Pastor Mark Hughes, Church of the Rock Sermon, 2013/08/12

[90] http://www.cnbc.com/id/101120054?_source=yahoopercent7Cfinancepercent7Cinlinepercent7Cstorypercent7Cstory&par=yahoo&doc=102035539# Accessed 2014/29/09

[91] https://ca.news.yahoo.com/nearly-36-mln-people-slaves-qatar-focus-global-134217592.html accessed 2014/18/11

[92] Stenger. *Hypothesis*. p. 201

[93] http://en.wikipedia.org/wiki/Solon accessed 2013/10/8

pederastic relationships in Athens; this has been presented as an adaption of custom to the new structure of the *polis*.[94,95] Now there is some question as to whether or not this is factual or an outright fabrication, but I question whether anyone should suggest that a purported child-molesting, pedophile, be revered for what he did to shape the laws that governed ancient Greece. If someone is to be revered, their reputation should be completely unblemished.

Are the Hebrew laws crude? Let's examine that position. Yes initially God gave Moses Ten Commandments in Exodus, the second book of the Bible. The book of Leviticus (third book in the Bible) is part of the Pentateuch and a compilation of instructions given to Moses on Mt. Sinai. There are also other rules spread throughout the OT and a plethora of new ones in the NT. To say the laws are crude is completely false. All-in-all there is well over six hundred thirteen laws given by which we are to abide in the OT alone.[96] Intriguingly, sin is discussed six hundred thirteen times in the Bible. In addition to this there are approximately six thousand oral traditions from the scribes that provide a rule specifically designed for almost every conceivable living situation or circumstance.[97] Unfortunately, a person cannot sit down and find a specific list in one place, but many laws can be found in Leviticus as the central teaching is to be holy (Lev. 11:44).

Since the Code of Hammurabi displays only 282, the Biblical laws/rules should be displayed and not the Hammurabi laws, as suggested, by Mr. Stenger.[98]

As for the existence of a god that hides himself from all but a few specifically chosen people being unworthy of worship, I agree wholeheartedly; there is absolutely no evidence for such a god.[99]

Our society is growing away from God exponentially. It is not politically correct to mention Jesus. In our public schools it is forbidden, by a believing teacher, to mention creation in a science class about evolution, unless a student broaches the subject.[100] If the teacher is pro-evolution the student can be chastised for having the audacity to bring up

---

[94] Bernard Sergent, "*Paederasty and Political Life in Archaic Greek Cities*" in *Gay Studies from the French Culture;* Harrington Park Press, Binghamton, NY 1993; pp.153-154
[95] Thomas Francis Scanlon *Eros and Greek Athletics* p.213
[96] http://www.jewfaq.org/613.htm accessed 2013/10/8
[97] Pate, C. Marvin. *Age has Come.* p. 20
[98] Stenger, *Hypothesis. p.*201
[99] Ibid. p. 241
[100] Creation Magazine. *Winning Against Suppression.* Creation Ministries International. Vol. 35 No. 3, 2013

the 'myths' and 'fairy-tales' of the Bible. While God's sovereign glory is paramount, it is poignant, and some will be lost through complacency. Ben Stein recently questioned the idea: since evil is rampant and bad things happen to good people either there is no god or he does not care about people. Jay Leno recently mused about the abundance of natural disasters and with all the potential epidemics threatening man-kind along with the perceived threat of terrorism, if this was a good time to remove God from the 'Pledge of Allegiance'. Anne Graham, Billy Graham's daughter, astutely responded, when interviewed on the Early Show and Jane Clayson asked her about Hurricane Katrina:

> "I believe God is deeply saddened by this, just as we are, but for years we've been telling God to get out of our schools, to get out of our government and to get out of our lives. Being the gentleman He is I believe He has calmly backed out. How can we expect God to give us His blessing and His protection if we demand He leave us alone?"

But this is not God hiding Himself. Knowledge of the Bible is not required for the knowledge of God. The term for this is General Revelation. God is the source of this knowledge (Prov. 1:7; 3:5; 9:10; Job 28:12; Eccl. 7:24). It is man's own obduracy that prevents him from accepting the truth (Acts 7:51-53; Heb. 3:7-8; Ps. 95:7-11).

Abraham Lincoln said: "*I can see how man can look upon the earth and be an atheist, but I cannot conceive how a man can look up into the heavens and say there is no God.*" King David said the Heavens clearly show God's handiwork (Ps. 19:1). Barnabas and Paul reiterated that God has given us all the proof we need (Acts 14:17). Everything we see around us all point to a benevolent God that provides all that is needed.[101] This is evident if people are willing to see the proofs. People who try to suppress the evidence through denial are not without knowing.

Paul is saying that everyone has some internal knowledge or perception of God's existence (*a priori*). On the last day everyone will be held accountable (Rom. 3:19). No one will be able to complain that God has been unfair.[102] The presence of a conscience, even in unbelievers, points to the proof of God. This is where General Revelation occurs by observing nature, through an inner evidence of God. An unbeliever may

---

[101] Pate, C Marvin. *End of Age*. p. 56
[102] Grudem, Wayne. *Theology*. p. 1147

incorrectly respond it is a moral upbringing that manifests in a conscience.

Let's explore that idea. David Suzuki aired a show entitled "*Babies: Born to be Good*" on CBC television, Thursday July 4, 2013; produced by Gail McIntyre & Amélie Blanchard. Directed and written by Eileen Thalenberg, babies as young as three months old were subjected to various experiments. They watched mini-plays and magic shows while being observed. Three-month old babies were able to tell the difference between 'good guys' and 'bad guys', showing an obvious preference for the 'good guys'. Six-month old babies were able to understand rewards and punishment based upon actions. Nine-month old babies appeared to recognize the concepts of justice and fairness.[103] How is this possible? Watch it and you will be amazed. There is only one possible explanation. Children are born with knowledge of God within themselves (Eccl. 3:11). It is with time, in our immoral evil world, that they can grow desensitized to that knowledge. Mahatma Ghandi realised this when he said:

> "I have also seen children successfully surmounting the effects of an evil inheritance. That is due to purity being an inherent attribute of the soul."

What did Blaise Pascal have to say on the subject?

- "Instead of complaining that God had hidden Himself, you will give Him thanks for not having revealed so much of Himself".
- "There is a God shaped vacuum in the heart of every man which cannot be filled by any created thing, but only by God, the Creator, made known through Jesus."
- "There are two kinds of people one can call reasonable; those who serve God with all their heart because they know him, and those who seek him with all their heart because they do not know him."
- "It is the heart which perceives God and not the reason. That is what faith is; God perceived by the heart, not by the reason."
- "That we must love one God only is a thing so evident that it does not require miracles to prove it."
- "Men despise religion. They hate it and are afraid it may be true."

---

[103] http://www.cbc.ca/natureofthings/episodes/_search_results/6e7c67449247f6964ef648ceb51ceb05/ accessed 2018/24/02

Evolution cannot explain these inherent abilities. Evolutionist Jaron Lanier retorted:

> *"There's a large group of people who simply are uncomfortable with accepting evolution because it leads to what they perceive as a moral vacuum, in which their best impulses have no basis in nature."*

How does Professor Dawkins answer this challenge?

> *"All I can say is; that's just tough. We have to face up to the truth."*

Now that is a succinct, logical argument (sarcasm intentional).

Another argument is about unbelievers who are not trained theologians, but know the basic theology for God.[104] I am not a trained physicist. I do not have a Ph.D., a Masters or even a Bachelor's degree in physics. But I understand Newtonian laws of motion. I understand the basics of the first and second Laws of Thermodynamics. I have a working knowledge of:

- Ohm's law
- Kirchhoff's law
- Lenz's law
- Boyle's law
- Charles' law
- Pascal's law
- Gaye-Lussac's law
- Bernoulli's principle

So does this extremely limited knowledge give me the credentials to write a book on Physics? I would not even aspire to undertaking such an endeavour. I am woefully under qualified.

Professor Dawkins suggests that all species on planet earth show the illusion of being designed.[105] This means that every species displays a powerful illusion. Why is it an illusion and a powerful one at that? If it was an illusion, it should not be shown by the ten million species. The odds of all these species displaying the same illusion are astronomical. Is it not more reasonable that it is not an illusion but it is actual design? Could it be the something mysterious giving rise to the origin of the universe, was a creator? This comment is quite mystifying. Does this mean evolution is the confounding part of the story? This would be quite out of character for him. He is a dyed-in-the-wool proponent of evo-

---

[104] Stenger, *Hypothesis*. p. 264
[105] Dawkins, *Delusion*. p. 139

lution. It is empirical fact in his mind. There is no doubt about it. Belief in God cannot be justified given the strong contradictory evidence. The theory of evolution can be doubted no more than the earth revolves around the sun. Words cannot do justice to the fact life evolved ten billion years ago out of literally nothing, according to him. So from where does this powerful illusion come?

If the evidence for evolution is so persuasive how can there even be an illusion of design. The evidence should leave no doubt and not even an inkling of another answer. Obviously the evidence is not that crystal clear and there is evidence that contradicts evolution and the origin of the universe.

I cannot let this next quoted statement go by. I enjoy Professor Dawkins' quotes. He has given credence to Christianity, even though I know it is not his purpose. Let's look at the quote about evidence for evolution. *"We don't need evidence for evolution; we know it to be true"*. That is quite the statement. If evidence was not needed for verification, the back log in the criminal justice system would disappear; no drawn-out trials would be necessary. All the Crown Attorney would have to say to a jury is: *"we do not have any evidence the accused is guilty, nonetheless I am asking you to convict since I know he/she did it"*.

Christians are eager to discover this wonderful creation. They rejoice to be part of it. What of the unbeliever? How do they answer the challenge of the meaning of life? If life has no meaning for them, what is the purpose? Why live a good and moral life? Why not lie, cheat, steal and do everything you can to make this life as pleasant as possible, stepping on anyone who gets in your way if there is no reward or punishment at the end? Why not observe Darwinian law? Let the weak, the infirmed and the unintelligent die and stop taking up space and wasting valuable resources. That would be a pretty sorry world in which to live. But these are the natural progressions of thought without God.

In his book "*The God Delusion*", Professor Dawkins proposes many things that tend to lean towards this type of thinking. What do some of his fellow atheists think about his latest book? Fellow atheist Michael Ruse, author of "*Darwinism and Its Discontents*" said of "*The God Delusion*": the book made him, as an atheist, embarrassed to admit his leanings.[106] I can only wonder why Professor Dawkins has such an apparent hate for someone who does not exist.

---

[106] McGrath. Alister et al. *Dawkins Delusion* (Front jacket cover)

Finally, the Bible is used to ridicule Christians and show that Jesus did not come to save the whole world as proclaimed. Paul did not invent the idea of taking the Jewish God to the Gentiles, as opposed to Professor Dawkins claims. We have already discussed the Great Commission where Jesus sent His Disciples out to the whole world. Ten days after Jesus reminded His Disciples of the promise of the Father (Acts 1:4-8), the power of the Holy Spirit descended at Pentecost (Acts 2:1-4). People from most nations were living in Jerusalem at the time (Acts 2:5). The people came to hear the message and they were amazed as they heard the Gospel in their own native tongue, even though it was spoken by Galileans (Acts 2:6-8). After this happened and the astonishment overtook everyone, Peter got up to speak. While preaching to the multitude Peter used the words "*to all who that are afar off*" (KJV), and "*even as many as the Lord our God shall call*" (Acts 2:39). The words "*to all who that are afar off*" would also refer to the Gentiles.

When forecasting future events, the prophet Isaiah said the Gentiles would be brought to Salvation (Is. 49:6). Simeon, a righteous and devout man from Jerusalem, allowed for Salvation to the Gentiles (Luke 2:32a). The Apostle John, when he was speaking of the Word becoming flesh, (John 1:9) reiterated Jesus would die to gather into one, the children of God (John 11:51b-52).

These events took place sometime before Paul even came onto the scene. It was Barnabas who brought Paul to Antioch to preach to the Gentiles (Acts 4:36). Samaritans were despised by the Jews, but Philip went there anyway obeying the command of Jesus. This was about the same time Saul (Paul) was persecuting the Church. Cornelius, a Gentile centurion, saw a vision from God that instructed him to send for Peter. Before the messenger from Cornelius arrived Peter had a vision. In this vision he saw both clean and unclean animals. Peter could not understand how he was to eat an unclean animal as it violated the Mosaic covenant. God was showing Peter that He was doing away with the old covenant and that he was to now go to the Gentiles and witness to them (Acts 10:9-20). When fellow Disciples questioned Peter about associating with Gentiles he retold the story there was no distinction between Jews and Gentiles (Is. 11:10). Anyone who accepted the Word would be able to enter into the presence of God (Acts 11:3-18). Jesus gave the initial command and it was His Disciples that carried the message to everyone, not just the Jews.

Hebrews 8:1-10:18 teaches that Abraham's seed will be shown through all believers, not just Jewish believers. Hebrews is a book written for all people and not just the Jews. The idea that it was Paul that began this practice, although he was quite veracious about Jesus telling him to take the message to the Gentiles (Acts 9:15), is sheer nonsense. What does all of this say about the atheistic argument?

> "*Overwhelmingly strong proofs of intelligent and benevolent design lay around...the atheistic idea is so non-sensical that I cannot put it into words*"[107]

While the Bible is not a scientific book, the events recounted are factual science. The most intelligent and best educated atheists and/or agnostics are some of my favourite people for quotes. I have included many of them in this book. They can be counted upon to say things that, due to their lack of knowledge of what Scripture really says, provide unintentional veracity for the Bible. We shall see in the next chapter the differences between the theories touted by scientists and God's telling of how things happened.

---

[107] Lord Kelvin. *Journal of the Victoria Institute*. vol. 124 p. 267

Chapter 3
Is Genesis Scientifically Accurate?

(All ages given in the next chapters of hundreds-of-thousands, millions or billions-of-years are long-age, evolutionary ages, not mine. Ma= million years ago. Ba=billion years ago)

Today's so-called educated population have dismissed the Bible as myths, fables, allegories and metaphors. They maintain for a person to believe in the Bible, they must ignore science and the proofs brought forward, believing only through blind faith. These feelings were made by satirist Bill Maher in his movie *'Religulous'*. He was dumbfounded leaders of the U.S.A. believed in talking snakes in the Garden of Eden and that Jonah spent three days in the belly of a whale (sic). He just could not believe persons who had risen to such a place in power could accept such fairy tales. What arguments are used try to debunk the Bible?

The age of the earth is approximately four billion years old, in its present form and the universe is nearly fifteen billion years old according to Big Bang theorists. In 1929 Edwin Hubble determined the universe was expanding proportional to the distance across. This gave rise to the Big Bang Theory. Theoretically at the beginning of the universe, a singularity exploded, sending all known matter outward from the blast site. The singularity was an infinitesimal small point where all the mass in the universe was concentrated.

The universe supposedly began with no structure and was in a state of complete disorder/chaos. This should show strong scientific evidence for God if the universe was not expanding.[108] The problem is Professor Stephen Hawking disputes the idea of a singularity at the begin-

---

[108] Stenger. *Hypothesis*. p. 121

ning,[109] and allowed for the beginning to be chaotic while the finished product was ordered. [110]Professor Hawking's view on God is not that of a loving and saving God, but it appears he and Mr. Stenger are at opposing positions on this one. Prominent physicists hypothesize that the universe could have come from nothing, but are unable to provide any proof. When the Big Bang began, the energy needed to start the expansion would have created very high temperature within the first few milliseconds. One second after the Big Bang, the temperature could have fallen to about 10,000,000,000°.[111] The universe at this point was unstable and with expansion, the universe continued to cool.[112] When the universe had cooled enough, electrons and nuclei began to form atoms. The universe would continue in this manner until stars and planets formed. Although the Big Bang happened about 15Ba, the earth did not start to form until about 11Ba. The timing is debated.

After forming, the earth went through many changes until we have current conditions. Life would begin to flourish and evolve into the millions of species we have today. Now, this is an extremely simplistic explanation of the Big Bang, as it is infinitely more complicated than this, but suffices to say, it is theorized, that it happened naturally without the input of any external force. The universe then, by extension, is a closed system.

This idea is further postulated when people who claim to be men-of-God try to debunk the Bible in its entirety. It is their claim that while the Bible is accurate in its description of the way to Salvation, the remainder, dealing with scientific and historical accuracy, can be treated with skepticism.[113] This does little to increase the faith of the church's followers and aids those who say church attendance is no longer necessary or meaningful.

Albert Schweitzer theorized that, in fact, the Jesus spoken of in the Bible was non-existent. The historical Jesus only had life in theological circles.[114] Martin Dibelius, a German theologian and a professor for the New Testament at the University of Heidelberg, noted for skepticism, questioned the possibility of describing Jesus with historical authority.[115] All the accounts we have in the Bible are not accurate and the writings

---

[109] Hawking. *History* p. 57
[110] Hawking. *Everything*. p.100
[111] Hawking. *History*. p. 129
[112] Stenger. *Hypothesis*. p. 148
[113] CEBW. *The Gift of Scripture*. Catholic Truth Society (Sep 15 2005)
[114] McDowell, *More Evidence*
[115] http://en.wikipedia.org/wiki/Martin_Dibelius accessed 2013/20/8

were designed only to win converts, according to Dibelius. Rudolf Bultmann, theologian, suggests the NT is mythological. How can an ordinary person accept the Bible, as the inspired Word of God, when those who are supposed to be showing the truth, vilify Scripture?

Unfortunately or fortunately, depending on your perspective, historical discoveries continue to show that the Bible is in fact, true. Some non-believers say no scientists believe in any of the Genesis account. Charles Templeton went as far as to say:

- No physicist in the world accepts the creation story [116]
- Every eminent physicist in the world accepts evolution [117]
- Every anthropologist in the world states that the fossil record shows incontrovertibly life on earth evolved over millions-of-years [118]
- No geologist will admit there is any evidence for a world-wide flood [119]

Let's examine these statements. If true then it would be hard for a Christian to explain their faith in Scripture. If false, the argument is completely meritless. Below is a list of prominent scientists with their field of expertise. There is not one, who could be called a radical, but there are sixty out of a surfeit that staunchly defend their faith in the Bible.

Dr. Steve Austin-Geology; Dr. Thomas Barnes-Physics; Dr. John Baumgardner-Electrical Engineering, Space Physicist, Geophysicist, expert in supercomputer modeling of plate tectonics; Professor Sung-Do Cha-Physics; Dr. Eugene F. Chaffin-Professor of Physics; Dr. Xidong Chen-Solid State Physics, Assistant Professor of Physics, Cedarville University; Professor Chung-Il Cho-Biology Education; Dr. Harold Coffin-Palaeontology; Dr. David A. DeWitt-Biology, Biochemistry, Neuroscience; Dr. Don DeYoung-Astronomy, atmospheric physics; Dr. Leroy Eimers-Atmospheric Science, Professor of Physics and Mathematics, Cedarville University; Professor Dennis L. Englin- Geophysics; Professor Carl B. Fliermans-Professor of Biology; Professor Robert H. Franks-Associate Professor of Biology; Dr. Roger G. Gallop-P.G. Geology; Dr. Robert Gentry-Physics; Dr. Steven Gollmer-Atmospheric Science, Professor of Physics, Cedarville University; Dr. Charles W. Harrison-Applied Physics, Electromagnetics; Dr. John Hartnett-Physics and Cosmology; Dr. Neil Huber-Physical Anthropology; Dr. Russell Humphreys-Physics; Dr. James A. Huggins, Professor and Chair, Department of Biology; Dr. Pierre Jerlström-Molecular Biology; Dr. Arthur Jones-Biology; Dr. Dean Kenyon-Biology; Professor Gi-Tai Kim-Biology; Dr. John W. Klotz-

---

[116] Templeton, Charles. *Farewell* p. 29
[117] Ibid p. 230
[118] Ibid p. 30
[119] Ibid

Biology; Dr. Leonid Korochkin, M.D.-Genetics, Molecular Biology, Neurobiology; Dr. Heather Kuruvilla-Plant Physiology, Senior Professor of Biology, Cedarville University; Professor Jin-Hyouk Kwon-Physics; Professor Lane P. Lester-Biology, Genetics; Dr. Jason Lisle-Astrophysics; Dr. Heinz Lycklama- Nuclear physics and Information Technology; Dr. Ian Macreadie-Molecular Biology and Microbiology; Dr. John Marcus-Molecular Biology; Dr. James Mason-Nuclear physics; Dr. John D. Morris-Geology; Dr. Graeme Mortimer-Geology; Professor Douglas Oliver-Professor of Biology; Professor Chris D. Osborne-Assistant Professor of Biology; Dr. Gary E. Parker-Biology, Cognate in Geology (Palaeontology); Dr. Terry Phipps-Professor of Biology, Cedarville University; Dr. Jung-Goo Roe-Biology; Dr. Marcus Ross-Palaeontology; Dr. Ariel A. Roth-Biology; Dr. Alicia (Lisa) Schaffner-Associate Professor of Biology, Cedarville University; Dr. Joachim Scheven-Paleontology; Dr. Saami Shaibani-Forensic Physics; Dr. Mikhail Shulgin-Physics; Dr. Emil Silvestru-Geology/Karstology; Dr. Harold Slusher-Geophysics; Dr. E. Norbert Smith-Zoology; Dr. Andrew Snelling-Geology; Dr. Timothy G. Standish-Biology; Dr. Dennis Sullivan-Biology, surgery, chemistry, Professor of Biology, Cedarville University; Dr. Larry Thaete-Molecular and Cellular Biology and Pathobiology; Dr. Ker C. Thomson-Geophysics; Professor Walter Veith-Zoology; Dr. Joachim Vetter-Biology; Dr. Tas Walker-Mechanical Engineering and Geology; Dr. Keith Wanser-Physics; Dr. John Whitmore-Geology/Palaeontology; Dr. Kurt Wise-Palaeontology; Dr. Sung-Hee Yoon-Biology; Dr. Daiqing Yuan-Theoretical Physics; Dr. Henry Zuill-Biology.

So much for that argument! There are also many scientists from the past that were Christians. Let's look at some famous scientists who believed what the Scriptures say. (I have included their reported I.Q. in brackets).

Kepler, Johannes (175):
- Mathematician and astronomer.
- Founder of physical astronomy
- Discovered the laws of planetary motion, proving the heliocentricity of the solar system
- Established the discipline of celestial mechanics
- An extremely devout Lutheran, he wrote extensively on how celestial bodies along with the space continuum represented the Trinity.
- More astounding was the historical fact that he was allowed to remain as a professor in Catholic Graz while other Protestants were removed.

Deluc, Jean:
- Coined the term geology
- With his father developed the mercury thermometer and hygrometer
- Defended Creation and the world-wide flood

Bacon, Francis (180):
- Established the now widely used method of using experimentation and inductive reasoning to prove or disprove a theory once said " *It is true, that a little philosophy inclineth man's mind to atheism, but depth in philosophy bringeth men's minds about to religion; for while the mind of man looketh upon second causes scattered, it may sometimes rest in them, and go no further; but when it beholdeth the chain of them confederate, and linked together, it must needs fly to Providence and Deity.*"[120]

Pascal, Blaise (195):
- Established math behind conic sections, differential calculus and theory of probability
- Father of Hydrostatics and one of founders of hydrodynamics
- Without hydraulics we would not have:
    1. Brakes for automobiles
    2. Clutches & Automatic transmissions for modern automobiles
    3. Snow ploughs for clearing snow
    4. Cranes to lift objects to great heights
    5. Garbage compactors
    6. Needles for insulin and medications and many other devices for everyday use (There are many more examples)

Proposes the "Wager of Pascal":

> "How can anyone lose who chooses to become a Christian? If, when he dies, there turns out to be no God and his faith was in vain, he has lost nothing- in fact, he has been happier in life than his non-believing friends, If, however there is a God and a Heaven and Hell, the he has gained Heaven and his skeptical friends will have lost everything in Hell".

Lister, Joseph:
- Instrumental in development of antiseptic surgery using disinfectants

---

[120] http://www.godandscience.org/apologetics/sciencefaith.html accessed 2013/20/8

Leibnitz, Gottfried Wilhelm (205):
- One of the world's most gifted mathematicians and philosophers
- Aided Newton in discovery of calculus, the scientific principle and conservation of energy
- Introduced the binary notational system and foresaw the Boolean system of logic

Boyle, Robert (185):
- Father of modern chemistry
- Experimented with gases. Experiments paved way for the discovery of Boyle's Law. Boyle's law is used in everyday use. If anyone has ever used, driven or ridden in a car, truck bus or anything with an engine, he/she has experienced Boyle's law.
- Great contributions in physics and chemistry while being called one of the greatest physical scientists of his day
- He is also known for lectures against the atheists of his day. He did this by showing that the study of nature was a duty to all those who felt a religious duty.

Newton, Sir Isaac (190):
- Theory of Gravity
- Three laws of motion leading to the principle of dynamics
- Development of calculus
- Foresaw the law of energy conservation
- Developed the light propagation particle theory
- Constructed the first reflecting telescope
- Refuted atheism and defended the Bible's scientific and historical nature
- Espoused the Flood as the cause of geological occurrences; namely fossils
- Said: "*We account the Scriptures of God to be the most sublime philosophy. I find more sure marks of authenticity in the Bible than in any profane history whatsoever*"
- To reinforce his beliefs he stated in "*Principia*": "*the most beautiful system of the sun, planets, and comets, could only proceed from the counsel and dominion of an intelligent and powerful Being.*"

Parkinson, James:
- Recognised the signs and dangers of the perforated appendix
- Parkinson's disease named after him as he first recognised the condition
- First to recognise plant origin of coal
- Proponent of the flood and its geological effects

Davy, Humphry (185):
- Developed the motion theory of heat
- Invented the safety lamp
- Demonstrated that diamond is actually carbon

Faraday, Michael:
- Michael Faraday was brilliant in that his discoveries and experiments related to electricity and magnetism have made the modern world what it is today. Without his advents computers, cars, telephones, radio, and television would be all science fiction.
- Regarded as one of the greatest physicists of all time
- Faraday was a devout Christian, originally in the Presbyterian domination. He defected to another sect, one more devoted to following a Christian faith more resembling the teachings of the New Testament in its entirety.

Brewster, David (142):
- Founded science of optical mineralogy and invented the kaleidoscope
- In one paper he described finding a nail embedded within a large quarry stone. Discovery was totally ignored by scientific world; he was captivated with ancient geological ages.

Riemann, Berhard:
- Non-Euclidean geometry
- Theory of relativity developed on his geometrical proofs

Sedgwick, Adam:
- Nineteenth century geologist who identified and named major rock formations called Cambrian and Devonian
- Predicted that evolutionary ideas would be *"devastatingly harmful to the world"*

Whewell, William:
- Named the Eocene, Miocene and Pliocene geological epochs
- Defined the terms anode, cathode and ion
- Coined the terms scientist, physicist and catastrophism
- Staunchly defended against uniformitarianism

Joule, James:
- Discovered the mechanical equivalent of heat constant for conversion of heat and mechanical energy leading to the law of energy conservation: called the chief founder of thermodynamics

Virchow, Rudolph:
- Father of pathology and cellular diseases
- First to recognize leukemia
- Purported that the Bible was historically accurate

Pasteur, Louis:
- Studies in germs as cause of disease and bacteriology
- Demolished the idea of spontaneous generation
- Developed vaccines for rabies, diphtheria, anthrax, as well as many others
- Initiated process for sterilization and pasteurization
- Strongly opposed Darwinism

Fabre, Henri:
- Opposed spontaneous generation and evolution
- Father of entomology
- Once said "*I regard atheism as a mania. It is the malady of the age*"

Huggins, Sir William:
- Astronomer
- First to show that stars are mostly hydrogen
- First to identify the Doppler Effect, leading to the idea of an expanding universe

Kelvin, Lord William Thompson (185):
- Infant and teen-age prodigy
- Physicist and mathematician
- Develop the scale of absolute zero leading to temperature given in degrees Kelvin
- Wrote the First and Second laws of Thermodynamics in exact terminology
- Calculated the age of the earth as not being old enough to support evolution

Ramsay, William Mitchell:
- Archaeologist concentrating in Asia Minor
- Proved that the statements in the book of Acts were completely historical
- Wrote over twenty books showing veracity of NT

Maxwell, Joseph Clerk,
- Further developed the theory of electromagnetic fields
- "*Maxwell is regarded by most modern physicists as the scientist of the 19th century who had the greatest influence on 20th century physics; he is ranked with Sir Isaac Newton and Albert Einstein for the fundamental nature of his contributions.*" [121]
- Albert Einstein said of Maxwell "*the most profound and fruitful that physics has experienced since the time of Newton*". Quite an accolade.
- Maxwell was a devout Christian that believed in a creationist earth, although his timelines were a bit skewed.
- Able to, through mathematics, refute atheist LaPlace's nebular hypothesis.

Plank, Max:
- Max Planck was best known for his theories regarding quantum physics. These theories would lead to an understanding of how the atomic and subatomic properties of matter acted. We all know where this would eventually lead.
- He would eventually state that "*both science and religion wage a tireless battle against skepticism and dogmatism, against unbelief and superstition with the goal toward God!*"

Next, we look at Albert Einstein; widely known as one of the most intellectual men who ever lived. Einstein never had an IQ test but it has been estimated to range from 160-180. Although he did not believe in a personal God, he said the following:

> "*Everyone who is seriously interested in the pursuit of science becomes convinced that a spirit is manifest in the laws of the universe-- a spirit vastly superior to man, and one in the face of which our modest powers must feel humble*"

Lastly let's look at Professor Stephen Hawking. No-one can doubt or question his brilliance, with any legitimacy. Professor Hawking is not a Christian, or believes in a personal saving God, but if we look at

---

[121] Encyclopaedia Britannica 2009

some of his writings we can get an idea where he stands on the issue. Professor Hawking states that God may have created the universe sometime in the past and since the universe is expanding this indicates a beginning.[122] Professor Hawking is confirming what I said earlier. The universe had a beginning and has not existed forever. Since we have seen the evidence for the expanding universe we know from this, why a beginning was necessary. He also postulates that the absence of primordial black holes points toward a smooth and uniform formation.[123] Since the Bible says God created the universe from a chaotic void in only one day, this would show a controlled, uniform and smooth creation explaining black holes and why dark matter/energy has never been found. The anthropic principle points to a conscious action to have the universe to be hospitable to human-like beings.[124] Life on earth was difficult for evolution to take place since God created us, in opposition to what Mr. Stenger points out. This makes sense, since the early evolutionary world was so inhospitable.

Professor Hawking's book "*The Theory of Everything*" is a fascinating read. After discussing the anthropic principle, background radiation, the Big Bang, black holes, general relativity, the inflationary model, the Laws of Thermodynamics, quantum dynamics and mechanics, the space time continuum, string theory and the uncertainty principle he concludes with what I consider a very provocative statement. If anyone was able to understand fully all of the physical laws or principles mentioned, they then would be able to understand the thought process of God's creation.[125]

Personally I would never suggest any of these scientists should have been subjected to an I.Q. test, as advocated by Bill Maher. Are naysayers actually saying they are so unbelievably arrogant they actually believe they are smarter than those I have listed? Many pro-evolutionists make these bold claims about the intelligence of anyone who believes Biblical teachings, yet as shown some of the smartest people who have ever lived had complete faith in the Holy Scriptures. If I was to question someone's intellect, I would be sure my cerebral superiority was beyond doubt.

Let's explore in more depth the Big Bang Theory. We have already discussed how the First and Second Laws of Thermodynamics

---

[122] Hawking, Stephen . *Everything. p.11*
[123] Ibid p.67
[124] Ibid p.80
[125] Ibid p.124

strike a fatal blow to this theory. A major flaw in this theory is that the expansion is purely an assumption without an explanation as to the cause of the primordial singularity's explosion. Some have theorised when the Big Bang happened, space and time came into existence. Others speculate that our universe was one of many that originated at the beginning. This goes back to the argument there are many universes and that some of the universes may have different physical laws. A serious flaw in the theory is, since science works in the present and has no direct access back to the beginning, it cannot be observed. As the event cannot be recreated, we can only infer what may have happened based solely upon assumptions.

If you recall Edwin Hubble determined that the universe was expanding. He was able to determine the farther the galaxy, the greater the redshift. This is used today to determine distance between stars and galaxies. The explosion was the result of thermonuclear effects, postulated nuclear physicist George Gamow. With the explosion, all the matter in the universe raced outward, later combining to form galaxies, stars, planets, and asteroids. If the rate of expansion had varied, galaxy formation and subsequent human life would not be possible. Subsequently if the expansion rate had been larger the universe would now be empty. But if we assume a perfect beginning, magnetic monopoles formed. Strangely, none have been detected.

As all this happened, an infinite series of other universes also formed and anti-matter also developed. This is a serious problem for the Big Bangers. When matter is generated in a laboratory there is always a pair. If we get an electron we obtain a positron. If a proton is produced, so is an antiproton. Why is this a problem, you ask? When the two touch each other they annihilate the other and revert back to pure energy.

Our universe consists of ordinary matter. We do not see equal amounts of matter and anti-matter. The only manner in which matter can be produced from energy is through quantum pair production, resulting in equal amounts of each. The only possible solution is that either an anti-matter galaxy formed at the same time or the anti-matter and matter collided after the Big Bang, with the anti-matter annihilated by the abundance of matter. Very convenient, but that violates the rules of physics. If the anti-matter formed other galaxies, would that solve the problem? Since galaxies are known to collide or merge with each other, a violent explosion would occur. Such an explosion should be seen by astronomers. It would appear that no anti-matter was formed contrary to all experiments conducted otherwise.

After about 10^{-43} seconds (Planck time) subatomic particles commenced forming. Then almost miraculously at 10^{-36} seconds, the universe expanded by a factor of thirty. This seems to suggest that a second bang was needed to cause the acceleration of a bewildering process into an even more indescribable process.[126] At this stage ordinary atomic matter takes shape. Hydrogen, helium, lithium and deuterium are the main ingredients. Expansion would continue for eons. As the expansion continues the temperature drops, allowing atom formation. After approximately three hundred thousand years the explosive power seemed to be diminishing. The uniformity of the CMBR (Cosmic Microwave Background Radiation) is quite evident at this point. After about one billion years, the stars and galaxies take form. But what physicists cannot explain is what caused the expanding gases to retreat through collapse. Lastly, about 5Ba the Milky Way formed with the sun, planets and life on the earth began to appear.

What about dark matter? The term dark matter refers to matter that is not readily visible. Anything that cannot be explained can be attributed to dark matter. It cannot be easily shown having a causal effect, it is just assumed. For example, when studying spiral galaxies, an unusual thing is observed. The speed of the moving objects should vary between the centre and the outer edges. When studying Andromeda, this is not what is seen. The rotational speeds are similar in both locations. This is obviously a result of dark matter respond Big Bang theorists. Dark matter is postulated to also be responsible for the clusters of galaxies that formed over 14Ba and should not be in the close vicinity of other galaxies; but this is not the case. The galaxies seem to be congregated fairly close to each other.

So how much dark matter is there in the universe? Varying opinion exists on this matter, but approximately ninety percent has been postulated. That means for every visible star there must be nine more similar masses floating around in inter-stellar space explaining every inconsistency within the Big Bang proposal. This reminds me of Professor Dawkins statement about evidence for evolution. Cosmologists do not need to prove anything or present any evidence, they know dark matter is present and answers all queries into the validity of the Big Bang.

As we have seen, with the Big Bang model, all stars and planets formed from collapsing clouds of gas. Gravity should cause these particles to collide with each other and the gravitational attraction maintains

---

[126] Williams, Alex et.al. *Dismantling*. p. 117

the physical contact. Unfortunately, this is not what lab experiments show. The particles either bounce off each other or they pulverize each other. Since the gas temperature is approximately 10°K (-263°C), and since we know higher temperature causes expansion, lower temperatures cause contraction. Density fluctuation exerts an inward compressive force allowing gravity to overtake the expansive force. This is a circular argument. To produce shock waves we need supernovae to explode; but we also need shock waves to make stars. This means the stars must die quickly and have a short life span to produce the recycling process needed to accommodate the Big Bang time frame.

Why though have scientists not observed measureable amounts of remnants of the explosions and why have they not observed many new stars forming? If the universe began almost 15Ba and there are billions of stars, would you not think that a significant number of them would have died and exploded? These deaths should have been observed. If a star, 'X' billion light years from earth exploded 'X' billion years ago we should be seeing it now. What are the odds numerous stars have exploded, and given the Big Bang time frame many should have died, we have not seen the effects of these explosions?

On average, a galaxy like our own should produce one supernova every twenty-five years.[127] Let's look at predicted supernovas.

Remnant Stage	Billion Years	7000 Years Old	Actual
1st	2	2	5
2nd	2260	125	200
3rd	5000	0	0

What are the three stages mentioned above? As stage one begins remnants of the star accelerate outward from the centre of the supernovae at about twenty-five million kilometres per hour. Obviously the debris does not maintain the initial speed. The second stage is estimated to expand for around one hundred twenty thousand years. Since it has been expanding for such a long period of time, the temperature should start to decrease dramatically. By this time, it is calculated; just fewer than fifty percent would be visible. This means about two thousand, two hundred sixty for Big Bangers and one hundred twenty five for creationists. Although two hundred have been observed; that number is within

---

[127] http://creation.com/exploding-stars-point-to-a-young-universe accessed 2013/22/8

close proximity of the creationist model, it is nowhere near the Big Bang model.

Lastly, the third stage lasts for one to six million years. At this point the S.N.R. debris is so dispersed it possesses no usefulness, or it would collide with other S.N.R's. This would allow about five thousand observable in the Big Bang time-table and zero for the creationist, as the universe has not existed long enough. How many do we observe? The answer is zero. Seems the Big Bang model does not quite fit with the observed.

The Big Bang also relies on the idea that the universe is approximately fifteen billion years old. This is a serious problem for Christians. Their reading of Scripture points to only a few thousand years. That is quite a substantial difference. They both cannot be correct and they do not share much commonality. To further postulate the creationist position, the idea of age must be explored. Different people using different methods can arrive at wildly varying values.

Take for example Professor John Joly who used the accumulation of sea salt to arrive at an age of eighty-nine million years for the earth, while Claire Patterson used isotope ratios to arrive at 4.55 ± 0.7 billion years.[128] They both cannot be accurate. They both made assumptions that cannot be verified. One of the assumptions proven false is: "*Time is a constant*". Scientists now know it is not a constant. Time slows down when subjected to strong gravitational forces and at extremely high velocities. Clocks must be adjusted when the force of gravity changes. The intriguing aspect of this is the observer is unaware time has changed when experiencing it. A person travelling in space would experience different passages of time compared to earth. When traveling near the speed of light, time also slows down, according to Einstein's theory. Theoretically a person travelling at the speed of light in the near vacuum of space could return in a few weeks to him, but years later on earth. How can we know how many years passed in the distant part of our galaxy when one year passed on earth?

The universe also appears to be expanding away from its starting point according to Big Bangers. Unfortunately, the Bible does say the universe is expanding. God stretched out the cosmos when He created it (Job 9:8; Ps. 104:2; Is. 40:22; 42:5; 44:24; 45:12; 48:13; 51:13; Jer. 10:12; 51:15; Zech. 12:1). Many skeptics use the argument that God

---

[128] Williams, Alex et al. *Dismantling* p. 165

created a firmament around the flat immovable earth.[129] What does the word firmament mean? According to my dictionary it means: *"the arch of the heavens; sky"*.[130] Some online dictionaries use the word *"expanse"*. I checked the different versions of the Bible I have and could find the word firmament in only the KJV, ASV, AMP and NKJV. It does not show up in the ESV, NIV, GNT, Living, NSAB, NET, NLT and only two times in the NRSV. The Hebrew word for firmament is *'raqia'*, which can also be translated expanse. The most modern version of the Torah I own (1999) uses the word *"expanse"* in Genesis 1:6,7,8,14,15,17,20, while using the word sky when talking about the area above the earth where the birds fly. Why is this so important you may ask? It is important because significant advances have been made in the past fifty years with regards to biblical archaeology and recovery of the languages in the ANE.[131] As discoveries are made, the meaning of the written words become more apparent. Think in modern terms. What meaning do you think someone in the year 6015 would assign to common colloquial words or phrases used today (Like- *"Sick" "Phat" "SHOTGUN!"*). I am sure they would be uncertain as to the meaning if they saw some in print. Translating can be extremely difficult if the mannerisms are unfamiliar. The more recent translations using *"expanse"* seem more accurate, reflecting a truer intention.

Getting back to the importance of this; expanse would seem to suggest a very large area. Also, when the KJV was written in 1611 there were approximately 15,000 words in the English language. There are now over 250,000 including technical and medical dictionaries. Firmament was the best description they had. As far as being used throughout the Bible, the term firmament is only used in Genesis, Psalms, Ezekiel and Daniel; four out of sixty-six books, and only the older translations. That does not seem to be throughout.

According to Lenny Flank, the word firmament refers to a hard, clear wall or divider. It refers to the ancient belief that the stars and planets were held in the sky by a huge transparent wall or roof. Needless to say, there is no firmament that holds rainwater or stars up in the sky. Ancient writers, having no knowledge or understanding of gravity, simply postulated that this hard clear sphere must be there, or else the stars and planets would all fall down and that the firmament must have windows to let the rain through[132] according to Flank. Since the Earth hangs

---

[129] Stenger. *Hypothesis*. p.175
[130] Winston Dictionary of Canadian English
[131] *The Torah. The Five Books of Moses*. Jewish Publication Society. Philadelphia PA. 1999
[132] http://www.huecotanks.com/debunk/genesis.html accessed 2013/22/8

on nothing (Job 26:7), the other planets and stars must do the same thing. Job is saying that the earth just hangs in space, which we know is true. So there is no necessity for a hard clear sphere to keep the earth in position. They also knew that the clouds provided the rain (Eccl. 11:3, Jdg. 5:4) and the water for the clouds came from the oceans (Eccl. 1:7), not windows to let the rain through. It seems almost all atheists use the same tired arguments and it is easily shown they are wrong. What they say the Bible says, it does not say. True maybe uneducated, naïve, simple man did not know these things, but those in tune with God did know. If there is no God, how do the atheists explain this scientific knowledge, unknown to the pagans and polytheists?

Another important consideration is Hebrew and Greek has masculine and feminine nouns. This is common-place in European dialect and not English. Although translators try to make it understandable, there could also be a slight difference. The old adage "*it loses something in the translation*" holds true here. It is also imperative that the reader remember for whom the words were originally written. It would not be reasonable to write the text in modern-day vernacular. People of the ANE would have no concept of the universe, galaxies, nebulas etc. If someone is going to criticize the wording they should be sure to read the original text. A perfect example is trying to read Shakespeare. The speeches in his plays would be obvious to Elizabethan people, but I remember not having a clue what he was trying to say when I was in high school. To be sure the interpretation is correct; it would be erudite to use a commentary along with the author's words. His or her intent would be more pellucid.

The stars and planets were made on day four. When God made all the other stars and planets in the cosmos He would have had to stretch it out in order to accommodate all the celestial constructs. Now this can lead to some interpretative issues. Exactly what are the waters above and below (Gen 1:6-7)? It refers to the fact that at this time the earth was just water (2 Pet. 3:5). Dry land had not yet appeared. So the water below refers to the water on the earth and the water above would refer to water in the rest of the universe (Ps. 148:4). Water in the rest of the universe cannot be denied by long-agers, as that is how evolutionists tell us water came to be upon the earth. It seems when a person does not cherry-pick one or two verses but incorporates the entire Bible, these arguments fade into the abyss, as modern science is again showing the

Bible's accuracy. God was able to create a universe, billions of light years across in just one day.

Having the dry land appear (Gen. 1:9-13) would produce the super continent known as Pangaea. Geologists confirm the earth was once a single land mass. Moses knew millennia before current geology students about the single super continent. This action would have also most likely caused enormous forces from the moving waters. This should have produced huge deposits of sediment. Obviously since there was no animal life on the earth, there would be no fossils in these deposits. This has been confirmed by geological studies. The deepest deposits, worldwide contain no fossil records. So it would seem God is making the planet habitable for life as creation progresses. What I find most fascinating is that this was not completely accepted by modern geologists until 1960 although it was proposed by a creationist scientist, Antonio Snider, in 1859.

God goes on to create all living creatures on the earth including man; created in God's own image. He gave man dominion over the earth and blessed him, requiring him to fill the earth (Gen. 1:24-28). God rested on the seventh day after seeing everything He had created was very good. This is where theistic evolution is obliterated. How could there be death and suffering in the world if everything was *"very good"*?

We have seen that the Big Bang does actually agree with some things shown in the Bible. The Big Bang and Bible agree that the universe is expanding. The chaotic universe was created in a very short time. The Big Bang has a long-age before morphology caused the original chaos to transform into our complex cosmos. Geology agrees with the single continent at the beginning. But does the universe show any evidence supporting the cosmology of the Bible?

Paul tells us in Rom.1:20, the universe shows God did create everything in it. Ancient people would have to observe daily occurrences. Some of these would be difficult for them to explain without the knowledge of modern science. They would struggle to explain why the sun rose every day. They were able to observe the movement of the stars, but the causes would elude them. The sun would provide heat, but it would not consume its power source as wood, olive oil, etc. To them this would show God's awesome power. But man has become jaded and now ignores these same things and tries to explain it all away. The sun does continue to shine and provide warm to the earth from a temperature of $15,000,000°$ C.

The ozone layer surrounding the earth protects us from the daily eruptions of the sun, ultra violet and infra-red radiation. The sun is just the right distance from us so that the earth is not too hot or too cold. The chances of the earth forming as described in Genesis 1:1 accidentally, is approximately 1 in 12 X10^{62}. To better understand this number let's look at a few other statistics. The odds of being hit by lightning are 1 in 6 X10^5. The odds of thoroughly shuffling a deck of cards and dealing them so the cards come up in proper suited, numerical order for all four suits is 1 in 8 X 10^{67}. Yet we are to believe the universe just happened to form with the earth in its present state?

So how do cosmologists explain away the evidence of divine design? One of the most used methods is termed the 'anthropic principle'. It basically says if the universe did not appear to be designed then we would not be here to observe it. They postulate the multiple universe idea and we just happen to be in the one that is most conducive to life. They maintain this position even though there is absolutely no evidence for multiple universes.

A perfect example for intelligent design is water. Water is considered to be an anomaly. All liquids except water display an inverse relationship between density and temperature. Ice is less dense than water and as a result it floats upon the surface of water. This allows the lakes, streams, ponds etc. to freeze over in the winter yet life will continue below the surface. Water in its liquid form is composed of ice relicts, quasi-crystals, and fluid. The components vary in proportions directly related to its temperature. Quasi-crystals and the fluid are equally present at 37°C, or the natural temperature of the human body. Wow, what a lucky happenstance for us.

The universe started out chaotic and reverted to a state of controlled order. Let's look at the different descriptions as to this formation:
- And the earth was without form and void (KJV)
- Now the earth was formless and empty (NIV)
- The earth was without form and void (ESV)

The only other place this is mentioned is in Jeremiah 4:23. It suggests that the earth lacked any order or content. It means that the earth was not completed and was empty. The Hebrew wording suggests it was a desolate wasteland. This most certainly sounds to me that it was in a chaotic state and had not realised its final form. All the raw materials were present but had not yet taken final shape. But whenever there is ambiguity, the only reasonable thing is to look at the original text. The original Hebrew uses the words *"tohu wabohu"*. This actually means total chaos.

When translators put things into another language it is done so the readers will comprehend. But, *"tohu wabohu"* is exactly what Big Bangers say existed. It annihilates their argument about the universe being chaotic at the beginning, but the Bible saying it was in its final organized state.

"Tohu wabohu" is the same as the Big Bang paradigm which says all the matter was just floating around waiting to join together to make the final order. The difference is creation does it all in one day whereas the Big Bang takes billions-of-years. Unfortunately the Big Bangers do not have anything to explain anyway the Second Law of Thermodynamics. Creationists do have an explanation. Before the creation of the earth and the cosmos there was nothing; no day, no night, no time and no space. At this point the physical laws of the universe are not present. God spoke the universe to be and when God's spirit moved over the faces of the water (Gen. 1:2) everything came into state of control. So the Biblical model fits.

Another problem here is some atheists use this verse to try to confuse things. There are some questions about this translation. According to Flank the original Hebrew text uses a plural noun for God i.e. Elohim, meaning the 'gods' created the universe in the beginning. He maintains Biblical scholars say this is from when the Jewish faith was polytheistic like all other religions of the time. Yahweh was a storm god.[133] These statements are blatantly false. Saying that the word is the plural form only confirms what I said about the Trinity earlier. The Gods would include God-the-Father, God-the-Son and God-the-Holy Spirit. Knowledgeable Biblical scholars recognize this speaks of the Trinity; God's three separate-yet-single personas. Jesus was 'The Son' sent to earth (Gal. 4:4) to take human form to provide the final sacrifice for sin. The Holy Spirit caused Jesus to rise from the dead and is the entity that lives within believers, guiding them in their daily lives. Jesus taught about the Trinitarian nature (John 14-16), showing that the members of the Triune God displayed a selfless love for one another.[134] Both Jesus and the Holy Spirit give all the glory to the Father (John 12:49-50).

It can be understood why this is can be problematic to many people. But if it is approached in purely scientific manner some of the

---

[133] Ibid accessed 2013/21/8
[134] Lockyer, Herbert et. al. *Dictionary*. p. 1073

impediments should dissipate. Let's first look at some mathematics answers to how this could be.

$N = [0,1,2,3,4,...]$
$N_1 = [1,4,7,10,...]$ where $3x + 1$ and $x = 0$ to ∞
$N_2 = [2,5,8,11,...]$ where $3x + 2$ and $x = 0$ to ∞
$N_3 = [0,3,6,9,12,...]$ where $3x$ and $x = 0$ to ∞

N_1, N_2, N_3 are subsets of N. There is no commonality. Each has the same degree of infinity as others, but each also has same degree of infinity as N; i.e. the sum of all three. Each of four sets is countable infinite; i.e. there is a one-to-one correlation between each set and the set of all positive numerals. The fullness of infinity which resides in the sum of all three distinct sets also resides in each of the three sets individually.[135]

Another example is in the realm of physics. I have already discussed the First and Second Laws of Thermodynamics. There is a law in thermodynamics known as the Triple Point. This is where an element or a compound can exist in three states-of-matter simultaneously. But first we must understand a few more simpler laws of physics.

Robert Boyle was a genius who worked with gases. His law says (in simplified terms): *"If the temperature of a gas remains constant, the pressure of a gas will vary inversely proportional to the volume of that gas"*. The formulae is expressed as $P_1V_1 = P_2V_2$. Charles' law states that: *"If the pressure of a gas remains constant the volume will vary directly proportional to the temperature of the gas"* ($V_1 \times T_1 = V_2 \times T_2$). If the temperature of a gas doubles, the volume will also double if the pressure remains constant. To visualize this, think of a hot air balloon. To make the balloon rise, the operator in the gondola will increase the intensity of the flame under the balloon opening. This causes the temperature of the air in the balloon to increase thereby increasing the volume in the balloon. If we have pressure also included we see changing results. For one thing, pressure directly affects the boiling point of a liquid. The cooling system of your car uses a pressure cap on either the radiator or the recovery tank. As the temperature of the coolant heats up, it expands. The radiator cap prevents it from expanding exponentially. This causes the pressure in the cooling system to increase. This also causes the boiling point of the coolant to increase.

---

[135] Fowler, Dr. Stan. *Introduction to Theology I*. Lesson 5. Heritage Bible College

This brings me back to the Triple Point. The Triple Point is where the element/compound can exist as a vapour, liquid and solid in equilibrium all at the same time. If the temperature and pressure are both at a specified point we can see this occur (see chart below).

Element/Compound	Temperature °C	Pressure kPa
Carbon	4,492	10,132
Arsenic	820	3,628
CO_2	-56.60	517
Acetylene	-80.7	120
Nitrous Oxide	-90.81	87.85
Xenon	-111.8	81.5
Neon	-248.58	43.2
Hexafluoroethane	-100.07	26.60
Nitric Oxide	-163.65	21.92
Deuterium	-254.52	17.1
CO	-205.05	15.37
Hydrogen Chloride	-114.19	13.9
Nitrogen	-209.97	12.6
Iodine	113.50	12.07
Methane	-182.47	11.7
Hydrogen	-259.31	7.04
Ammonia	-77.75	6.076
Helium-4 (Lambda point)	-270.96	5.1
Formic Acid	8.25	2.2
Sulphur Dioxide	-75.46	1.67
Chloroform	-97.72	.870
Water (H_2O)	0.01	.6117
Oxygen	-218.79	.152
Ethylene	-169.2	.12
Zinc	419.50	0.065
Titanium	1,668	5.3×10^{-3}
Palladium	1,552	3.5×10^{-3}
Ethane	-183.26	8×10^{-4}
Butane	-138.6	7×10^{-4}
Platinum	1,772	2.0×10^{-4}
Iso-butane	-159.60	1.9481×10^{-5}
Ethanol	-123	4.3×10^{-7}
Mercury	-39	1.65×10^{-7}
Argon	-189.34	68.9

If we observe water we see at a temperature of 0.01°C, just slightly above freezing, and at a pressure of .6117 kPa, water can actually be in three states at the same time. Since earth has a standard pressure of 101.325 kPa the water must be under a partial vacuum.

I could imagine some will question how this is possible. Since a pressure increase, increases the boiling point; the inverse is also true. A pressure decrease will decrease the boiling point. To understand this, just think of the air conditioning in your auto.

When the refrigerant gas is compressed the temperature increases. As it passes through the condenser, the temperature decreases. As it passes through either the orifice tube/TXV/Expansion Valve the pressure decreases; causing a temperature drop. The cold refrigerant then enters the evaporator to cool the air. So under exacting conditions a specific refrigerant can be a fluid and a vapour at the same time in the same container. We can have three distinctive states of matter coexisting at the same time. It is actually quite fascinating to see this happen.

Water, at 0°C is ice. At 0.01°C it would still be a solid unless left at that temperature for a long period of time. As we apply a vacuum the boiling point decreases. With a quantity of ice at the temperature just above freezing, the ice will still melt and if the pressure is low enough the liquid will start to boil. Under the correct conditions we could have solid ice that is melting and changing to a vapour almost immediately, hence the term Triple Point. Since it is not an anomaly for an element or compound to be in three states of matter simultaneously, why would people be so concerned about God, a non-corporeal Being, having three distinct personalities yet be one God, as He created the laws of physics?

Judaism also was never polytheistic (Deut.6:4). Judaism is based on the belief of the one and only true God. True, Abraham was a polytheist before he was called, but after he went to the Promised Land he worshiped only God. He was the first to practice Judaism and the Jews are descended from him. Additionally it was Moses who wrote the Pentateuch. He worshipped only God. He would not write as a polytheist. For those who challenge this saying, Moses would have been illiterate; I only have one comment. Would a child raised in the house of the Pharaoh of Egypt be totally unschooled and unable to read or write? Does that make any logical sense whatsoever? Lastly the storm gods of the people in the OT were: Ba'al- Philistines, Ada- Akkadian's, Ishkur- Sumerians, and Hadad- Aramaic. The arguments made to the contrary, are outright falsehoods.

Now at this point some Christians veer off. Theistic evolutionists say there is a gap between verse one and two. This allows for the long ages of the earth to connect creation with evolution. They should be very careful here. They are trying to equate creationism with evolution. This is just "*barking mad*" according to Professor Dawkins. They accept the old age of the earth and in doing so open up a can of worms that cannot be re-sealed. Genesis 1:1 and 1:2 are joined by a *"waw"* disjunctive in Hebrew. It means that it was created this way and did not become that way at a later date. Gap theorists say the original creation was destroyed by Satan's rebellion and became formless and void. This allows for a second creation that can fit within the long-age timelines of evolutionary thought. But Jesus taught God created in the beginning (Mat. 19:4). Christians must believe what Jesus taught or they defeat everything He did.

Another problem faced, because of skeptics, is misinterpretation. Old Hebrew is not written in the same manner as modern English. The syntax and style is quite different. Reading Genesis or any other part of Scripture as modern script, will most likely lead to inserting things not intended and omitting important concepts. Jesus confirmed the authority of Scripture (John 5:46-47; 10:35; Mat. 5:17-18; Luke 24:25; 4:44; Mark 10:2-8). It is not wise to try to read things into Scripture what is not there, nor intended. It can only lead to erroneous interpretations. So how does a person know how the universe came to be?

We have already seen God created everything in the beginning (Gen. 1:1-2). There was no time, no space, no energy, in the sense we understand, and no matter. God commanded the universe into being through His spoken word, *"ex nihilo"* (Heb. 11:3; Ps. 33:6, 9). The universe appeared out of nothing. Does this sound familiar? It should. But their argument breaks down here as time, space and mass cannot exist without the other.[136]

During the creation story the word *"day"* is used (Gen. 1:3-5). Now, this is where some people go astray. The word day can have many uses. To know which one to use we must look at the context. Taking verses out of context cause people to go off kilter most times.

Since the sun is not yet made, it cannot mean from sunrise to sunset or sunset to sunset. The rest of the chapter uses the word day the same, so it is not an indefinite period of time. It can only mean the full rotation of the earth on its axis. We can then hypothesize that, at this time, the earth was spinning in space. Additionally if this was shown to anybody they would in most likelihood interpret this to mean one twenty-four hour day. Arguing long-age day only makes sense if trying to incorporate theistic evolution into the text. God also confirms that it is just one

---

[136] Williams, Alex et.al. *Dismantling*. p, 225

day when He gave the Ten Commandments to Moses. God commanded the Israelites to observe the Sabbath since God made Heaven, earth, sea, and everything in them in six days (Ex. 20:11). Since the earth was spinning and God had created the light, not the sun, to rule the day, it is only reasonable to assume it was a twenty-four hour day. If the earth spun much slower, life would not be possible since the dark side would cool too much from facing away from the light. If it spun too quickly life on earth would also be drastically affected by cyclonic winds. Since the sun had not yet been created the light source must have been the same that will provide light for the new creation (Rev. 21:23; 22:5)

Another theory about the day four controversy comes from the use of the Hebrew word 'c'sh'. This term is used many times in the Bible, but nowhere does the context refer to manufactured.[137] Either interpretation can explain how there was light before day four.

In the discussion on the Big Bang I have kept it simple as all aspects of long age theory can get quite complicated. Let's look at easy-to-understand aspects of science that help to confirm the Bible and short-age time of the universe. Everyone should be familiar with comets. Comets are balls of ice and dirt which circumnavigate the solar system in highly eccentric orbits. The nucleus of the comet is solid. The area surrounding the comet that looks sort of like fog is called the 'coma'. During their orbit as it approaches the sun the comet increases in speed. The gravitational pull causes the comet to slingshot around the sun. With the close proximity to the sun a tail develops. This is a stream of vapour following the comet, pointing away from the sun. This vapour is actually part of the comet melting, to form the visual vapour. This means that the comet is losing some of its mass. Each orbit around the sun reduces the size of the comet and therefore will limit the time the comet can exist. It has been estimated that in general a comet can continue this orbit for, at most, ten thousand years before losing all of its material.

The best known comet for us is Halley's Comet. It orbits the sun and returns to the earth approximately every seventy-six years. It appears that this comet loses about one percent of its mass every revolution. This provides a maximum of seven thousand six hundred years for Halley's Comet. Since it is still quite visible today and does not appear to be anywhere near diminishing to the point of extinction we can assume it has not been around for that long.

---

[137] Walton, John H., *Genesis Commentary*. p. 125

Obviously a comet cannot exist for billions-of-years. So why do we still have comets today? Astronomers have a ready answer. They point to new comets being formed or current comets gaining new material through the 'Oort cloud'. This is a vast reservoir of ice material. But no-one has seen the 'Oort cloud'. There is absolutely no evidence whatsoever for the 'Oort cloud'. It is purely conjecture. If we can see stars that are billions of light years away why has no-one seen this phenomenon that must be within or just outside our solar system? Another suggestion has been the Kyper belt. Unfortunately it is not in the correct location or has the proper mass to fuel comets.

Let's look at other fascinating coincidences. The sun is about four hundred times further from the earth than the moon. Coincidentally it is also four hundred times larger. This allows the sun and the moon to appear to be the same size in the sky. The earth takes almost three-hundred sixty-six days for one trip around the sun. The earth is three-hundred sixty-six percent larger than the moon. It takes 27.32 days for the moon to orbit the earth. The moon is 27.32 percent the size of the earth.[138] Genesis 22:17 tells us that Abraham's descendants would be as the stars of the heaven and the sand on the seashore, both about 1 X 10^{22}.[139] Let's explore that number a little; 10^{22} stars. There are 31,536,000 seconds in every non-leap calendar year. If you could count a number every second without stopping, it would take 3.17 X 10^{15} years to do reach this quantity. When we look into the night sky, on a good night, we can count about three thousand stars. How did the authors of the Bible know about the quantity of stars in the universe? Although not conclusive, it is interesting.

The distant starlight issue can be seen as a problem for both Big Bangers and creationists. Who has a better answer for the question? Scientists tell us there are stars, billions of light years away. Since we see this light does this mean that the light has been travelling for billions-of-years to get to the earth? We have already discussed that time and the speed of light are not constants as once thought. It has also been suggested that maybe the speed of light is actually slowing down. Also if the stars were closer to the earth at the time of creation and they expanded away from the earth since the universe is expanding, how does anyone knows for sure how long it actually took for the light to arrive? The light would be travelling toward the earth at about three hundred

---

[138] Knight, Christopher & Butler, Alan
[139] Lisle, Jason. *Astronomy*. p. 33

thousand km. /sec while the star was expanding away at a similar speed according to astrophysicists. If God did create the universe through supernatural means, how can natural men even begin to explain the causalities?

The Big Bang has a serious issue called the 'Horizon Problem'. After the initial explosion temperatures would be extremely high. But quickly the temperatures would start to deviate from one another. Unfortunately, it can be shown the temperatures throughout the universe are quite similar, as displayed through the CMBR. This radiation has a temperature of 2.7° K with a deviation of about 1 in 10^5. The only acceptable explanation is that two distant parts must have exchanged energy to be at the same temperature. Light also has not had enough time to get from one outer edge of the universe to the opposite edge of the universe. Remember the two are expanding away from each other in opposite directions. They are twice the distance from each other than the time elapsed. Do not forget a light year is a measurement of distance not velocity.

This is explained away with the inflationary model. The inflationary model allows for two different expansion rates. After the initial explosion the expansion rate was extremely high. Almost immediately the expansion rate increases dramatically. Magically, the expansion rate then slows back to the original rate long before any planets or stars have had the chance to form. I can only assume then, since scientists think the expansion rate is increasing; it must have reversed and sped up again. This means that the speed of light would have to be accelerated to faster than the inflationary expansion rate. But how do you get the rate started and how do you stop it?

So it seems that there is a problem that is unexplained for both. One cannot denigrate the other for a problem with which they themselves have to deal. Big Bangers cannot criticise the Bible until they can solve their own problems first, since creationists also have a hypothesis, but cannot prove their position. The difference is creationists present their beliefs as faith-based and do not ridicule people who believe something else.

How has the idea of a long ago formed earth taken hold of our society? It comes from dating methods. The best known method is Carbon dating. Many people erroneously think that fossils millions-of-years old can be dated using this method. Carbon-14 (^{14}C) can only be used for short-time scales because of its relative short half-life.

All life on earth is based on Carbon. When something dies ^{14}C is released. The half-life for ^{14}C is five thousand seven hundred thirty years. That means that after five thousand seven hundred thirty years only half of the original carbon remains. After another five thousand seven hundred thirty years only twenty-five percent of the original remains and so on. After ten half-lives of decay there is approximately 0.1 percent of the original ^{14}C remaining. So this method is only effective for dating things less than about fifty thousand years old. It is used to date wood, charcoal, bone, shells, plants etc. Interestingly ^{14}C can form from cosmic rays bombarding the earth's atmosphere. When high energy particles from outer space collide with gas molecules in our atmosphere they can produce unattached neutrons. These neutrons are then free to bond to ^{14}N (Nitrogen-14) resulting in the formation of ^{14}C. Remember your basic chemistry from high school.

^{14}N + Neutron → ^{14}C + Proton

The ^{14}C atoms fall to earth and are able to combine with O_2 (Oxygen) to form CO_2. Included with this is a stable ^{12}C isotope and quantitative amounts of radio-active ^{14}C. This is not the problem you would think since there are approximately 1×10^{12}, ^{12}C atoms for every one ^{14}C atom. This allows about 1×10^{24}, ^{14}C atoms across the face of the earth every year. Since plants and trees inhale CO_2 as part of the photosynthesis process, it will become part of the cellular structure of the living organism. People will absorb this into their cells since we eat plants or eat animals that eat plants. After the organism perishes ^{14}C decays back to the original Nitrogen.

^{14}C → $14N$ + Beta (β)

To determine the age, the value of ^{14}C present is compared to an initial known sample. This is valid as long as the initial content is known. If it is incorrectly assumed, the measurements can vary wildly as we are about to see.

Coal, for example, is mostly comprised of Carbon. Most coal is dated to the *Pennsylvanian* or late *Carboniferous* period about 300Ma. Since this coal is said to be hundreds of millions-of-years old there should be no detectable ^{14}C inside. Coal samples were selected from the U.S. Department of Energy Coal Sample Bank. Three hundred samples from across the geological time frame including *Palaeozoic, Mesozoic* and *Cenozoic* periods were collected. Using an accelerator mass spectrometer (AMS) these samples were analysed for ^{14}C content. The total amounts of ^{14}C found in these samples averaged 0.25 percent of ^{14}C in the atmosphere today. Ten half-lives or fifty seven thousand three hundred years would produce 0.1 percent. So the coal samples that are supposed to be from 1.8Ma to 4.6Ba test out to be around fifty thousand years. Perplexingly, the sample from Kentucky should have tested at three hundred to three hundred eleven million years, according to the Geological Column Chart; yet it came out at forty five thousand six hundred years. That does not appear to me to be a very accurate result. The other results varied wildly from 0.13 percent ± 0.02 for *Palaeozoic* to 0.35 percent ± 0.03 for *Mesozoic* strata. While it is significantly more than the proposed six to ten thousand years of the Bible, it is most certainly much closer than the long-age proposal.

A completely bewildering example comes from my alma-mater, Brock University in St. Catharines, Ontario, Canada. The Department of Earth Sciences at Brock University tested a large bore hole in Oak Island, Canada. After repeated attempts the calculated age was approximately positive three thousand years. This would mean that this particular piece of wood died sometime in the early 5,000's A.D. Given that it was tested in the early 2,000's A.D. this would seem to suggest that there is something terribly wrong, especially as it was tested repeatedly. I guess the reasons these are never reported in the general media is a comment from J.O. Brew: *"If a ^{14}C date supports our theories, we put it in the main text. If it does not entirely contradict them, we put it in a footnote. And if it is completely 'out of date', we just drop it"*. Now, that is good science. Are there other examples of testing that is obviously just plain wrong?

The following are examples of other tests that are not even close to the actual age:
- A fresh seal skin tests to be one thousand three hundred years old
- A living mollusc tests at two thousand three hundred years
- The antler of antelope tests at five thousand three hundred forty, nine thousand three hundred ten and ten thousand three hundred twenty years at different spots
- A mastodon tested at seven hundred fifty years more on the outside than on the inside

Are there any tests that suggest a young earth? They are listed below
- A bristle cone pine is approximately four thousand three hundred years old—dated via tree rings.

- The Great Barrier Reef is less than four thousand two hundred years old—dated via measuring the growth rate for twenty years.
- Niagara Falls' erosion rate (four to seven feet per year) indicates an age of less than eight thousand four hundred years.
- A relatively small amount of sediment is now on the ocean floor, indicating only a few thousand years of accumulation. This embarrassing fact is one of the reasons why the continental drift theory is vehemently defended by those who worship evolution.
- Ice accumulation at the poles indicates less than five thousand years[140]
- Deposits at the mouth of the Gulf of Mexico show about four thousand five hundred years of mud deposits. All major rivers show the same result
- If four and one half billion years old the oceans should display dozens of miles of mud. They do not.[141]
- Sodium content of the oceans do not correlate to four and one half billion years
- Diamonds from Namibia which are supposedly billions-of-years old showed levels of ^{14}C. Interestingly artificial diamonds can be formed from graphite in a matter of minutes if exposed to the conditions scientists say are necessary for their formation.
- ^{14}C in coal that was supposedly hundreds of millions-of-years old.
- ^{14}C is found in almost every fossil tested, even those dated to hundreds of millions-of-years.[142]
- Spiral galaxies tend to become twisted due to the varying rotation rates of the inner and outer regions. After a few hundred million years it should be so tightly wound, the spiral would be non-existent.[143]
- The magnetic forces of Jupiter, Uranus and Neptune should be extremely weak if actually billions-of-years old[144]
- Since magnetic fields decay at a rate of about five percent per century, the field would have precluded any life millions-of-years ago.[145]

---

[140] http://www.creationtoday.org/evidence-from-earth/ accessed 2013/22/8
[141] Dr. Russell Humphreys. Louisiana State University, Baton Rouge, LA, 1972
[142] Sarfati J. *Greatest Hoax*. p. 199
[143] Lisle, Jason. *Astronomy*. p. 66
[144] Ibid .p. 60

- Although virtually all secular scientists believe that stars form spontaneously, the physics behind this alleged process is riddled with difficulties. According to the standard model of star formation, stars form from a collapsing nebula. When gas is compressed it heats up. This higher temperature creates extra pressure which resists further compression. The collapse would have a tendency to stop before the star ever formed. Formula $P=nkT$ ($P=$ pressure $n=$number density of particles $k=$ Boltzmann constant $T=$ temp in degrees Kelvin[146])

Quite interestingly Abraham Loeb from Harvard's Center for Astrophysics says, when speaking of star formation, that if the existence of stars was unknown there are plenty of reasons as to why a person could think star formation is impossible.[147]

The next surprise that confounds long-agers is Helium. Helium is one of the most abundant elements in the universe. On earth it can be found within granite, deep underground. When tests are performed, Helium is found in places where it should no longer exist. In 1974, bedrock in Fenton Hill, New Mexico was drilled. The Granodiorite rock from this area was formed when molten magna was cooled, forming Zircons. Combining with close-by electrons, Helium atoms formed. Helium atoms are very small in size and tend to escape the rock quite easily. This particular rock formation was classified as *Precambrian* by using the Geological Column Chart. This makes the formation about one and one half billion years old, based upon lead-lead dating. After such a long period of time all the Helium atoms should have disseminated from the rock and escaped into earth's atmosphere. When tested, large amounts of Helium were still present in the zircons. At a depth of one thousand metres fifty-eight percent of total Helium was present. But to confound the technicians the escaped forty-two percent had remained in the surrounding biotite material.

To be sure this was not an anomaly; readings were taken at just under three thousand metres. At this depth, seventeen percent of the Helium was retained. It is quite reasonable to assume the difference was due to the amount of heat being generated by the surrounding material. Think back to high school physics. Heat causes atoms to increase in ve-

---

[145] Ibid p. 59-60
[146] Ibid p. 85
[147] Tyson, N. deGrasse, *Death by Black Hole; And Other Cosmic Quandries*. W.W. Norton & Company, 2007 p. 187

locity. If atom action was increased and helium is an element that easily passes through objects, it should be obvious that more of the element would indeed escape and move upward. This is a serious problem. Increased temperatures for millions-of-years would have completely depleted the helium stores; yet this is not what we see. Mathematically the measured rates actually confirm an age of six thousand ± two thousand years. Isn't true science, namely mathematics, wonderful?

How are rocks dated? One method is to use the age of the fossils contained within. The age of the fossils tells us the age of the rock and the age of the rock tell us the age of the fossils. I am not making this up. Let's check the World Book Encyclopaedia. Volume fifteen, page eighty-five says the following: "*age of the rocks may be determined by fossils found within them*". Volume seven, page three hundred sixty-four says: "*scientists determine when fossils where formed by finding the age of the rocks in which they lie*". Now, tell me that is not circular reasoning. But we shall give the scientists some latitude here. Many use the geological column to determine age of the fossils. This means that wherever the fossil is found, that layer of sediment is compared to the geological column. If the chart says one hundred million years, then that is the age of the fossil. On the surface that seems to be sound reasoning. The problem is if the geological column chart is compared to any formation on earth the two do not match. How can this be? As Sherlock Holmes would say "*Elementary*". It should be obvious that the geological column is a fabrication of imaginative minds. But, is there any factual way to determine age?

Igneous rocks are dated via radiometric dating. Igneous rock forms when lava cools and is hardened. This is when Potassium begins to decay into Argon. Dating is then accomplished. Since scientists tell us all of their statements are known, we can assume that if a rock is dated then that will be the actual age of the rock. There should be no samples that provide wild exaggeration of age since this is the preferred method of dating.

Samples were sent to Geochron Laboratories in Massachusetts, as well as other reputable labs. They were not told who requested the testing only that rocks needed to be dated.

- In 1990's five rocks from the Mt. St. Helen eruption were collected. This was about ten years after the eruption. So the rocks should have dated to about ten years. The results were: 1) three hundred forty thousand years 2) three hundred fifty thousand

years 3) nine hundred thousand years 4) 1.7 M years 5) 2.8 M years.
- Mt. Hualalai in Hawaii erupted in 1801. Twelve samples from this eruption were also analyzed. The testing should have shown about two hundred years. The results ranged from one hundred forty million to 1.41 billion years
- Eleven samples taken in New Zealand known to be from 1954 and 1990's were analysed. The results ranged from hundreds of thousands to 3.5 Million years

More examples of dating gone wrong:
- What about the Grand Canyon. Rock strata from a lava bed at the top date to 2.6 billion years. Lava bed from the bottom dates to 1.1 billion years
- Santo Domingo rock formation in Argentina was dated at two hundred twelve million years in 2002 via Argon/Argon method. Recently rechecked due to bird-like footprints and dated to thirty-seven million years using Lead/Uranium.
- Fossil KNM-ER 1470 (Kenya National Museum-East Rudolf specimen # 1470) dated at two hundred twelve to two hundred thirty million years. Richard Leaky disputed that saying it was two to five million years old because of the *australopithecine* and mammal fossils within. His testing returned the results he wanted, 2.61 million years. Recent testing provides a date of 1.9 million.

Do fossil fuels take millions-of-years to form? It is said that oil being pumped from the ground are fossil fuels from dinosaurs. It has been under the ground all that time. Well, there are some problems with this also. On April 16, 1999 The Wall Street Journal published an article *"Oil Field Grows as It is Tapped"*. The article referred to the Eugene Oil Field operated by the PennzEnergy Co. In 1989 it was pumping four thousand barrels per day. Suddenly it started to pump thirteen thousand barrels per day and reserves have increased from sixty million barrels to four hundred million barrels. On September 26, 1995 The New York Times ran an article that said "*Geochemist Says Oil Fields May Be Refilled Naturally*". In Halifax, Nova Scotia Canada, a processing plant converts 508,030 tonnes of waste sewage into seven hundred thousand barrels of oil per annum. The process is also being used in Israel by *Bio Petrol* to reduce the amount of imported oil they use.

If it takes millions-of-years for fossil fuels to form from dead organic life, how is the above possible? It cannot be discarded as creationist propaganda. The Wall Street Journal and Geotimes are most certainly not creationist supporters. This evidence cannot be dismissed.

Next we'll look at Polonium Halos in Granite. Dr. Robert V. Gentry is a nuclear physicist who worked thirteen years for the Oakridge National Laboratory. He has studied the creation vs. evolution debate and while he worked at Oakridge, he was known as the world's leader in Polonium Halos. Polonium-218 has a half-life of about three minutes. When the rock is heated the halo disintegrates. Evolutionary geology tells us halos contained within granite formed as hot magma was slowly cooled over long ages. But since the low half-life, the Polonium would have disappeared long before the magna could have cooled the necessary amount to form the granite rocks.

We have already discussed this with the igneous rocks above. So the question that begs asking is *"How in the world did they get there"*? Dr. Gentry is so convinced that this gives credence to creationism and utterly destroys the Big Bang Theory, on March 22, 2000 he wrote a letter challenging any scientist at the National Academy of Science to debate him on live Prime-time TV to refute his suppositions. ABC, NBC and CBS all declined the invitation. To date no scientist has accepted his offer. USA Today refuses to print his challenge. Dr. Gentry has been censored to the point he filed a lawsuit for discrimination.

Why do they refuse to debate Dr. Gentry? If creationism is pseudo-science, as said by many of the long-agers, it should be quite simple to refute all of his evidence. Of what are they so afraid? If they feel his evidence is wrong or inadequate, refute it and put the matter to rest. Is it possible the evidence is so irrefutable they hope ignoring it will make it go away? Creationists try to answer queries of people, who are confused about the evidence, not sweep it under the rug.

The Geological Strata also poses some problems for billions-of-years. According to the Geological Column Chart, layers of ground have been building for hundreds-of-millions-of-years. Each layer on the surface was deposited over time. Mud being placed there would dry forming these layers. This should tell us how long it took since each layer would correspond to a known time period.

But here is where the problem begins. Cut vertically the layers display no erosion, no gopher or rabbit holes, of any kind. There are areas of the strata that are still bent tightly. If the layers took millions-of-years to form, the mud should have straightened out from gravity and other exterior forces acting upon them. It is almost as if the layers were laid upon each other over very short periods of time.

In the Grand Canyon, trees have been found standing upright through millions-of-years of deposits. When Mt. St. Helen erupted the force caused the bark of trees to be stripped making them look like hydro poles. As the trees became water-logged, they inverted. They would eventually sink in the water and imbed into the bottom of a river. This is the exact appearance in the millions-of-layers of earth. Kind of suggests something radically different from millions-of-years of soil build-up.

Does all of this prove Genesis or the creation story? It does not. Does it call into question the long-age theory? Absolutely! We can only look at the evidence and see which hypothesis makes the most sense. The Big Bang just seems to have too many flaws. Big Bangers also use their theory to vilify the creationist position. They say the creation story is wrong because the Big Bang says this happened. Well, that is not valid evidence. The evidence only qualifies the Big Bang because the Big Bang explains how the evidence should look.

Presenting what the Bible says is fine. But the evidence must be scrutinized with an objective mind; difficult to do. But if the evidence is look at quantitatively it seems that long age just does not cut the mustard.

Chapter 4
Creation or Evolution?

Evolutionists state there are millions of fossils all over the world showing how evolution took place. You can actually see the species changing through time, according to evolutionary proponents.

Let's see what these people hypothesize. (All evidence said to further evolutionary thought is that of the long-agers and not mine. My arguments against evolution will be presented showing it to be the worldview it is). Evolution, through Natural Selection, shows that all living things in the world arose from a single inorganic source. Man in particular arose from an ape-like ancestor that lived a few million years ago. Man did not come from apes as some people say. This was accomplished by a series of changes or mutations as a result of environmental and genetic factors. Apes evolved on a totally different evolutionary path. Although his father proposed the idea of evolution years before Charles Darwin, it was he that brought the idea into the mainstream with his book 'On *The Origin of Species*', even though it had been proposed as far back as ancient Greece (Epicureans). Darwin just beat out Alfred Russell Wallace who was almost ready to publish his theory. The basis for Darwin's book came from his five-year voyage around the world on the HMS Beagle. It was his observations that led the way for evolution to become a paradigm, said to be proven as absolute fact.

Without doubt, all living beings have the ability to pass genetic information to their offspring by reproducing. Evolutionists say there are two ways this happens; either micro or macro-evolution. Micro-evolution shows that when mutations happen, it is in the genetic sequence. A mutation is a random, naturally occurring mistake that is displayed through reproduction. There are external forces such as chemicals or radiation that can effect these changes. Natural Selection is environmentally caused changes, where the species' fittest members survive, and the weaker members die off. The third aspect to evolution is 'Speciation'. This happens when some of the species mutate to the point where they are unable to reproduce with other members of their species. This only allows reproduction with like beings.

The evidence for evolution is theorized to be not hard to find. It is everywhere; in anthropology, palaeontology, zoology and molecular biology, depicted through the tree of life. Each discipline in itself is not solid proof, but collectively they are said to be undeniable. The original theory does have some problems and when discovered are dismissed, while the new evidence hones the theory, sticking to its roots. These discoveries have caused a number of scientists to disagree with mistakes that cannot explain the evolutionary tree completely, but small changes do not change the absolute fact of evolution.

'Homology' has caused some minor problems due to the similarity between species. It does not necessarily mean the species are related. These features can come about as the result of different gene segments converging through unrelated species. All this shows, humans did evolve from lower life forms over millions-of-years and were not created by a designer in six days a mere six thousand years ago. With all the overwhelming evidence, how can anyone doubt evolution?

Dr. George Wald, winner of 1967 Nobel Peace prize said that there is only two possibilities for life to have originated on the earth; creation or spontaneous generation, i.e. evolution. He maintains that spontaneous generation was disproven over one hundred years ago. This only leaves design by an intelligent creator. Since this is unacceptable to evolutionists, purely for philosophical reasons, they believe what is impossible; life on earth is by chance.[148] American engineer Henry Morris had his own take after reading Darwin's book. His analysis of the book stated that evolution cannot be proven or subjected to scientific testing. The result is that a naturalistic position is the only possible explanation, short of a Supernatural Creator.

The science refuting evolution is quite in-depth and complete books have been written in rebuttal. Here I shall try to keep it fairly simple. Anyone wishing to explore it further should investigate the books listed in the bibliography. According to evolutionists, life began from inorganic matter. Through the eons, all life has evolved to the current level of sophistication. Anaximander of Miletus, an ancient Greek philosopher,

---

[148] Huse.S. *Collapse of Evolution*. p. 3

decided that organic life can develop on its own from a non-organic source. This theory has since been disproven via the law of biogenesis (interesting choice). The idea came from maggots 'magically' appearing in spoiled food, namely meat. It was the experiments of Redi and Pasteur that proved maggots did not just spring forth from inorganic material but was actually hatched fly eggs laid within the meat, proving that life can only come forth from life. At the 1985 conference attended by Sandage, another world renowned scientist, Dean Kenyon, a biophysicist from San Francisco State University, spoke. When discussing how the first living cell would almost miraculously appear from non-living matter he stunned the audience. He was of the opinion that cell complexity and the amount of information contained within DNA was not an accident, but the universe came into being through a designer of life. Sandage would later say that many evolutionary scientists are now engaged in faith-driven endeavours. Evolutionists now avoid any discussion on how life came from inorganic material like the plague; because they know it is impossible. Some go as-far-as to say it is not part of evolutionary teaching. My question is *"then, from where did the first life arise?"* Life from non-life would then be termed a miracle.

Evolution relies on mutations that eventually form a new species. Obviously these mutations must be positive and further the ability of the species to progress to a more complex organism. In order to change from the parents, there must be a change in the genetic information. This is where problems can arise. Humans have twenty to thirty thousand genes.[149] In order to get a new species the genes from the parents must change to the same configuration. If we take fifty genes and mutate them, the chances of the two results being exactly the same are 1 in 3×10^{64}. But when we look at DNA, there are three billion letters stored in each human cell and there are trillions of cells. This is known as specified complexity. A single human could produce 2×10^{1675} different sperm or egg cells.[150]

DNA is also responsible for the two hundred bones, six hundred muscles, ten thousand auditory nerve cells, two million optic nerve fibres, one hundred billion brain-cell nerves and four hundred million feet of blood vessels with capillaries, in the typical human being.[151] Since evolution is supposed fact, the odds are truly mind-boggling of changes on the scale shown by the fossil records according to evolutionists. Statistically

---

[149] This can vary depending on source used and ranges from 20,000 up to 40,000
[150] Safarti, Jonathan. *Greatest Hoax.* p.44
[151] Blanchard. J. *Evolution, Fact or Fiction?*

the chances of a single protein molecule being able to complete what evolutionists tout is 1 in 10^{158}. There are 4.73 X10^{17} seconds in fifteen billion years. So these changes would have to occur over 10^{141} times every second for the entire fifteen billion years, the universe is said to have existed, just to arrive at the correct combination, statistically.

These principles are combined to form the core of the evolutionary model. The traditional Darwinian outlook holds that small incremental changes in structure and behaviour, brought about by the Natural Selection of variations, produce, after a long period of time, organisms that differ so greatly from their ancestors, that they are no longer the same organism, and must be classified as a separate species. This process of Speciation, repeated over the three and one half billion year span of time since life first appeared on earth, is said to explain the gradual production of all of life's diversity.[152]

This is what scientists call macro-evolution; the dramatic change in species. What has been supposedly observed is what is termed Natural Selection. Even creationists agree this does occur. The best example is Adam and Eve giving rise to the many different 'races' on the earth. But this is not evolution per se, it is simple genetics. Some evolutionists have proposed that the races are at different points on the evolutionary time scale. Thankfully that is not the position of all evolutionary proponents.

How do creationists explain the 'races'? It is actually quite simple. Remember your genetics' classes from high school. There are recessive and dominant genes. Again let's keep it simple. Say Adam and Eve were both olive skin (does not matter where we begin). If they had the genes AaBb to give this skin colour their offspring could retain the AaBb characteristics. A and B are the dominant genes, where 'a' and 'b' are the recessive genes. This combination allows for sixteen variants. That is quite a few variations and could easily explain why we have so many people who look differently but are still the same species. But the ethnicity of the world's population is more than skin deep. How do we explain this?

In April 2005 this was unequivocally confirmed. Kian and Remee Hodgson were born to Kylie Hodgson, nineteen and her partner Remi Horder, then, just seventeen. What is so unusual about twins? Kian who weighed in 2.69 kg is black and her sister Remee who was born one mi-

---
[152] http://www.huecotanks.com/debunk/intro.htm accessed 2013/15/08

nute later weighed 2.73 kg is Caucasian.[153] Mr. Holder and Ms. Hodgson are both children of black fathers and white mothers. It should be quite apparent that Kian would have inherited the dominant black genes while Remee the white genes. Both had beautiful blue eyes, while Remee has blonde-as-blonde-can-be hair and Kian has dark black hair. Ms. Hodgson's mother remarked that most likely Remee's skin would darken with time. The exact opposite occurred. As time progressed she became even lighter. Kian's eyes also changed from blue to brown. Since skin pigmentation is controlled by seven separate genes, the egg and sperm normally will contain a variety of the genes. But there will be times when only the single dominant gene will be within the cell or egg. If sperm containing just the white genes impregnates a similar egg and a sperm with just black skin genes fuse with a similar egg, two babies of different colour will result. The statistical odds of this happening are 1 in 1,000,000. This would allow for all the possible variations we see today. Given the myriad of different skin tones amongst the races, we can see there are many different possibilities. This oddity has also happened to:

- A Ghanaian woman and German father in Berlin. Fraternal twins were born that appear to be of different races.[154]
- A Mexican mother and black father have twins. One is black, the other Hispanic in appearance.[155]
- Cheryl and Karen Grant of Chelmford, England are daughters born to a Caucasian mother, and a Jamaican father. Karen appears to be black, verses her sister who looks white.[156]
- Triniti and Ghabriael born to Khristi and Charles Cunningham, of Akron, Ohio. 'Triniti' has all the classic features of an African American. 'Gabe' is ivory-white with steely blue eyes and blonde hair.[157]
- Leah and Miya Durrant, appearing mixed, were born to mixed-race parents Dean Durrant and Alison Spooner. This is the second set of twins to display this curiosity. Lauren is white with

---

[153] http://snopes.com/photos/people/mixedtwins.asp accessed 2012/30/09
[154] http://www.huffingtonpost.com/2008/07/25/biracial-twins-born-to in_n_115037.html accessed 2013/30/09
[155] http://community.babycenter.com/post/a24105555/bi-racial_twins?cpg=3 accessed 2013/30/09
[156] http://bifactor.wordpress.com/2009/01/05/new-year-new-biracial-twins-mystery/ accessed 2013/30/09
[157] http://www.dailymail.co.uk/news/article-1360424/Ohio-twins-Triniti-Ghabriael-Cunningham-The-black-white-rulebook.html accessed 2013/30/09

blue eyes and red hair. Hayleigh had black skin and hair like her dad.[158]

Recent analysis has shown that ancient Europeans had blues eyes and olive coloured-skin. Obviously this trait has since ceased through Natural Selection. Anyone who claims any racial diversity is pitifully uninformed.

Molecular biologists tell us every human alive is a descendant of an African woman who lived about two hundred thousand years ago.[159] Anthropologists contradict this when they say Homo erectus fossils older than two hundred thousand years found outside Africa could not be related to this individual. Why the disagreement if evolution is science?

The next question would be, "*did Adam and Eve really exist, and all humanity originate from a single pair?*" These questions are the cornerstone of the Christian faith. Mitochondrial DNA analysis seems to indicate humanity can be traced back to a single female ancestor as already shown. Similarly, the Y-chromosomal DNA indicates that humans trace their origin back to what could be interpreted as a single man.[160,161] Evolutionary biologists quickly assert that Eve and Adam could not be the first humans. They suggest many Eves and Adams existed.[162] This Adam and Eve were the lucky ones who, by pure happenstance, survived and actually procreated. What is most amazing is 'Mitochondrial Eve' lived about two hundred thousand years ago and 'Y-chromosome Adam' lived about three hundred forty thousand years ago. These timelines seem highly suspicious. We now know, through undeniable scientific analysis, at the very least, an 'Adam' and an 'Eve' did exist, contrary to what Professor Dawkins[163] and his cohorts contend. The question we must ask is "*Which account seems more coherent*"? Looking only at the timeframes, the biblical account is the more prudent elucidation. The scientific case for the biblical Adam and Eve seems to stand firm. Why are evolutionists so conflicted with each other? Fact should be fact.

Mutations do occur and can be more detrimental than beneficial. Remember the Second Law of Thermodynamics. Can this have a detri-

---

[158] http://www.mailments.com/2012/05/the-bi-racial-twins-in-europe/ accessed 2013/30/09
[159] Johnson, Philip. *On Trial* p. 99
[160] http://www.icr.org/article/7899/ accessed 2014/22/02
[161] http://www.newscientist.com/article/dn23240-the-father-of-all-men-is-340000-years-old.html#.VQrgc47F854 accessed 2014/22/02
[162] http://www.sheffield.ac.uk/news/nr/putting-adam-in-his-rightful-place-1.342467 accessed 2014/22/02
[163] *The Unbelievers, What are you willing to Believe*. DVD documentary. Directed by Gus Holwerda. Revelation Films. 2014

mental effect of the human genome? Plant geneticist Dr. John Stanford and some of his colleagues used computer simulations to show that the human genome would be fatally flawed if we have been here for thousands of generations.[164] This is confirmed in Richard Lenski's experiment that lasted nearly one decade. The results show, a loss of information, not the gain that is necessary for evolution. Through the thousands-of-generations of mutations, the result was a germ that was essentially the same. This tells us that mutations did occur, but without the addition any new genetic material. Mutations do make changes, but they do not add to the species, let alone cause a transformation. So if additional information is not added to the genome how did we get from single-celled amoeba-like material to the complex organisms needed for evolution?

Does this display itself in humans? Michael Woodley, a psychologist, of the Umea University in Sweden has performed studies to determine if reaction times are decreasing, increasing or remaining stable amongst humans. He measured reaction times prevalent today and compared it to those of the 1800's. Reaction times measured by Francis Galton[165] taken in 1889 were compared to those taken in the last decade. The average male response in 1889 was one hundred eighty-three milliseconds while the female was one hundred eighty-eight. The result in 2004 provided a male response of two hundred fifty-three and a female of two hundred sixty-one milliseconds. The men were 38.25 percent slower and the women were 38.83 percent slower. In addition to the one hundred new progressive mutational degradations per generation that have been studied, it appears that we are not evolving, but if you accept naturalized evolution, we are actually de-evolving. Humans are decaying (Rom.8:19-22) at an alarming rate. This should be called Reverse Natural Selection.[166]

Do fossils then prove evolution? Are there any out-of-place fossils? The following are examples of out-of-place fossils. First let's look at *Archaeopteryx*. This has been presented as an intermediate step between dinosaurs and birds known as the *'Cursorial'* theory. But if the evidence was so conclusive, why do even palaeontologists so vehemently disagree over this? Dr. Storrs Olson, who happens to be the curator of birds at the National Museum of Natural History of the Smithsonian Institution in Washington D.C., has written an open letter saying that the postulation of dino-to-bird evolution is a scientific hoax. A confirmed evolu-

---

[164] Safarti, J. *Greatest Hoax*. p. 58
[165] Charles Darwin's first cousin and a founding member of Eugenics
[166] www.dailymail.co.uk accessed 2013/13/05

tionist calling another evolutionist's work a hoax is to say the least, quite fascinating, especially when it has been suggested the article was a complete fabrication. There also seems to be rampant chicanery, as palaeontologist Kraig Derstler of the University of New Orleans in Louisiana said most displays have had reconstruction performed to make it prettier and the deceptions are getting harder and harder to spot.[167] So controversial are these claims that two opposing papers were published only a few days apart by Chinese scientists. Xing Xu et al. wrote in Nature magazine about finding the smallest known *Theropod*. It was a crow-sized bird termed *Microraptor Zhaoianus*. Apparently it lived in trees about 125Ma. But near the same time, and I am sure to their consternation, Fucheng Zhang and Zhonghe Zhou published a report in Science magazine about *Protopteryx Fengningensis*; apparently the true flying bird fossil. Extinct birds, known as the *Enantiornithines*, date to about 120Ma. Their fossil displayed imprints of downy feathers in addition to a structuralized pelvis; i.e. the *procoracoid* process and is a strong indication of how modern birds are able to fly. A plethora of secular headlines arose with titles such as *"scientists say 'Fossil Shows Birds Came before Dinosaurs"*.

    The museum in Milwaukee WI., actually displays them together. Is this a deliberate attempt to pull-the-wool-over-the-eyes of the general public? Now it should be noted, I am not condemning all evolutionists based solely on this. As shown above there are many who do not hold to this so-called paradigm. But there is much dissension on the subject. The experts cannot seem to agree on much. I am left a bit bewildered. How can there be opposing opinions on something that has been proven as fact?

    Archaeopteryx is claimed to be one hundred fifty-three million years old. Its cousin *Confuciusornis* is dated at one hundred thirty-five million years. But miraculously their common ancestor *Sinosauropteryx* and *Caudipteryx* are both dated at one hundred twenty-five million years. This is like being born before your great-grandfather. How can they have lived before their common ancestor? Remember what was said about evidence being found out of place.

    Archaeopteryx also had the unique bird lung design. Birds have a design that allows for maximum oxygen intake; presumably because of the higher altitudes at which they fly. Reptiles though, use a bellows-like respiratory system. Reptilian design would countermand the avian de-

---

[167] Jeff Hecht, *"F is for fake"*, New Scientist **165**(2226):12, Feb. 19, 2000

sign. This paradox works against Natural Selection; so it seems, in this case, the reptile-to-bird evolution does not seem feasible. Remarkably a bird's brain is three times that of an equivalent sized dinosaur. The *Archaeopteryx* also had auditory improvements needed for flight. So if the *Archaeopteryx* lived about twenty-eight million years before its ancestor the *Sinosauropteryx* and *Caudipteryx*, this seems to me to be de-evolution.

A parrot's beak, that had been fossilized, found at the University of Berkeley, was determined to be from the *Cretaceous* period. The problem for evolutionists is this is when dinosaurs lived, whereas if birds evolved from dinosaurs they were not alive at this time. Examination of the beak showed it was near identical to that of a modern-day parrot. Loons, frigate-birds and assorted other birds have been found in the same rock formations. There are many other examples of anomalous evidence from artefacts. There are in fact not only out-of-place fossils; there is evidence that seems to refute the other position. How does a person know what is real? Bulleted points below show the artefact, location and where in the geological strata it appears.

- A metallic man-made sphere in South Africa at 2.8 billion years
- Metal vase, belly shaped. 11.43 cm X 16.51 cm X 6.35 cm X .3175 cm thick, Dorchester MA. Six hundred million years[168]
- Iron nail embedded in sandstone found 1844 in Scotland. Three hundred sixty to four hundred eight million years
- Gold thread twenty cm deep inside rock, found 1844/22/06 in Tweed U.K. three hundred twenty to three hundred sixty million years[169]
- Iron cup inside centre of broken chunk of coal. Found 1912, Wilburton OK. Three hundred twelve million years
- Carved stone with diamond shaped etching found at Webster IA. 1897/02/04. Two hundred eighty-six to three hundred sixty million years[170]
- Bones of male skeleton found on coal-bed capped with 5.08 cm slate rock below surface, Macoupin IL. Two hundred eighty six to three hundred twenty million years.[171]
- Barrel-shaped block of silver in Wilburton IL. Two hundred sixty to three hundred twenty million years

---

[168] Reported in Scientific America 1852/05/06
[169] Reported in London Times 1844/22/06
[170] Daily News. Omaha NE. 1897/02/04
[171] The Geologist. Dec 1862

- Gold chain found in Carboniferous coal at Morrisonville IL. Two hundred sixty to three hundred twenty million years.[172]
- Smooth, polished concrete blocks 30.48 cm³ forming a wall found 1.2 km. below surface, Heavener OK. Two hundred sixty to three hundred twenty million years
- Semi-ovoid tubes found in *Cretaceous* rock at Saint-Jean de Livet, France. Sixty-five to one hundred forty-four million years.
- Chalk ball found seventy-five metres below surface, Laon, France. Forty-five to fifty-five million years[173]
- 24.13 cm X 24.13 cm X 5.715 cm piece of carved stone displaying chopping like marks in Barton Cliff U.K. Thirty-eight to fifty-five million years
- Complete Human skeleton found sixty-two metres below mountain brow in Tuolumne Table Mt. CA. thirty-eight to fifty-five million years
- Bone that has incision marks, Billy France twelve to nineteen million years
- Human jaw found fifty-five metres below surface near mastodon debris, Tuolumne Table Mt. CA. Nine to fifty-five million years
- Human bones found in tunnel under lava Placer County CA. 8.7+ million years
- Complete buried human skeleton Midi de France, France. Five to twenty-five million years.
- Bones fractured longitudinally allowing marrow extract. Bone with engraving and a flint flake. Dardanelles Turkey. Five to twenty-five million years.
- Seventy-five bone fragments displaying methodical fracturing allowing marrow extract. Pikermi Greece. Five to twelve million years.
- Incised bones along with stone tools, pieces of hard, burned clay and slag from fires hotter than a campfire. Entrerrean Formation, Argentina. Five to twelve million years
- Human humerus bone found beside crude stone tools. Gombore, Ethiopia. Four to four and one half million years.
- Human vertebra, hearths, slag, burned bones and crude flints. Monte Hermoso, Argentina. Three to five million years.

---

[172] Morrisonville Times. 1891/11/06
[173] The Geologist. April 1862

- Partial and full human female skeleton found covered by clay with coral & shell fragments. Castenedolo Italy. Three to four million years.
- Human skeleton found in the 1850's three metres below surface. Savona, Italy. Three to four million years.
- Human femur found in limestone quarry. Sterkfontein, South Africa. 2.2 to 3 million years
- Incised bones showing signs of butchering made with a flint blade. Monte Aperto, Italy. Two to three million years
- Human lower jaw bone with two molars. Miramar, Argentina. Two to three million years.
- Shark teeth displaying signs of drilling reminiscent of necklaces used by South Sea Islanders. Red Crag UK. 2 to 2.5 million years
- Shell carved into the shape of a human face. Red Crag UK. 2 to 2.5 million years
- Human jaw with debris from flint workshop, five metres below surface and infused with iron oxide 1855 Foxhall UK. 2 to 2.5 million years.
- In 1899, a clay model of a small human found ninety two metres below surface Nampa, Idaho. Two million years.
- Bone tool used for leather work. Olduvai, Tanzania. 1.7 to 2 million years
- In 1932, five human jaw fragments, human femur, stone hand-axes found in fossil-bearing beds. 1.7 to two million years.
- In 1974, human talus identical to modern humans Koobi Fora, Kenya. 1.5 to 1.8 million years.
- Third molar of human jaw found in stream bed. Trinil, Java. 1.1 to 1.9 million years.
- Splintered animal bones, charcoal and a hearth foundation found. Trinil Java, .836 million years
- Piece of sawn wood found by S.A. Notcutt, Cromer Forest Bed UK. .4 to 1.7 million years. Metal coin found thirty-six metres below surface Lawn Ridge IL. .2 to .4 million years. [174]

It is not creationists that are saying the fossils are out of order, but so are secular scientists, archaeologists and universities; only they are not pub-

---

[174] Cremo, and Thompson. *Hidden History (All bulleted points in this above section are from their book. The book is quite long and has a chart to simplify their findings.)*

lically admitting it. The findings show that modern man was on the earth much sooner than the geological strata would have us believe.

Here is some other evidence of more out-of-place artefacts with geological dates given:
- Sulfur Springs, Arkansas. Nov. 27, 1948: iron pot inside the centre of lump of coal. Coal dated Mid-Pennsylvanian. 295Ma.
- In 1944 brass bell found encased inside a lump of coal 300Ma. Bell contains mixture of metals totally different from modern alloy production. Bell embossed with a figure similar to the Babylonian Southwest Wind Demon, Pazuzu.
- A hammer head found inside a piece of limestone rock in June 1934. The rock has been dated to the *Cretaceous* period. The hammer is made from an iron mixture with chlorine.
- June 11, 1891 in Illinois, a circular-shaped gold chain about twenty-five cm. long was found contained within a lump of coal. Interestingly the artefact has since disappeared.
- Mount Roraima in Venezuela 2,810 metres above sea level, laid down about 1.7Ba (during Pre-Cambrian period); spores and pollen fossils found in the Roraima formation.[175] Seed bearing plants date from Devonian period 380Ma. These fossils then are 1.3 billion years 'out of date'.
- At the Grand Canyon Hakatai Shale (Pre-Cambrian) nine samples showed cryptograms. Minimum two hundred million years out-of-date.
- In Canada a fresh unfossilised wooden log containing the original cellulose, within a 'kimberlite pipe', i.e. volcanic rock that is a natural source for diamonds. The rock is estimated to be fifty-three million years old.[176]

Out-of-place fossils are found quite often. Archaeologists, palaeontologists and geologists just revise their interpretation to fit evolution, even if it means saying diametrically opposing things right after one another.

A university student found what he thought was belemnite[177] in Warwick UK. He took it to the leading palaeontologist at his university for identification. The professor identified the sample as an iron-concretion.

---

[175] Stainforth, R.M. *Occurrence of pollen and spores in the Roraima Formation of Venezuela and British Guiana*, Nature 210(5033): p. 292–294, 1966/16/04.
[176] www.plosone.org accessed 2012/19/09
[177] An extinct fossilized squid-like creature.

He thought it was from Warwick, Queensland Australia. The professor explained it is easy to be duped, as iron-concretion can do peculiar things. It takes an expert to properly identify the substance. After talking for some time, the student reaffirmed the sample was from Warwick UK. At that point the professor changed his identification and said yes it was belemnite. His opinion changed only when the place of the find changed.[178] Taking this statement into account and given the evidence presented in Michael A. Cremo and Richard L. Thompson's book, they have completely decimated evolutionary theory.

One of Professor Dawkins' best quotes is: *"Evolution has been observed. It's just that it hasn't been observed while it's happening"*.[179] What a strange comment. It has been observed, just not while it is happening. Does that not mean then that the observation is open to interpretation? After-all, seeing something after the fact can be subjected to scrutiny, and if observed after the fact, there must be undeniable evidence the interpretation is factual. Could it also be this is more a faith-based position? Since it violates the principles of science, I would say yes. Faith is the confidence that what we want, will actually happen. (Heb. 11:1). Henry Morris had an interesting take on this hypothesis. He said:

> *"Creation is not taking place now, so far as can be observed. Therefore, it was accomplished sometime in the past, if at all, and thus is inaccessible to the scientific method"*

If it has been observed, where are all the transitional fossils? The intermediate forms seem to be missing and have not been since the days of Darwin. What about the Cambrian Explosion? How do evolutionists explain the vast phyla that appeared at this time, but have not surfaced since then? How do they also explain the apparent stasis of some species?

It has also been said the evidence for evolution is air-tight even without fossils.[180] What evidence is there without fossils? The whole premise is that fossils show the progression from single-celled organisms to complex life-forms and Darwin admits that absence of evidence is evidence of absence; i.e. absence of transition forms show there was no transition. Professor N. Heribert Nilsson who worked at Lund University in

---

[178] Story relayed by Taz Walker
[179] Moyers, Bill. *Battle Over Evolution.* Interview with Richard Dawkins. Now on PBS network. Dec. 2004. See www.pbs.org/now/transcript/transcript349_full.html
[180] Dawkins, Richard. *The Greatest Show on Earth.* p. 146

Sweden decided after forty years of studies, the missing transition fossils will most likely never be found.[181]

Cambrian Explosion refers to the large number of fossils that appeared during this Cambrian period. It appears that all of the phyla were deposited during this time about 542 to 488Ma. There has been some reputed missing link fossils discovered; reputed, due to the controversy surrounding them. Jay Gould wrote that the absence of intermediary stages of the transitions between species is a never-ending problem for the theory of evolution.

One of the biggest problems seems to be the human/ape evolution. The common argument is that humans evolved from apes, which is not what evolution teaches. Evolution says that all apes are part of the *Homininae,* as are humans. Humans and apes supposedly evolved from a common ancestor millions-of-years ago. An argument for this has been that humans and chimps, for example, share about ninety-five percent similarities in their genetic code; although some evolutionists claim it is as high as ninety-nine percent. Humans have twenty-three chromosome pairs, whereas apes have twenty-four. The maximum similarity could then be ninety-six percent, if everything else was the same. This theory goes back to 1975 before it was possible to compare base pairs through a process called hybridization. Since geneticists have now shown that human DNA has three trillion letters even a one percent difference is quite substantial. Recently this statement has been shown to be an unmitigated myth. In 2012 it was estimated that the actual difference is more likely thirteen to nineteen percent[182] and could be as high as thirty percent.[183] Additionally, Y-chromosomes are completely different between the two species.[184] Geneticists have also proven humans are ninety percent similar to a cat, eighty percent similar to a cow, seventy-five percent to a mouse, forty-four percent similar to a fruit fly, fifty percent similar to a banana, twenty-six percent similar to yeast and eighteen percent similar to Thale Cress (a weed).

The question that must be asked: "*is this a biological or a morphological condition?*" Biologically, most animals on earth will be similar since we have a common food source, i.e. plants and fruits. Also if the

---

[181] Blanchard, John. *Evolution.* p, 9
[182] Dr. Jeffrey Tomkins and Dr. Jerry Bergman. *Creation.* Vol. 26 # 1 p. 94-100 April 2013 cited in CMI Magazine. Vol. 36 # 1 p.36
[183] Dr. Jeffrey Tomkins. *Answers Research Journal.* Vol. 6 # 1 p. 63-69 Feb 2013. Cited in CMI Magazine. Vol. 36 # 1 p.36
[184] CMI Magazine. Vol. 36 # 1 p.36

animals varied dramatically then it would not be possible to digest the different amino acids, sugars and fats etc. Since humans and apes have a similar physical appearance does it not make sense they would be similar biologically? As human DNA has three billion base pairs, a four percent variation would be one hundred twenty million base pairs. Think about the math we did earlier with only fifty genes.

Large DNA sequences can be controlled by small control sequences. When sexual reproduction is compared, there are virtually no similarities in the rearrangement of DNA fragments through chromosomal interaction. To say that a mutation was able to cause transmigration from apes to humans seems impossible. There are other examples of apparent close genetic make-up. The haemoglobin in reptilian crocodiles is 17.5 percent similar to chickens while 5.6 percent similar to vipers (also a reptile). Camels and nurse sharks also have the same structured antigen receptor protein. I doubt many would say this makes them common ancestors.

The so-called missing link has also been reputed to display in the formation of embryos. When a human embryo is becoming a baby, it was said that it went through stages exemplifying the evolutionary path. Humans were said to have gills like fish, a tail like a monkey etc. This fallacy is perpetrated by abortion clinics upon unsuspecting women. As a bit of an aside, and I am sure will generate a great deal of hate for me, Planned Parenthood founder Margaret Sanger was a staunch eugenicist. She believed in the proper order of humans. Australian Aborigines were only one step more evolved than chimpanzees and not quite on the level of blacks, Jews and Italians.[185] Abortionists reassure the person, it is not a baby, but a fish, or a reptile or something less than human. Falsely termed the biogenetic law (which ironically was disproven by von Baer even before Haeckel envisioned it); it was disseminated by Ernst Haeckel. So pervasive is this notion, many text books still contain these drawings. Basically, Haeckel showed, through his drawings, that the embryo retraces an evolutionary path from the beginning, to the current state of the species. Remarkably L. Rutimeyer, professor of zoology at the University of Basel and William His, a professor of anatomy at the University of Leipzig, demonstrated it to be a complete and unmitigated fraud in 1874. They were able to show without any doubt the drawings were modified to make them look more similar. So why is it still in modern text-

---

[185] Weiland, Carl. *One Family* p. 65

books almost one hundred fifty years later? Why are some evolutionists so unsure of their position they have to commit outright fraud?

It has become so common place that in 2001, one hundred twenty-seven cases of misconduct was lodged with the Office of Research Integrity, US Department of Health & Human Services. This was the third annual increase in unscrupulous behaviour.[186] Why the need for such fraud? The answer is not scientific but philosophical; outright greed! There is a great deal of money to be made furthering the case for evolution. The saddest thing is that these blatant lies are still being taught to unsuspecting and unknowledgeable young people in our schools, sometimes by ingenuous teachers, even if it means being disingenuous to students. With time they will sort out the inaccuracies. This is much preferred to them being Creationists retort unbelievers.[187] They are only reiterating the nonsense they were taught.

von Baer's law states the youngest embryos tend to look similar due to the generalized features shared. As they age to the pharyngeal stage they look similar, but this is the very basic form at the earliest stage. This does not mean that as they age they still appear the same. As the specialized features appear the similarity disappears. But, there are exceptions. Vertebrate embryos look similar at the pharyngeal stage but remarkably different before and after this stage. Amphibian toes develop from buds through a growth outwards, while mammals develop from a plate as the material between the toes disappear; totally opposite. Mammals could not have evolved from amphibians according to this evidence. Sir Gavin de Beer, embryologist and past director of the British Museum of Natural History, was able to demonstrate while there was an apparent correlation; it was not consistent with a common ancestry. Embryo development points away from evolution and towards a designer.

Along with the missing link connection, evolutionists point to vestigial organs, showing man has evolved from a lower life form to the more complex life form of today. Less than one hundred years ago scientist's maintained man had one hundred eighty vestigial organs. They now know that this was completely false and without fail almost every one of these have been removed from the list. It is now accepted that these organs do actually perform a needed task. A few more problematic examples are:

---

[186] Check, E., *Sitting in judgment*. Nature **419**, 2002; p. 332
[187] Zivkovic, Bora (aka "Coturnix"), *Why teaching evolution is dangerous*. Scienceblogs.com
    25 August 2008 cited on http://creation.com/evolutionist-its-ok-to-deceive-students-to-believe-evolution. accessed 2014/08/12

1. The appendix is not useless but is part of the immune system and is an important part of the lymphatic system. [188]
2. The tonsils have a similar function in the entrance to the pharynx. The pineal gland secretes melatonin which is a hormone that regulates the circadian rhythm and has other functions.
3. The thymus is part of the immune system, related to T-cells. HIV attacks T-cells, rendering them ineffective and for this reason is eventually fatal.

Even if there were a few vestigial organs, that would not prove evolution. As S.R. Scadding, a confirmed evolutionist, said: *"vestigial organs provide no evidence for evolutionary theory"*.

Some of the finds claimed to be intermediate stages and now totally rejected are:

- *Homo sapiens- Neanderthalensis* (Neandertal man): These people stooped like we would expect an ape-man to stoop. It is now accepted this may have been due to diseases like rickets. They were fully human and had many of our cultural diversities
- *Ramapithecus*: Now proven to be an extinct orang-utan
- *Eoanthropus* (Piltdown man): Fraud that used a human skull cap with an orang-utan's jaw bone. Although a poor forgery it was hailed as a missing link for forty years.
- *Hesperopithecus* (Nebraska Man): This missing link was drawn to show a close resemblance to man only later to be shown it was based completely on a pig's tooth.
- *Pithecanthropus* (Java Man): Now accepted to be fully human and termed *Homo erectus*
- *Australopithecus Africanus*: No longer accepted to be a missing link. Accepted as completely ape-like
- *Sinanthropus* (Peking man): Reclassified as *Homo erectus*, fully human.
- Nutcracker Man: Found in east Africa in 1959 was proclaimed by National Geographic as a missing link between man and apes. Now known to be skull of extinct ape.
- Lucy: Found in 1974 by Donald Johanson in the Great Rift Valley, Ethiopia, she was touted as the proverbial missing link between man and apes. Famed anthropologist Richard Leakey

---

[188] Frederic H. Martini. *Fundamentals of Anatomy and Physiology*, Prentice Hall, Englewood Cliffs, New Jersey, 1995. p. 916

said of the find, most of it is imagination.[189] In 1987, Dr. Charles Oxnard, Professor of Anatomy & Human Biology at the University of Western Australia, determined Lucy belongs to *Australopithecines*. They are neither human nor ape but are a unique species according to Dr. Oxnard.
- A fossilized elbow, plus *Laetoli* footprints are exactly similar to modern man, four million years before the first Neandertal.[190]

It appears that every missing link that has been found has either been shown to be a fraud, fully man or fully ape.

Neandertal man was supposedly the predecessor of modern man. It has been suggested that a Vitamin 'D' deficiency would produce the same appearance. Recent finds though have shown Neandertal and modern man to be identical kinds. They not only lived together, they interbred.[191] This is a poor choice of words. Since they are not evolutionary relatives, they cannot interbreed.[192] They are both fully human.

Are there any missing links from other creatures? *Pakicetus*, found in Pakistan, was known as the 'walking whale'. Dr. Philip Gingrich said this fossil showed a direct correlation between a land mammal and a modern whale. The proposed fossil reconstruction seemed to show this to be acceptable. That was until a few years later; more found bones proved it to have no similarity to the 'walking whale' depicted.

Tiktaalik was touted as the final unshakable link between fish and amphibians. This was the very first creature to leave the ocean and crawl onto dry land. But an unusual footprint found in Poland showed a four-legged creature that walked on dry land eighteen million years before *Tiktaalik* left the ocean. This brings us to the confounding fact of stasis.

Stasis is where evolution seems to have taken a holiday, as opposed to punctuated equilibrium, where sudden development occurs. The animals have displayed significant changes over millennia but suddenly, just stop evolving. In Hertfordshire U.K. an *ostracode crustacean*

---

[189] *The Weekend Australian*, May 7–8, 1983, Magazine section, p. 3.

[190] Tuttle, R. 1990. *The Pitted Pattern of Laetoli Feet.* Natural History. March Issue, 60-65. Quoted in Lubenow, *Bones of Contention, p.* 170.

[191] Walker, M. et. al. 2008. *Late Neandertals in Southeastern Iberia: Sima de las Palomas del Cabezo Gordo, Murcia, Spain.* Proceedings of the National Academy of Sciences.

[192] Duarte, C. et al. 1999. *The early Upper Paleolithic human skeleton from the Abrigo do Lagar Velho (Portugal) and modern human emergence in Iberia.* Proceedings of the National Academy of Sciences. 96 (13): 7604-7609. Cited on http://www.icr.org/article/neanderthal-were-modern-men/

was found mostly intact, although fossilized. It was put into the category of living crustaceans. Remarkably it is quite similar to *myodocopids*, even though it demonstrates virtually no change in the last four hundred twenty-five million years. So I guess this particular animal has reached the pinnacle of its evolutionary change. Another example is the army ant. Thought to have evolved on different continents and evolving several times, the modern ant resembles the one from 100Ma. A fossil of a shrimp/prawn that is reportedly one hundred fifty million years old was termed *Antrimpos*. It lived during the *Triassic* and *Jurassic* time periods. This organism seems to display change and no change at the same time. Unfortunately it is now extinct so we can make no modern comparisons, but no change over two separate periods suggests some serious problems.

How is stasis explained away? Living through an unchanging long-term environment, has been proposed. There is nothing to cause the necessary changes so everything remains status-quo. So for millions-of-years everything remained stable, then suddenly an undetermined amount of time shows drastic changes caused the creatures to evolve to combat the environment? It should be obvious that climatic changes can be dramatic, but to have a climate that remains virtually unchanged for eons seems to stretch the imagination.

An extinct fish, the *Coelacanth*, was caught near Indonesia in 1938, even though it was said to have gone extinct sixty-five million years ago. This fish has apparently remained the same for all that time. There have been some dramatic changes in earth's biosphere during the same time. Why did the *Coelacanth* remain unchanged while scores of other animals made dramatic strides in evolutionary changes?

Stephen Jay Gould said about stasis, that there does not appear to be much of a change between the appearances and disappears of species. There also does not seem to be a transitional transformation. Any new species appears in its final state according to Mr. Gould. It seems that stasis has been shown over and over again as a routine occurrence and is not an exception to the rule, as many evolutionists attempt to make it. An excellent example of this is the Bighorn Basin in Wyoming, U.S.A. During the early stages of mammal formation, reportedly 5Ma, a complete record was laid down. Palaeontologists were excited that this would produce a complete record of the transition. Unfortunately this was not the case. While the apparent record remained unchanged for around one million years, it was at this point the species vanished. Stephen Stanley uses a bat and whale to show bats and whales are evolved from a common mammal ancestor around 10Ma. So it seems that evolution happens in a way that cannot be detected, and remains a mystery as to how it actually occurs; but it has been observed? Stasis and punctuated equilibrium seem to be diametrically opposed to Darwinian Theory. The only thing that explains the quick disappearance of species is catastrophic occurrences.

The *Permian* extinction, about 245Ma, wiped out around ninety percent of all species and the K-T extinction that ended the *Cretaceous* era about 65Ma are the best known examples. The biggest problem with these mass extinctions is in order for evolution to continue, the older less advanced mechanism must die out slowly so that a new and better version can be formed. But this is not what is seen. What the record shows is sudden appearance of a new species followed by eons of stasis. Niles Eldridge retorts that "*Most palaeontologists were aware of the stability, the lack of change we call stasis*". Palaeontologists brush this off as no results, rather than contradictory evidence. The absence of gradual changes continues to be dismissed as gaps in the record. How convenient is that? The importance of the fossil record is diminished as more and more evidence is found.

Next we shall look at living fossils. This is a term used to describe animals alive today that should be extinct. I have already mentioned the C*oelacanth*, but is this an anomaly? Let's first look as a small animal called *Gansus*. It had wing claws, not uncommon on a few modern birds, but it looked just like a duck or a loon. According to the strata it is one hundred twenty million years old. But this is not possible as ducks had not yet evolved. So Geographical News stated that although it looked like a duck and acted like a duck, it was not a duck. I guess the old axiom "*if it looks like a duck and walks like a duck*" should now be finished "*does not mean it is a duck*".

Other examples of living fossils are:
- Fossil resembling Purple Heart Sea Urchin (*Spatangus*), renamed *Holaster*
- Gladiator insect
- *Cryptobranchid* salamander
- *Pleurotomaria*
- *Athedon*
- *Penaeus*
- *Mesozoic* Squirrel

The pygmy whale is the final ancestor of ancient whales believed extinct. "*The living pygmy right whale is, if you like, a remnant, almost like a living fossil,*" said Felix Marx, a paleontologist at the University of Otago in New Zealand. "*It's the last survivor of quite an ancient lineage that until now no one thought was around.*" This whale grows to just six and a half metres. They live in the southern hemisphere and are rarely seen. An arched, almost frown-like nose makes it quite odd looking compared to other whales. When analyzed via DNA testing it appears that this whale evolved from the Humpback and Blue whales about 17-25Ma. But their skeletal remains actually resemble *Cetotheres*, a species of whale that died out around 2Ma and appeared around 15Ma. So why are they still here? In addition to this frogs, salamanders, boa constrictors, lizards, sharks, rays, sturgeons, paddlefish, salmon, herring, flounder, bow fish, hagfish, box turtles, soft-shelled turtles, alligators, crocodiles, gavials and lamprey that completely resemble modern fish have shown up in dinosaur layers.

What are some of the other dinosaur-layer finds that stymie evolutionary scientists? The answer is parrots, owls, penguins, albatross, sandpipers, avocets, Tasmanian Devils, squirrels, possums, hedgehogs and beavers. In total, four hundred thirty-two mammal species have been found in dinosaur layers[193] but strangely, none of the mammal or bird fossils have ever made it into any museum display. I wonder why this is.

To finish this off, we'll examine a previously unknown species of mammal found in China that is supposed to be large enough to eat young dinosaurs. This is remarkable since palaeontologists tell us that the only mammals around when the dinosaurs roamed the earth were rat or mice size in stature. This fossil is reportedly one hundred thirty million years old and therefore lived during the *Mesozoic* era. It was discovered in the Liaoning region of China. It should be apparent that as more research happens and discoveries are made the theory of evolution looks less and less probable.

What about the dinosaurs? Do they not prove evolution and millions-of-years? The K-T extinction that ended the *Cretaceous* era about sixty-five million years ago was said to have wiped out the dinosaurs. Geologists tell us that a huge meteor crater in the Chicxulub region of

---

[193] Kielan-Jaworowska, Z., et al. *Mammals from the Age of Dinosaurs*. Columbia University Press, NY, 2004. Cited by Dr. Carl Warner, interviewed by Don Batten.

Mexico's Yucatan Peninsula was discovered showing that it was a meteor getting through the earth's atmosphere that caused their extinction. It was not immediate events like many people suppose, but it was the catalyst that led to their supposed demise over thousands-of-years. We have already discussed the reliability of dating methods used to validate this claim. Let's explore the subject of dinosaurs in some detail.

The word *dinosauria* (dinosaur) was first used by Dr. Richard Owen M.D. in 1841. It comes from the Greek meaning *deinos* (fearfully great) and *sauros* (a lizard). The common vernacular now is dinosaur and literally means fearfully great lizard. Did they not die out sixty-five million years ago and was it actually more recent? Are there any texts before the age of paleontology that speaks of dinosaurs? Are there are any eye witness accounts of dinosaurs? Is there any evidence that dinosaurs survived the K-T cataclysm? Does the Bible mention dinosaurs? The astonishing answer to all of these questions is a resounding YES!

First we must ask if there are any words or descriptions of dinosaurs used elsewhere. The word dragon comes to mind. Now many people think of the cartoonish, mythological drawings we have all seen. But if a person objectively looks at the renderings for dragons they do resemble what artists have reconstructed from dinosaur fossils. Remember fossils in museums are renderings done by artists based on the paleontologist's suggestions. Fossilized bones are found and then the being is reconstructed often with much of the finished product missing. Look at the *Brontosaurus*. It may not be common knowledge to many people but the *Brontosaurus* never really existed.

At the height of archaeology in the nineteenth century there was extreme pressure to produce fossils. Two major players in the game were Othniel Charles Marsh and Edward Drinker Cope. They were bitter rivals who were always trying to upstage the other. Their feud was termed the 'Bone Wars'. This rivalry led to the findings of hundreds of new fossils. Historians tell us that this competition began around 1868. It seems, Cope reconstructed a fossil and named it *Elasmosaurus*. The problem is that since no-one had seen an aquatic reptile whose proportions were out of the norm, he placed the skull at the end of its short tail instead of its long neck. Apparently, although unconfirmed, Marsh humiliated him about his error. But, it is more likely the war began when Marsh scooped Cope by paying excavators to send a massive find to him rather than Cope. This is considered totally uncouth since Cope was the one who found the *Hadrosaurus* rich area, and the war was on. Marsh would take advantage of every opportunity to profit from every mistake Cope made.

During the pinnacle of their war, around 1877, Marsh found a partial skeleton that showed an animal with a long neck, a long tail but a missing head. As is commonplace amongst many so-called scientists, to get the discovery on record the skull of another dinosaur was used and the find was termed *Apatosaurus*. About two years later he was sent another skeleton that he assumed belonged to another dinosaur that he named *Brontosaurus*. Unfortunately for Marsh it was actually another *Apatosaurus*. I guess Marsh was unaware of the word patience. If he had exhibited some he would not have been shown to be completely wrong years later. In 1903 his error was discovered. It is interesting to note that even in 1932 the Carnegie Museum placed the wrong head on an *Apatosaurus* and called it *Brontosaurus*, almost thirty years after the artefact was proven erroneous. It was not until 1979 the skeleton was matched with an actual *Apatosaurus*, discovered in Utah in 1910.[194]

That's quite a gap in time. How many people were deceived during that time frame? But the problem is, factually inaccurate ideas remain ingrained in our culture. Think back to the Haeckel debacle discussed earlier. I guess, as archaeologist Ken Feder expresses, it is just easier to ignore evidence against evolution since accepting the evidence would require all the textbooks be re-written (paraphrase of his statement on 'William Shatner's-Weird or What').

Let us first look at the Bible. If the Bible is true you would think there would be some mention of dinosaurs. Does it mention these truly awesome creatures? In the Bible one of the words used for dinosaurs is dragon *(tannin)*. Remember the word dinosaur was first used in 1841. If dinosaurs were on the earth there would have to be a word for them. Although dragons are considered mythological they do resemble dinosaurs when the cartoonish exaggerations are removed. Job describes seeing a large creature he called *Behemoth* (Job 40:15-18). It is described as having a tail like a cedar (v.17), the bones like tubes of bronze and his limbs like bars of iron (v.18). Cedar tree trunks are usually quite long and thick when fully grown. If he was referring to a regular shaped tail, he most likely would have used a less towering tree as an example. If not a dinosaur what animal was it? An elephant could fit the limbs and bones metaphor, but it has a tail like a flyswatter. What about a hippopotamus? Its

---

[194] http://ca.news.yahoo.com/blogs/sideshow/brontosaurus-never-existed-tale-bone-wars-185524946.html accessed 2013/07/09

tail is, well, kind of gross. So it could not be that. Could he be describing a rhinoceros? Not likely, their tails are similar to many animals and not that long. So what was he describing? If you were to describe this animal completely out of context with no references, how do you think most people would respond if you asked them *"What animal did I just describe?"* I would venture to say the vast majority would say a dinosaur. Job goes on to say that the *Behemoth* is not afraid of a turbulent river (40:23). Very few animals are not afraid to cross a raging river.

Another word used to describe unknown other dinosaur-like creatures is *Leviathan*. This word is found six times in the Bible. It is used while referring to sea monsters (Job 7:12; Psalms 74:16; 104:26). The phrase sea monster/dragon is also found in other places (Is. 27:1; 51:9, Eze. 29:3; 32:2). Nehemiah, also speaks of a dragon spring (Neh. 2:13). Malachi 1:3 says: *"I hated Esau and laid his mountains and his heritage waste, for the dragons of the wilderness"* (KJV). Isaiah 43:20 tells us *"The beast of the field shall honour me, the dragons and the owls; because I give waters in the wilderness"* (KJV). Strange the writer uses a well-known animal with a mythological creature. That stretches the realms of logic to the breaking point. How did they know about these monsters? Let's explore the term dragon a little more. Are there any more examples of the word dragon in the Bible? Dragons, plural use: Deuteronomy 32:33; Job 30:29; Psalm 44:19; 74:13; 148:7; Isaiah 13:22; 34:13; 35:7; 43:20; Jeremiah 9:11; 10:22; 14:6; 49:33; 51:37; Micah 1:8; Malachi 1:3

I find it absolutely fascinating that the Chinese still have a dragon on their zodiac chart that originated just over four thousand seven hundred years ago. Chinese paleontologist Doug Zhiming says dinosaurs have been part of the Chinese culture back to before Christ. All other animals are regularly seen, living breathing animals alive and thriving today. With all the other mythological creatures available why was the dragon the only one chosen? Remember back where I spoke of a translation where serpent can also mean dragon. In years past sea serpents were drawn on maps. These sea serpents were mythological creatures that were able to sink entire ships, according to folklore. But if sea dinosaurs such as a *Plesiosaur* are closely examined they do resemble the supposed sea serpents. So is it possible that these dragons were actually dinosaurs?

It is fact that every continent has stories of dragons and remarkably the stories most often describe the same type of animal. The odds against a myth taking the same form are huge. Carl Rose is an expert in mythology and has written a book entitled *"Giants, Monsters, and Dragons"*. In this book a cohesive image from all over the world emerges. He tells us that the European dragon is quite similar to the Oriental dragon. The creature is humungous, drawn-out, has scales similar to an alligator/crocodile with wings like a bat. They also have large legs like a lizard with sharp claws. Some have a toothed dorsal ridge that continues to a barbed serpentine-like tail. The head resembles the lizard or alligator and can be green, red or black in colour. There is the odd instance where they can also be yellow, blue or white. So, similar stories from cultures vast distances apart just happened magically? *"A myth is far truer than a history, for a history only gives a story of the shadows, whereas a myth gives a story of the substances that cast the shadows"* (Annie Besant). Some dragon legends can be traced to just five hundred years ago. So it is not just the primitive man of millennia ago that had these stories. Even in North America there are legends of large dragons. One was named *Angont*. The Huron Indians tell it lived in rivers, lakes and forests. The Seneca Indians have the *Doonongaes* that displayed the reptilian trait of lying beside a river or lake sunning itself. In the highlands of Peshawar, Pakistan the *Apalala* lived in the Swat River. Switzerland had a dragon called *Elbst*. It was seen from 1584-1926 in a lake near Lucerne. The *Gargouille* inhabited the River Seine near Normandy. Sussex England is home to the *Dragon-of-Saint Leonard's Forest* according to John Trundle. He reports that in 1614 this dragon was the cause of cattle and men's disappearances. Not to be outdone the Irish have *Peiste*, a water dragon last seen in 1954. Japan has *Tatsu*, while China boasts of *Ti Lung*; the Great Water Dragon. Malaysia has the *Bujanga*, which lived in the jungle. *Scitalis* and *Safta* are European, while *Ying Lung* is a long-lived legend from China. The Slavs speak of *Simargl* and Estonia has *Tuliband*. Now, I am not saying all of this is actually true, but it seems strange that these animals are so wide-spread and so alike. As the 1973 World Book Encyclopaedia wrote:

> *"The dragon legends are strangely like actual creatures that have lived in the past. They are much like the great reptiles (dinosaurs), which inhabited the Earth long before man was supposed to have appeared on the earth".* [195]

---

[195] Vol. 5, p.265

Even Carl Sagan recognised the similarities between dragons and dinosaurs.[196]

Huge flying reptiles have been described through history by well-respected historians. Josephus recounts the story of serpent-like creatures with the ability to fly. Pliny-the-Elder tells of serpents large enough to completely encircle an elephant. Herodotus spoke of winged serpents, like water-snakes, that were able to fly with wings of a bat. This winged creature was sans feathers. Even the famed explorer Marco Polo claimed to have seen a dinosaur.

After leaving the city of Yachi, China he and his compatriots travelled in a westerly direction for about ten days, they arrived at Karazan. Here he witnessed what he termed a large serpent about nine metres in length with a breadth of about two metres. The creature had two short legs in the vicinity of the head with three claws similar to that of a tiger. Its eyes were exceedingly large. With large sharp teeth it was large enough to be able to swallow a man whole. While observing this monstrosity he observed it would hide within caverns during the high heat of the day. After dining on a tiger, wolf or other choice of meal, they would meander toward a lake or river for a drink of water. Walking on the shoreline causes deep impressions from their massive weight. To catch these animals, hunters use hidden pits lined with sharp iron spikes that impales it rendering it dead. Parts of the creature are used for medicinal purposes, with the meat being a delicacy.[197] Now read that description again and tell me honestly that Marco Polo did not see a *Megalosaurus,* an *Albertosaurus* or some other dinosaur. How were these reputable historians able to accurately describe creatures that so closely resemble dinosaurs millions-of-years after their apparent demise?

There are reports that there are in excess of eighty worldwide artefacts that show an intimate knowledge of dinosaurs. In the U.K. at the Carlisle Cathedral there exists an engraving of Bishop Richard Bell (1410-1496) in his priestly robe. Interestingly though, a nine and one-half foot piece of brass shows what can only be described as both a *Shunosaurus* & a *Vulcanodon*, over four hundred years before the first dinosaur was dug up. What is most interesting about this is that at the time the Church of God maintained that all the animals created in Genesis and that survived the flood were alive at the time. Extinction was completely unthinkable to them.

---

[196] Sagan, Carl. *The Dragons of Eden.* Ballantine Books. 1977 cited in Isaacs D. p. 24
[197] *The Travels of Marco Polo.* Book 2, Chapter XL, 1948, p. 185-186

The Chinese were able to correctly fashion and display the skin type of a duck-billed dinosaur two thousand five hundred years in the past. This is remarkable since skin was only understood by palaeontologists in the past few decades. The Moche Indians who inhabited Peru from approximately 100-800 A.D. depicted a dinosaur on an early vase. Between 206 B.C. and 220 A.D., during the Hans Dynasty, a replica of a dinosaur was constructed from bronze that is amazingly similar to the vase. Deep in the interior of Cambodia can be found the temples of *Ankor* that were built between 50 & 140 A.D. An accurate depiction of a *Stegosaurus* that is currently on display in the Glendive Dinosaur & fossil Museum in Montana can be found on one of the pillars. It is proportionally accurate to current depictions.

Below is a more worldwide complete list of "dragons"

USA: (Depictions from Native Americans will be dealt with separately)
- Elephant-like creature called Moab Mastodon (Moab Utah)
- Creatures resembling Dinosaurs, *Pterosaurs*, & Mastodons (S.W. US)
- *Sauropod*-like animal on the Kachina Bridge

Mexico:
- Near Guatemala a depiction of a *Hypacrosaurus* engraved between 250 & 900 A.D.
- In the Mayan jungles a drawing of a pig, a bird, humans and a *Hadrosaur*.
- At Bonampak, a full colour picture of a part of a *Deinonychus* being used as a head-dress

U.K.:
- In St. Andrew's Hall a carving of a T.Rex as architecture
- A gold coin minted during the reign of Edward IV with a *Carnotaurus sastrei* on one side

Peru:
- In Lima, from the Wari culture (500-900 A.D.) on the side of a vessel a drawing of a *Protoceratops*.
- A Chancy (1000-1450 A.D.) figure resembling a *Mussaurus*.
- More art resembling a *Pteranodon*
- A Chimuan burial cloth with a replica of a *Brachylophosaurus*

Netherlands:
- In the Castle DeHaar a six hundred year old painting depicting St. George fighting a creature similar to a *Coelophysis bauri.*

France:
- Chateau de Chambord a hand-carved door with a *Messospondylus* depicted
- The Royal Chateau of Blois has stone carvings of a *Plateosaurus*
- On the pendant of Francois I what looks like a *Hypsilophodon*
- A tapestry, in the order of St. Michael, a wing devoted to Francois I depicts a being similar to a *Maiasaura peeblesorum.* So far these have only been found in Montana USA.[198]
- More of Francois I artefacts displayed in Azay-le-Rideau; on a table drawer, a carving looking just like an *Albertosaurus*

Spain:
- In Barcelona at the Palau de La Generalitat an altar cloth from the early 1600's showing St. George slaying a dragon remarkably resembling a *Nothosaurus*

China:
- Four thousand year old Hongshan jade pendant looks like a *Graciliceratops*
- Four thousand year old Hongshan nephrite pendant looks like a *Stegoceras*
- Four thousand year+ Hongshan Turquoise dragon resembles a *Centrosaurus*
- Another turquoise dragon resembles a *Protoceratops*[199]

Is it even remotely possible that the people actually saw dinosaurs and drawings are how they captured them?

If we look at cave drawings we can see they do resemble reality, but are somewhat askew. Cave drawings of dinosaurs have been found in Bernifal about five km. from Les Eyzies in the Vezere Valley, France. It

---

[198] Nelson, Vance. Dire Dragons. p. 90
[199] Ibid. I would strongly suggest anyone interested in seeing for themselves, get Mr. Nelson's book. It has many examples from all over the world including photos of the actual items and pictures of dinosaur reconstructions. It is a truly fascinating book.

is well known for its pre-historic cave paintings. Tour guides take visitors through three of the four caves and show the remarkably authentic drawings, but restrict which passageways they are allowed to venture into. Bernifal is the cave not routinely shown and this cave's location is not promoted. It is difficult to get a local to direct an outsider to its exact location. Although it is not restricted, lights are not provided to allow viewing and if a person wishes to see inside the cave they must provide their own illumination. The cave is said to be slippery, when guides are queried as if they are trying to dissuade anyone from entering. Officials decided to close the cave in 1982 even though tourism is a major money maker for the area.

People that do go into the cave and explore should be astounded to find actual dinosaur drawings. One of the drawings depicts a dinosaur-like animal head-butting a woolly mammoth. The dinosaur displayed small front legs/arms with vertical eyes. There was also displayed a small lower jaw under a large upper jaw. The dinosaur depicted resembled a *Theropod,* a creature that lived in the *Mesozoic* era two hundred thirty to sixty-two million years in the past. Since this painting is quite distinctive there are only two explanations. Either this was a copy of a rendering handed down or the painter actually saw these two creatures in battle. Another section shows a red ochre. How can a red ochre and a dinosaur be depicted on the same wall?

But this is not the only pictorial evidence of man and dinosaurs co-existing. The Inca Stones depict not only dinosaurs, but man living with dinosaurs. A depiction of this phenomenon was featured on 'William Shatner's: Weird or What' broadcast on the History channel in Canada and the Discovery channel. The Incas were Indians that lived in Peru until 1572 A.D. They were quite advanced for their time. The stones appear to be a collection of andesite, found in a cave near Inca, Peru, with these depictions drawn on them. There are apparently about fifteen thousand of the stones. The stones are all engraved with what appears to be extinct creatures. Andesite is a volcanic rock that is grey/black in colour whose characteristics would make etching extremely difficult due to the hardness of the surface. It would be even more difficult with primitive etching tools of the time. Near the location where they were reportedly found are bone fragments, millions-of-years old. Because of the composition, radiocarbon dating cannot be used. But the surface of these stones has build-up from bacteria and tiny organisms even in the grooves of the etchings, suggesting an origin of many years ago.

Dinosaurs interacting with humans, some of the Incas advanced technology, medical procedures and geological maps are just some of the depictions. Some people have hypothesized that these are the result of ancient astronaut influence. The maps in some instances are similar, but many are completely inaccurate, although this was not an uncommon event at the time. California was an island on many maps from the fifteenth and sixteenth centuries. Some also show unknown continents, again not that unusual for the time. Atlantis was said to have existed at one point in earth's history. How they came to be has been questioned and even suggested as a hoax by others. But the detail of the dinosaurs contained and the difficulty it would take with such a hard substance does present an intriguing conundrum. Additionally the Incas were not the only native people to do such a thing.

Not only the North American Indians have claimed to be eyewitnesses to dinosaurs, *Pterosaur*-like flying creatures and other animals that supposedly went extinct millions-of-years ago. The Native Americans have artwork that depicts dinosaurs, centuries before they should have even been aware of them. Their depictions are exceptionally accurate. They even got the *'Brontosaur'* right where modern scientists totally blew it for a while (this has already been discussed). Modern scientists argue against the 'legends of the Indians' as they are done from memory and cannot be accurate.

In 1812 a Seneca chief named Red Jacket had a dispute with Daniel Tompkins, the then governor of New York State. The governor's argument was that since his position was recorded on paper it must be accurate and since Red Jacket was arguing strictly from memory it could not be regarded as factual. In the end the governor was proven wrong and Red Jacket's recollection was proven accurate.[200] It is with great pride the detailed stories are retold to generation after generation. Interestingly, it also appears that if an error is made the error lives on through the story.[201] But the point here is, the artefacts from Native Americans do strongly resemble dinosaurs and given their dedication to preserving their heritage it can be almost guaranteed they actually saw them.

Nearly two hundred years ago, the Dakota Sioux stories of 'thunderbirds' were well known. They knew where the creatures lived and that their nests contained the remains of serpents. What is most intriguing about this whole affair is that in modern times *Pteranodon* fossils have

---

[200] Isaacs, D. *Dragons*. p.68 citing Adrienne Mayor, *Fossil Legends of the First Americans*. Princeton Press 2005
[201] Isaacs. D. *Dragons*. p. 68

been found in this exact same area of the Black Hills. They understood the flight patterns of the *Pteranodon,* something that did not come to light to modern-day scientists until just recently. They also knew about the nesting habits. How did they know that it laid eggs? It was not until 2004 that fossilized eggs found in China finally ended the debate as to whether not the *Pteranodon* actually laid eggs.

The Sioux Indians also have a tale of a humungous creature that supposedly lived in their area. This is where the fallacy of the *Brontosaurus* (Thunder Reptile) began. It has been suggested that the name came from their ability to whip their tails at supersonic speeds thereby breaking the sound barrier. Dr. Nathan P. Myhrvold and Dr. Philip J. Currie were able to show through computer simulation that an *Apatosaurus* would be able to flick its tail fast enough to create a sonic boom.[202] This could cause the moniker thunder to be applied. Unfortunately this is only a hypothesis as we do not have them around to test the theory. In 1680, Father Hennepin recorded in his journal descriptions of another creature the Sioux called *Unktehi*. This mammal-like animal was similar in appearance to the buffalo yet the descriptions of it point to a much larger animal with four legs, long brown hair and a massive girth. In 1874 mammoth tusks and teeth were found in St. Anthony Falls (modern-day Minneapolis, Minnesota). If the mammoth became extinct ten thousand years ago how were the Indians able to describe such a creature? If we take the evidence already provided, we are starting to see a re-occurring theme.

A Crow Indian who scouted for General Custer went by the name 'Goes Ahead' (1850-1919). Apparently, he once saw a serpent-like creature that had wings, fall out of the sky. He retrieved it and completely mesmerized by it, left a record of his encounter by carving an image into a tree and autographed his depiction. In 1973 William Boyes went in search of the carving. The grand-daughter of 'Goes Ahead' was able to provide enough detail that he was able to find the carving. This goes to reaffirm Native's commitment to detail. One hundred years after-the-fact Mr. Boyes was able to find the figure that astonishingly resembled the *Meganeura-monyi,* a dragonfly-like being with a .75 meter wingspan. Why this is so remarkable is that according to evolutionary theory it died out about 300Ma.

The rebuttal of most evolutionists is that the Indians must have seen fossils and from here their legends spread. After digging up the fos-

---

[202] Ibid p. 87

sils they were able to reconstruct the dinosaur as it done today. What about the *Brontosaurus*? Are they saying the primitive Indians got it right and the modern, educated, knowledgeable palaeontologist got it wrong? These Indians were extremely superstitious people. They believed that the immortal soul was tied to the bones. They would never disturb a burial site. Burial sites are of ultimate importance. Look at recent events whenever an Indian burial site is uncovered.

A Crow Indian girl named Pretty Shield found a large skull buried in the ground. She and her friends dug up the skull and took it to her father who happened to be a medicine man. The Indians smoked a pipe with the skull as her father pleaded with it to forgive the intrusion. He tried feverously to convince the skull the little girl meant no harm. He then covered the skull with a cloth and buried it. This does not sound like people who routinely dig up fossils, but are petrified of them. They would not dig them up for study purposes. The only reasonable explanation is that the Natives actually saw the creatures and even interacted with them.

This is not the only evidence against evolutionary thought. The current worldwide population increase is 1.14 percent per annum. The average lifespan today in the heaviest populated countries is approximately seventy-eight years.[203] From the Bronze Age until the early twentieth century the life expectancy was from twenty-eight to forty-five years of age.[204] Before the Renaissance the age was much lower than after. From classical Greece until medieval Britain it was only twenty-eight to thirty years-of-age.[205] During the time from the Renaissance to modern times there were also serious plagues that depleted the population. The Black Death: twenty-five million dead, the flu epidemic of 1918: fifty million died; the Asian flu in 1957 killed two million and the Hong Kong Flu in 1968: one million dead. Let's can take a population increase of one half of one percent. I will stipulate that it is an assumption, but based on historical records a reasonable one (see following chart).

---

[203] CIA World Factbook 2009.
[204] Encyclopaedia Britannica 2009
[205] Ibid

Time Span	Population (Millions)	Increase (Millions)	Percent Increase
1000 A.D.	250		
1100	300	50	.2
1200	360	60	.2
1250	400	40	.22
1300	360	-40	-.2
1350	440	80	.44
1400	350	-90	-.41
1500	430	80	.23
1600	550	120	.28
1650	470	-80	-.29
1700	600	130	.55
1750	630	30	.1
1800	820	190	.6
1850	1130	310	.76
1900	1550	420	.74
1910	1750	200	1.3
1920	1860	110	.62
1930	2070	210	1.3
1940	2300	230	1.11
1950	2550	250	1.09
2000	6500	3950	3.1

This annual increase is less than approximately one-half of the current number. Therefore we should be able to calculate those on the earth at the present time. Suppose that the flood happened about four thousand two hundred years ago (Gen. 11:10-26 tells us there was two hundred ninety-two years between the Flood and Abram. Abram lived around 1875 B.C.[206]-2100 B.C.[207]). The encyclopedia Britannica, 1771 edition, has Abram being born in 1999 B.C. The same edition also has the great deluge[208] (Noah's flood) happening in 2351 B.C. Now their math is off a bit, but not enough to warrant any major concern. It should be obvious the dates are not exact, as recorded history from this time is a little ambiguous, but again it is in the ball park. To get a reasonable comparison we must take the recorded population increase. We can verify this increase from the beginning of the second millennium until today. This comparison is the only way to make a logical assumption. The chart

---

[206] Brimson, J. *Archaeological Data and the Dating of the Patriarchs*. In Essays on the Patriarchal Narratives. Ed. A.R, Millard and D.J. Wiseman p. 53-89 cited in Walton, *Genesis* p. 49
[207] Bietzel, B. *Moody Bible Atlas of Bible Lands*. p.85 cited in Walton p. 49
[208] Encyclopedia Britannica, 1771 edition p. 414

shows the population growth from 1,000 A.D. until the beginning of the twenty-first century. We will use this as our basis to arrive at a reasonable population growth number for the Biblical timeline of six thousand years.

There were eight people that survived the flood and if six of them were at child reproducing age, the mathematical calculation would give us a population today of about 7.9 Billion people. [*The formula for logarithmic human world population growth is $Pf = P_o e^{rt}$, where Pf = the current population, P_o = the initial population, e = the base of natural logarithms (2.718), r = the average annual population growth rate, and t = the time interval from P_o to Pf*]. That is larger than the number of persons currently inhabiting the earth, but since we are not sure of the actual population growth rate or the exact year of the flood it is a reasonable assertion. Depending upon the number of years we use since the flood this number will vary, similarly dependent upon the population increase percent we use. Since we can only guess at the population change and the number of years since the flood this is somewhat speculative, but reasonable given the population increase between 1,000 A.D. and today.

If we accept the theory that people have been on the earth for a much longer period of time, that number will grow exponentially. Say, hypothetically, there were two fertile people twenty-five thousand years ago. Sounds kind of ridiculous doesn't it? Using the same numbers we would now have 2.84×10^{54} people on the earth. Change that number twenty-five thousand years ago to say two thousand people the number balloons to 2.84×10^{57}. Remember at one point we could have been only two thousand people on the earth[209] according to the suggestion given by some. Now increase that to millions-of-years and the number is mind-boggling.[210] Obviously this is impossible since the entire area of the world cannot hold that many people. You can see how this is getting silly.

One argument long-agers give is that death, a high mortality rate amongst infants and diseases such as Rotavirus and Coronavirus caused a slow increase in the population over this time. Interestingly it appears the birth rate increased just before the mortality rate jumped significantly. What about all the animals. Their reproduction rate makes ours look diminutive. Yet animals have been evolving for millions-of-

---

[209] Stenger, V. *Hypothesis*. p. v
[210] If we take the idea of man-like people, namely "genus *Homo*", being on the earth for 2.4 million years to get 7,000,000,000 people now the population growth over that time period would be 0.000000009 percent or 0.00000225 percent of the historical rate of .4 per cent.

years? I have only two questions for the evolutionists. Where are all the animals that should be alive today? As man has been burying their dead for at least four hundred thousand years according to long-agers, where all of the human bodies?

So what do some of the world's best known atheists/evolutionists actually say in private about their sacred ~~fact~~ theory?

- No-one can say for sure how a bunch of chemicals transformed into life. [211]
- Darwinian explanations seem to be circular. Humans are egocentric except when they are altruistic. The propagation of the species comes from selecting the best mate, except when monogamy is preferred; quite difficult to test scientifically. [212]
- The necessary intermediate forms between species are not shown by paleontology. [213]
- Only a naturalistic explanation for life is possible. God cannot be allowed into the equation. [214]
- Nobody can say how life came to be on earth. [215]
- When viewing evidence a biologist must keep reminding himself life evolved and was not designed. [216]
- Biology is studying things that appear to be purposefully designed [217]
- Darwinism is untestable as a scientific fact. It is, in reality, metaphysical. [218]
- Many evolutionary theorists realise punctuated equilibrium is a stumbling-block to the evolutionary thought. [219]
- The biggest secret in the field of paleontology is that transitional forms are extremely rare; to the point of

---

[211] Davies, Paul, Australian Centre for Astrobiology, Sydney, New Scientist **179**(2403):32, 2003.
[212] Skell, P.S., *Why Do We Invoke Darwin? Evolutionary theory contributes little to experimental biology*, The Scientist **19**(16):10, 2005.
[213] David B. Kitts '*Evolution*' 1974, Vol. 28, p 467:
[214] Richard Lewontin. *Billions and billions of demons* The New York Review, 9 January 1997. p. 31
[215] Knoll, Andrew H , PBS Nova interview, *How Did Life Begin?* July 1, 2004
[216] Crick, F., *What mad pursuit: a Personal View of Scientific Discovery*, Sloan Foundation Science, London, 1988, p. 138
[217] Dawkins, R., *The Blind Watchmaker*, W.W. Norton & Company, New York, 1986. p. 1
[218] Popper, K., *Unended Quest*, Fontana, Collins, Glasgow, 1976.p. 151 cited on CMI.org
[219] Stephen Jay Gould and Niles Eldredge, 1993. *Punctuated equilibrium comes of age*. Nature, 366, pp. 223–224.

- never actually seeing the evolutionary process they report.[220]
- It must be conceded that there is actually no concrete evidence for evolution. It is only wishful speculation.[221]
- Evolution was a religion in the days of Darwin, and it is still a religion today.[222]

It would appear even some of the staunchest supporters of evolution know it is a worldview and not a scientific fact. So why do these scientists say these things about evolution? They seem to agree with Professor Dawkins. Faith is used so a person does have not to think. They can believe what they want regardless of the evidence or lack thereof.

God did not, make the planet easy for life to evolve[223] because it did not evolve. The correct response is that the earth is inhabitable because God went to a lot of trouble to make it so (Is. 45:12a). Evolution has been shown to be fanciful and not fact by using their own rules of scientific explanation. The timeframe does not fit. There are glaring examples that nullify their view, i.e. living fossils, fossils out-of-place and outright hoaxes; fresh or fresh-like fossils with soft tissue intact for supposedly sixty-five+ million year old samples. There are numerous examples of dishonesty to verify a theory that should not be needed, if it is a fact. Evolution, when studied with scientific methods, fails all the 'Tests of Reason' talked about earlier.

Unfortunately for Professor Dawkins and the others listed above, a recent survey shows that approximately thirty-three percent of Americans believe humans have existed just as they are since the beginning of time. Also, only thirty-two percent believe in naturalistic evolution, and about one-quarter believe God used evolution. That is a great number of ignorant, stupid, insane, or wicked people (Professor Dawkins' suggestion). The problem is that this mindset is so ingrained into proponents they refuse to even listen to the mountain of evidence that contradicts evolutionary theory.

---

[220] Gould, S. J., 1977. *Evolution's erratic pace.* Natural History, **86**(5):14
[221] Harold, Franklin M. (Prof. Emeritus Biochemistry, Colorado State University) *The way of the cell: molecules, organisms and the order of life*, Oxford University Press, New York, 2001, p. 205. Cited on CMI.org
[222] Ruse, M., *How evolution became a religion: creationists correct?* National Post, pp. B1,B3,B7 May 13, 2000
[223] Stenger, Victor J. *Hypothesis.* p. 145

This piece of evidence for me is 'a nail in the coffin' for evolutionary thought. An amateur archaeologist by the name of Alvis Delk from Stephenville, Texas discovered a loose slab at the Paluxy River just north of Dinosaur Valley State Park. On the slab he noticed a distinctive dinosaur footprint. He placed it with hundreds of other fossils he had collected over the years. An unfortunate accident, in 2008, left him somewhat debilitated. Thinking he could sell the rock, he started to clean it, to remove all foreign debris. He was astonished to find a human footprint underneath the dinosaur print. It was obvious to him that a human had stepped into the mud at one point and a dinosaur stepped into the mud immediately adjacent to the first print before the mud could change to stone. Mud from the dinosaur's middle toe was transplanted inside the human footprint. To verify his findings Spiral CT scans were used, generating images that allowed analyzing the footprints without causing any physical damage. This method of testing allowed him to see inside the rock, i.e. underneath the footprint. At Glen Rose medical centre eight hundred X-ray images demonstrated density changes within the rock corresponding to the underlying structures. If this was a hoax and the prints had been carved in a nefarious attempt to defraud, there would be no underlying structures. As contours beneath each footprint are present; there can be no doubt as to its authenticity. If the tracks made at Glen Rose TX were made one hundred million years ago, according to the evolutionary timescale, something is seriously wrong here. The CT and X-ray scans eliminate all doubt as to the authenticity.[224] There is only one reasonable answer. The tracks were made about the same time when humans and dinosaurs co-existed on the earth. Pictures of the actual slab can be found at website cited in footnotes. How do evolutionists explain this? You will be astonished at one idea. According to some evolutionists this proves time travel will be possible at some point in the future. Someone will go back in time and step into the mud where dinosaurs are common. Sounds like these individuals have never heard of Occam's razor.

If this is not enough, what about Dr. Mary Schweitzer, an evolutionary palaeontologist, whose discovery sent shock waves through her community? In a place called Hell Creek Formation in Montana she discovered a T-rex bone that contained blood vessels and whole cells inside the bone. A bone from a dinosaur that died over sixty-five million years ago had not completely decomposed? In addition to the blood cells she

---

[224] http://www.bible.ca/tracks/delk-track.htm accessed 2014/11/10

also noticed soft tissue, and a pliable brown material form within the bone. Jack Horner, a palaeontology expert used for the movie 'Jurassic Park', suggested she perform tests to prove what she found was actually not soft tissue that should have been gone for millions-of-years. Performing more tests she was able to detect Heme, which is a component of haemoglobin, in the bones. It provides the red colour from the protein that distributes oxygen in the blood. If you look at the pictures it also appears that there is something similar to ligaments in one of them.[225] This should be irrefutable proof that the bone was in fact not sixty-five million years old. It does not make any sense that human bones are gone, yet this tissue, blood vessels and even DNA from a T-Rex that died over sixty-five million years ago was found, completely intact. As Sherlock Holmes said "*Something is afoot*". Dr. Schweitzer not believing what she saw ran the tests multiple times thinking something must be wrong. She kept getting the same result. So she was unable to complete the challenge given to her by Mr. Horner.

Dr. David Menton tells that Mr. Horner was offered a substantial amount of money to run a ^{14}C test on the bone. He declined. Does it not make sense that after the original testing a ^{14}C test would be warranted? I guess it would unless you want your worldview (evolutionary fact) smashed to smithereens. Any ^{14}C present would date this bone to thousands-of-years. When this was initially discovered *Discover* magazine ran an article with the headline: "*Schweitzer's Dangerous Discovery*".[226] The same article spoke of Dr. Schweitzer's difficulty in getting her findings published. It seemed the scientific community was reluctant to believe her findings. She told *Discover:*

> "*I had one reviewer tell me that he didn't care what the data said, he knew that what I was finding wasn't possible,*" says Schweitzer. "*I wrote back and said, 'Well, what data would convince you?' And he said, 'None'*".[227]

Now that is good science. He did not care what the data said, it was wrong. Naturally evolutionists have found a way to explain everything and maintain their theory. That is their right, but the explanations are not at all convincing.

Even today dinosaur-like creatures have been reported in remote areas like Papua New Guinea. Additionally, scientist John Allen Watson

---

[225] https://www.smithsonianmag.com/science-nature/dinosaur-shocker-115306469/
[226] Yeoman, B., *Schweitzer's Dangerous Discovery*, Discover **27**(4):37–41, 77, April 2006.
[227] Ibid

has written a booklet entitled: "*Man, dinosaurs and mammals together*", describing how bones of all three have been found in Phosphate deposits in South Carolina, some side-by-side, in direct opposition as to what evolutionists maintain. So then, why do people believe the myth of evolution? Psychoanalyst Walter Langer said: "*People will believe a big lie sooner than a little one, and if you repeat it frequently enough, people will sooner or later believe it*". How then how are fossils explained since they are quite abundant around the world? The next chapter on the historicity of Noah's Flood will explain the complete fossil record.

Chapter 5
Did Noah's Flood Actually Occur?

It is an undeniable fact that nearly every culture on the earth has a flood story. By careful study it can be shown that almost every account of a flood are just slightly different recollections of the Biblical account.[228] The American Indian account of the Navajo Flood says the first world was destroyed due to the sinfulness of man; mostly sexual sin.[229] Even the Hopi and the Inca Indians have a flood story. Some might wonder why this would happen. If the people were all dispersed from the tower of Babel years after the flood, it would be reasonable that the flood account would go with them to their new locations.

The only account that seemed to vary widely was the story of Gilgamesh. There are a few similarities between the Genesis account and the Mesopotamian account, but the differences are far more substantial. This may seem to suggest that neither one is really based on the other as has been suggested by many anti-Biblical critics.

The Biblical account of the flood says that God made it rain for forty days and forty nights causing the entire earth to be covered with water. This was done to rid the world (Gen. 6:7) of all the evil that was in it at the time (Gen. 6:5). With the Biblical account there are many questions including some common fallacies.

What is the true account of the flood of Genesis? God chose to save Noah from His judgment due to Noah's righteousness (Gen. 6:8). God came to Noah and told him to build an ark to be saved from the coming deluge (6:14). He instructed him how to build the boat and what animals he would take into the ark. Noah actually took seven pairs of

---

[228] Strickling, J. *A Statistical Analysis of Flood Legends*. CRSQ Vol.9 # 3 1972 p. 152
[229] Leming & Leming. *A Dictionary of Creation Myths*. p.204 cited in Ashton J. et al. Big Argument p.245

every clean animal and two of every kind of unclean animal (7:2-3). The animals came to him. Rain fell for forty days and forty nights (7:12). The water was so great every point of elevation was completely covered to a depth of about eight metres (7:20). After one hundred fifty days the Ark came to rest on Mt. Ararat (8:4). After forty days Noah opened the window to check on the progress of the receding waters (8:6). Noah sent out a raven to see what would happen (8:7). The raven returned since it was just water to be seen. He waited for a while and sent out a dove; the dove returned (8:8). He waited seven days and sent the dove out again. The dove returned with an olive leaf (8:11). Noah waited another seven days. This time the dove did not return (8:12). Noah knew the water had abated so he let the animals go (8:17).

He came out of the Ark with his family and made a sacrifice to the Lord (8:20). It was at this point the new covenant was made (9:9-12). God promised to never flood the entire earth again (9:11) and gave the rainbow as a reminder (9:13), not a sign as many people seem to misrepresent. Noah and his family were told to be fruitful and multiply (9:1). Some people have problems with the Biblical account. But all of their questions or skeptical comments are easily answered.

One question that a skeptic may ask is "*How were Noah, his family and the animals able to survive with every mountain being covered with water?*" Since Mt. Everest in the highest point in the world it too should have been covered with water. People climbing Mt. Everest require oxygen tanks to breathe. Would not the passengers on the Ark also require such devices? This question presupposes that Mount Everest was the height it is now. Earth's highest mountains have fossils of sea creatures at their tops, showing they were once under the sea.[230] There are a few possibilities that could explain this. They are:
- the sea rose to cover the mountains
- the mountains were once under the sea and have since risen out of the sea,
- combination of the two.

Geologists currently think mountains such as the Himalayas were built by catastrophic movement of the Earth's continental plates. This is known as plate tectonics. This could have happened during or after the Flood. The rate of rise now measured is just the remnant of the processes which occurred much faster in the past. Mountain building occurred as a part of the geologic processes which deepened the oceans to take the waters off the land towards the end of the Flood. Some mountains could

---

[230] http://www.christiananswers.net/q-aig/noah-above-mts.html accessed 2013/01/10

have existed before the Flood, but none like the current Himalayas, Alps, or Andes in height. Even if the flood waters were nine kilometres deep, would Noah and company have had trouble breathing? Absolutely not!

Air pressure is caused by the weight of air above the point where the pressure is experienced. If the water was this height, the air pressure from the water surface to the edge of the atmosphere would increase since the volume of air was more tightly compacted. It is certain, therefore, that those on the Ark would have had no trouble breathing - without oxygen tanks.[231] After the waters subsided the problem would reappear. If Noah and his family were high on the mountain how did they get to the bottom without any of the necessary equipment? For starters the Bible says only that the Ark came to rest on Mt. Ararat, not at the top of the mountain. Even one thousand metres up the mountain would still be on the mountain. They could easily descend from that height. But we do not know how high up it was. So speculation should not be used.

Now consider the construction of the Ark. The Ark was one hundred forty metres long, twenty-three metres wide and thirteen and one half metres high; longer than the paying area of a Canadian football field including end zones. To verify the feasibility of an ark similar to Noah's, all one has to do is look at the fifteenth century fleet of Admiral Zheng He. Records show that the wooden boats in his fleet were between one hundred twenty-three and one hundred thirty-seven metres in length. These boats were able to navigate the rough waters of the world's oceans. Noah's ark would easily be seaworthy and not bend, twist, sag or break apart as skeptics try to suggest. Skeptics have also suggested that Noah would not be technologically advanced enough not build this boat. Mr. Templeton went as far as to say that at the time the tools needed to complete the task were non-existent.[232] So, according to Mr. Templeton, Noah could not build a wooden boat, but the Egyptians could build the pyramids; which modern engineers admit to not understanding how they were constructed, around the same time.

Noah built the Ark, basically, in the middle of the mid-east. Most likely, Noah had never seen a boat, let alone sail on one. Why did Noah build the Ark to these dimensions? To answer we must ask ourselves, "What is the dimension of most boats/ships for proper handling characteristics and floatability on a large body of water?" Modern ships that sail around the world have a ratio of length to width of between 5:1 and 6:1.

---

[231] Ibid
[232] Templeton, C. *Farewell* p. 55

What was the dimension of the Ark? Let's do the math. Length was three hundred cubits and width was fifty cubits. That is a ratio of 6:1; the exact ratio of today's cruisers. So how did Noah know this living in or near a desert and not near an ocean? He was most certainly not a master ship builder, just a righteous man. He must have had this knowledge given to him by an expert.

Skeptics claim that the flood narrative of Genesis is a rewritten version of an original myth, The Epic of Gilgamesh, from the Enuma Elish produced by the Sumerians. The flood of the Epic of Gilgamesh is contained on Tablet XI of twelve large stone tablets that date to around 650 B.C. Liberal scholars placed the Genesis written record between 1,500 and 500 B.C

An ancient clay Sumerian cuneiform was discovered that pre-dated the Gilgamesh story. The dating of the tablet could be reasonably inferred as it was discovered, by University of Pennsylvania archaeologists, in Nippur, an ancient Babylonian city. Nippur had been invaded and ravaged around 2100 B.C. by the Elamites. This means this fragment could not be a copy of the older one. What is most significant is that the text on this stone is eerily similar to ancient Hebrew text in the language and syntax. Also of most importance is what is missing. It does not have the polytheistic references contained in the Atrahais account. So, here we have proof that a flood story existed over four thousand years ago. Although the stone is not completely intact, there is enough that the text can be shown to be astonishingly similar to the Genesis account. First we should examine the similarities before we look at the differences.

J. Norris was able to determine after studying two hundred flood stories that the following similarities were found.

Event	Percent Containing
The cataclysm was a flood	95
It was a global flood	95
A favoured family was saved	88
The geography was local	82
Mention of a rainbow	75
Animals involved	73
A boat was used for survival	70
Animals were also spared	67

Event	Percent Containing
The flood was a judgement	66
Forewarning provided	66
Survivors landed on a mountain	57
Birds sent out	35
Sacrifice offered	13
Only 8 people were saved	9

Noah lived in what today would be the Iraqi/Turkey part of the world. So, which of the stories is true and which is based on the other account? This is shown in the following section for the reader to decide. A quick look at the text does show some key similarities between them, however there are also many pointed differences. I will show you both and let you decide whether there is or is not a connection?

Dissimilarities:

Genesis[233]	Gilgamesh[234]
Noah found favour with God due to his righteousness (6:9)	Gilgamesh asks Utanapishtim how he found favour with the gods
Noah reveals coming flood to his family	Utanapishtim reveals the coming flood to Gilgamesh
God decided to destroy mankind (6:13)	Anu, Enlil, Ninurta, Ennugi and Ea decided to flood the earth
Noah told to build ark from gopher wood (6:14)	Utanapishtim told to tear down his house to build boat
Noah to take two unclean animals and 7 pairs of clean animals (7:2-3)	Told to take all living things on boat
Size- 300X50X30 cubits (6:15) (stable. Dimension ratios used today)	Size- Cube one hundred twenty cubits all sides (unseaworthy)
Noah does everything God tells him (6:22)	Utanapishtim tells Ea, he will comply
No mention of what God told Noah to say to inhabitants.	Ea told Utanapishtim to lie about building boat. Told them great wealth was coming after he left.

---

[233] Genesis 6-9:17 ESV Study Bible. Crossway Bibles. Wheaton IL. 2008
[234] http://www.ancienttexts.org/library/mesopotamian/gilgamesh/tab11.htm accessed 2013/15/01

Genesis	Gilgamesh
Apparently only Noah and his sons build ark, though not recorded	Many craftsmen, children & the weak helped Utanapishtim build boat
Three decks plus a roof (6:16)	Six decks, seven levels
No mention.	Nine compartments
One hundred twenty years to complete construction (6:3)	Six days to complete construction? not clear
Launched after flood waters caused ark to rise. (7:17)	Launched backwards by hand using poles are runners
Only took sample of animals (7:2-3) and food (6:21)	Took every animal, silver and gold
Noah took only his wife, three sons and three daughters-in-law (7:6)	Took all his relatives and craftsmen that helped build boat
The Lord sealed them in (7:16)	Utanapishtim seals the entrance
No direct mention of black clouds only water came upon earth (7:10)	Seventh day, in morning black cloud arose
Water began seven days after ark was sealed (7:10)	Seventh day after warning rain began
God send flood waters (7:4)	Flood came from Adad, Shullat, Hanish, Erragal, Ninurta, and Anunnaki.
Rained forty days and forty nights (7:12)	Rained for six days and seven nights, calm during seventh day
After forty days & forty nights water covered mountains (7:19) Wind sent to dry up water (8:1)	Mountains covered by South wind on first day
Landed on Mt. Ararat (8:4)	Landed on Mt. Nimush
God was in complete control the entire time	gods frightened by flood and cowered liked dogs.
God anger soothed	gods wept with grief
Water prevailed for three hundred seventy days (8:3 8:4;8:14)	Water remained for seven days
Used some of the clean animals (8:20)	Sacrificed a sheep
God sad most humans died (8:21)	Enlil angry humans survived
God starts new covenant (9:9)	gods argue over flood
Noah's sons told to multiply (9:1)	Utanapishtim & wife granted immortality like the gods

Genesis	Gilgamesh
God saved Noah because he was righteous (6:9)	No reason given for saving Uta-napishtim
No mention of land on fire	Anunnaki set land ablaze
The Lord smelled pleasing aroma of sacrifice and vowed to never again curse the ground (8:21)	gods crowd like flies around sacrifice

Similarities:
- Both are set in Iraqi/Turkey area (Mesopotamia)
- A man is warned to construct a craft the survive coming flood
- He is told to save himself, his family and other living things
- Seal the boat with resin inside and out
- A set time is given for the flood
- Flood includes rain and water from the surface
- The flood covered the mountains.
- The boat came to rest on a mountain
- After the flood subsided a sacrifice was offered
- Birds were released to see whether or not the flood waters had subsided. The Biblical account has a raven and a dove. Gilgamesh released a dove, swallow and a raven.

We have examined the similarities between the Epic of Gilgamesh and Genesis flood account of the Bible. Although there are a number of superficial similarities between the accounts, the vast majority of similarities would be expected to be found in any ancient flood account. Only two similarities stand out as being unique - landing of the boats on a mountain and the use of birds to determine when the flood subsided. However, both of these similarities differ in important details. In addition, there are great differences in the timing of each of the flood accounts and the nature of the vessels. Why these details would be so drastically changed is a problem for those who claim that the Genesis flood was derived from the Epic of Gilgamesh.

There are a couple possible explanations for the existence of multiple ancient flood accounts. One - that Genesis was a copy of Gilgamesh - has already been discussed and does not seem to fit the available data. The other possible explanation is that the flood was a real event in the history of the world passed down through the generations of different cultures. If so, the Gilgamesh account seems to have undergone some rather radical transformations. The story is a rather silly myth that bears little resemblance to reality. In contrast, the Genesis account is a logical, seemingly factual account of a historical event. It lacks the obvious mythological aspects of the Gilgamesh epic.

Intriguingly, research at the Black Sea has shown some very interesting observations. In 1993 geologists William Ryan and Walter Pitman of Columbia University made some astounding finds. While sampling the sea bed they found the top-bed contained *Mytilus Galloprovincialis* molluscs. They only live in seawater. When excavating lower, a surprising result was had. To their utter surprise they discovered *Dreissena Rostriformis* molluscs; astonishing since these molluscs thrive only in freshwater. This proves without any doubt that the Black Sea was at one time a freshwater lake. This dramatic change was within approximately a few thousand years of the birth of Christ. This was confirmed by ^{14}C dating.

The question of how animals indigenous to only far-off parts of the world came to be on the Ark has been raised.[235] Sounds like a reasonable question. But ignorance of the facts is no excuse. For one, the vast majority of marsupial fossils have been found in Europe and South America not Australia. Secondly, I have also already discussed Pangaea.

The major continents we have today did not exist back then; this is confirmed by modern-day geologists. It would be easy for God to direct the animals to Noah. How the continents formed will be discussed shortly. He would have also had to get two or seven pairs of every type of animal. The current four hundred+ breeds of dog are descendant from the wolf. Another example is that all horse-like animals had the same ancestor. Every type of cattle is descendant from the *Aurochs*. All cats have the basic same genome and domestic cats come from the Lynx. Dinosaurs have been shown to be alive at the time. How did they all go onto the Ark? The same thing applies. Since the earth needed to be repopulated after the flood Noah would not take older adult dinosaurs but adolescent ones that could reproduce many times. They are much smaller than their adult counter-part.

It has then been estimated only eight thousand animals would be needed to repopulate the earth with land-dwellers. The question of eight thousand air-breathing, land dwelling creatures will surely be a bone of contention for some people. It must be remembered that aquatic animals would fare quite well in a flood. Insects and vermin would be able to survive on the resulting logs and trees that would be uprooted. Even if there

---

[235] Templeton. *Farewell.* p.55

were some small colonies (seven individual specimens) of insects on the ark, the space taken up by them would be miniscule. The Ark would provide approximately forty thousand cubic metres of space. This is more than enough for this many animals. This also leaves plenty of room for the needed food. As a person who grew up on a farm that raised hogs, I can assure you it would be a challenging task for eight people to feed this many animals, but not impossible. Many animals hibernate. They would need no care. Progressive farming methods allow one person to feed many animals at one time. Cleaning the stalls would also provide some challenges unless the floors were sloped to allow the refuse to just fall into the water. The stalls could have also used water to wash away the waste products. There was a copious amount of water around.

Many, even professing Christians, have tried to say it was a local flood and was not global. Does the evidence support such a claim? To begin if it was a local flood why did Noah spend one hundred twenty+ years[236] building an ark, not seven days as suggested by skeptics?[237] But this is again cherry-picking verses to make a point that is completely fallacious. The seven days refers to how long Noah and his family were inside the Ark before the flood began (Gen 7:1, 4).

He and his family could have just moved to a distant part of the world after being warned by God, if it were a local flood. Secondly why build an ark so large if only the local animals had to be taken aboard. It has also been well documented that animals flee impending catastrophes, often even before humans realize is it upon them. A local flood would not necessitate the need to take birds onboard. They could easily fly to another area where there was no flood.

If the flood was local, only the people in Mesopotamia would have died. People living elsewhere would have been spared. Are these people actually hypothesizing that for the fifteen hundred or so years after creation no-one moved to another part of the world? The purpose of the flood was to wipe man off the face of the earth (Gen. 6:9). Even Je-

---

[236] It has been suggested by some scholars that it took Noah 120 years to build the ark, based on Genesis 6:3. This seems reasonable. Shem went into the ark with Noah. Genesis 11:10 tells us he was 100 years old when he fathered Arphaxad, 2 years after the flood, making Shem 97 or 98 when the flood came. So it could only have taken Noah about 120 years to build the boat if Shem was born while the Ark was being constructed. Noah's 3 sons were born when he was around 500 (Gen 5:32). They entered the ark when he was 600 (Gen. 7:11) But, given the size of the boat it most certainly would have taken Noah's family a very long time to construct it. Additionally Shem was also married when the flood came. This shows that it possible all of Noah's children were born while he was constructing the ark. May he have done this to have help in the construction?

[237] Templeton, *Farewell.* p. 55. A 7 day construction time is from the Gilgamesh epic.

sus said that everyone not in the Ark perished in the flood (Mat. 24:37-39). This could not have happened if it was only a local flood and not global.

Here is a place where I have heard some objections. People object to God drowning millions of people. Given the longevity at the time there could have been a great many people on the earth. *"What kind of a loving God would do this"* is often what I hear. This is valid if you do not know the whole story. I am sure during the one hundred twenty+ years of Noah building a boat, in the middle of a desert; people would come up to him and ask what he was doing. Before the flood, rain was unreal to them (Gen. 2:6). So a man building a boat almost one hundred forty metres in length would garner some attention. Noah being the righteous man he was would have told them about God's warning. Since the people had one hundred twenty+ years of being warned of what was coming, and completely ignoring that warning, they have no-one to blame but themselves. I would hope that people would be receptive to this so they can avoid the next judgment that will be by fire (2 Pet. 3:6-7).

Another argument against a local flood is water's natural characteristics. Water always takes the shape on the container and finds its own level. Water could not rise to twenty-two feet (Gen 7:20) in one area, yet remain non-existent in another, unless blocked physically. The flood also lasted for about three hundred seventy days. That seems unlikely for a local flood. Are we to believe the Ark floated for over one year and never saw any dry land outside the flood area? There are also numerous references in the NT to a global, not local flood (Luke 17:27; 1 Pet. 3:20; 2 Pet.2:5; 3:6; Heb.11:7).

There is also a great deal of evidence for a global flood. I have already mentioned about the Black Sea. This is not an anomaly. Mt. Everest has marine fossils at its peak. How did the highest point on the earth obtain fossils of creatures from the sea/ocean? Fossils are embedded all over the world. The amount of the fossil remains, points to a rapid burial to prevent decay and scavenging. We have already discussed the evidence for quickly formed rock strata. Preservation of animal tracks, light marks, raindrop marks all point to this. Evidence for lack of erosion that should have happened over the millions-of-years postulated io missing.

A fossil was found in 1895, near Baylor Texas, with remains of its lunch still in its mouth. The fossil shows a reptilian creature trying to eat a *Cotylosaur.* How did eighty Baleen whales end up near the Pan-American Highway in the middle of the desert near Caldera, Chile or

Haplochromis desfontainesii, a tropical fish be found in the Sahara? What about a herd of twenty-five dinosaurs getting trapped in a crouched position possibly indicating they were trying to escape from a mud pit in Inner Mongolia? Ponder the Siberian woolly mammoth entombed in ice with its last meal still slightly undigested. Another example that cannot be easily explained is the case of the mother *Ichthyosaurs* giving birth. A fossil of one with just the beak still within the mother was discovered. The rest of the baby had been born. Are we to believe that the mother and child just laid there for thousands-of-years like this without being scavenged, before being covered with sand and silt? Still another fossil shows a mother *Ichthyosaurs* with several unborn babies still in her uterus and a newborn just a short distance away. There are many more examples that point to a quick, rapid complete burial that prevented decay or scavenging, only to be fossilized later.

On the 'Nature of Things', David Suzuki speaks of a marine fossil in the Arabian Desert hundreds-of-kilometres from the nearest body of water. He suggested a local flood placed it there. In December of 1992, Paul LeBlond, professor of oceanography at the University of British Columbia, discussed a recent discovery of a C*adborosaurus* in the stomach of a sperm whale caught in the Pacific.[238]

Recent exploration of the planet Mars via the Mars Orbital Camera has shown that in the distant past Mars was bombarded by a massive flood. This was not your garden-variety flood. NASA has estimated the volume was six hundred cubic kilometres of water. The flood occurred just north of the Martian equator. The evidence appears in the Cerberus Plains that is presently covered with lava. Scientists estimate this cataclysm occurred about 2Ba. According to researchers large passageways were also sculpted through *Chryse Planitia*, another part of Mars. Are people to believe Mars, a completely barren planet, had a massive flood; the only evidence is a single gorge, whereas earth whose surface is seventy percent water, and show twelve such canyons worldwide (listed next), did not? (These canyons are found all over the world as opposed to what Bill Nye touts)

- Todra Gorge- Morocco
- King's Canyon- Australia
- Taroko Gorge- Taiwan
- Copper Canyon- Mexico
- Colca Canyon-Peru

---

[238] New Scientist, January 23, 1993, 137:16

- Samaria Gorge- Crete
- Waimea Canyon- Kauai
- Gorge du Verdon- France
- Tiger Leaping Gorge- China
- Fish River Canyon- Namibia Africa
- Yarlung Zangbo Grand Canyon- China
- Burlingame Canyon- Walla Walla, Washington

A more recent example would be Mt. Saint Helens. The rocks formed from this eruption have proven quite a challenge for long-agers. The rock build-up from the eruption also caused some interesting phenomenon. Spirit Lake is close to Mt. Saint Helens. Rocks and debris from the eruption caused dam-like structures to form, preventing the normal water flow from the lake to be ebbed. When the dam could no longer keep the water contained, it burst with such magnitude that a wash formed forty-three metres high. The walls looked remarkably similar to the Grand Canyon. This clearly demonstrated that fluid dynamics can wreak havoc on earth's crust. Some geologists have openly stated that if they did not know this portent had formed rapidly, they would estimate that it had taken millions-of-years.

What about Burlingame Canyon in Walla Walla, Washington? It measures four hundred fifty metres long, up to thirty-five metres deep, and as wide, winding through a hillside. Six days of runaway ditch erosion removed around one hundred fifty thousand cubic metres of silt, sand and rock. Check it out. A mini Grand Canyon formed in only six days. Obviously millions-of-years are not needed.

We have already mentioned the super continent Pangaea. As early as 1960 the idea of moving continents was ridiculed. There were only a few proponents of this idea; the first in 1859. It should be noted that the first person to propose such a 'wild' idea was Antonio Snide; a creationist. He based his theory on Genesis 1:9-10. Geologists have confirmed its validity. Plate tectonics allow for the sea-floor to have caused Pangaea to break apart and the land masses we see today to form.

The earth's magnetic field would also cause the minerals within the earth's crust to be magnetised. Evidence seems to also suggest that the magnetic fields have reversed in the past. This reversal, if quick enough, would allow lava flows so thin, they would be able to cool within a few weeks according to Dr. Russell Humphreys. R.S. Coe and M.

Prevot have confirmed that the reversals of the magnetic field were, in their own words, astonishingly rapid.[239]

Dr. John Baumgardner has been able to produce a 3-D computer simulation of the results of plate tectonics. Without getting into the exhaustive details of his research, he has been able to demonstrate how Pangaea could have formed the continents today. It can be shown through these movements, collisions would occur between plates; the direct result would be the formation of mountains. Mount Ararat is at the junction of three different crustal plates.[240] Unlike geologists who suggest the movement was very slow, about two cm. per year, it could have happened during the one year period of the flood. This rapid movement would cause explosive results when collisions occurred and would completely explain the mountain ranges seen worldwide. Most everyone knows about the San Andreas Fault. It runs along the Pacific Ocean side of North America. Not far from this major fault-line are the extensive Rocky Mountains. Quite interestingly all major fault lines either intersect with land or are very close to land with mountain ranges not that distant.

But the paradigm of plate tectonics is complicated. As I write this a recent discovery shows there could be an amount of water, four hundred to six hundred km. beneath the earth's crust, equal to the total amount of water on our planet. This would explain how the water continued to grow after the rain ceased falling (Gen 7:11, 8:2).

Professor Graham Pearson from the University of Alberta Canada was excavating near Mato Grasso, Brazil. He found a content of one and one half percent water inside a sample of ringwoodite.[241] This is a material that is formed under extreme pressure within the mantle of the earth. This water content is said to possibly hold the key to understanding plate tectonics. It was the shifting land masses that formed the mountain ranges we see. As the plates shifted, the land separated and the mountains formed.

One of the biggest criticisms of the flood story was how all this water dissipated. According to Professor Pearson this shifting could have pulled the water into these chasms. This could explain how all of the water from the flood subsided. Professor Pearson theorizes that the water could have been sucked (sic) down into the mantle as the plates went through a shifting phase. If the water in the centre of the

---

[239] Batten, Don et. al. *Answers book*. p. 164
[240] Ibid. p. 169
[241] http://ca.news.yahoo.com/blogs/sideshow/new-discovery-suggests-oceans-of-water-beneath-earth-s-surface-192931291.html accessed 2014/16/03

earth is as massive as he suggests it lends credibility to the account of Noah's flood. Additionally Hans Keppler, a geochemist from the University of Bayreuth, stipulates that vast amounts of underground oceans are plausible.[242,243] While the depth is quite substantial, and this is not definitive proof of the Genesis account, it is not out of the realm of possibility that this is what happened to the copious amount of water that would exist after the cataclysmic flood event. From where else would all of this water originate?

Another major event that would have transpired as the result of a global flood would be a massive ice age. Scientists have hypothesized there has been at least one major ice age. Evolutionists maintain the age began about 2Ma and lasted until about eleven thousand years ago. Creationists maintain it happened after the flood and lasted for about one thousand years. The term 'Ice Age' describes the *Pleistocene* era. Long-age anthropologists say it was during this period that man reached his pinnacle of evolutionary development. The ice covered most of North America & Greenland, Northern Europe; the west coast of South America, Antarctica, and New Zealand & Tasmania. Ice could have also been on the peaks of S.E. Australia.

Geologists claim there were most likely four advances and retreats due to temperature fluctuations. Some have proposed as many as twenty cycles of advance and retreat. M. J. Oard suggests that the evidence more likely shows a single ice age after the global flood.[244] The reasons suggested for multiple ice ages just do not seem to make a great deal of sense.

People would have also have had to survive these difficult times. Anthropologists have found evidence that they did thrive near the edge of the glaciers, mostly in Western Europe. They had capitulated to creationist's ideals by saying Neandertal man, who would have been alive at this time, could have attained their brutish appearance because of the environment to which they were subjected. The dark, cold and humid conditions would result from lack of sunlight. Sunlight is a major contributor to Vitamin 'D'. Vitamin 'D' is necessary for proper bone development; lack of which would cause rickets, which has already been discussed. It is

---

[242] http://www.nature.com/nature/journal/v507/n7491/full/nature13080.html accessed 2014/16/03
[243] https://ca.news.yahoo.com/found-hidden-ocean-locked-deep-earths-mantle-181204475.html accessed 2014/13/06
[244] Oard M.J. *Ancient Ice Ages or Gigantic Submarine Landslide?* pp. 149-166

completely feasible they existed during the time of Abraham and his descendants.

The Jews lived in a part of the world that was unaffected by the ice age so they would have not been directly influenced. Archaeologists have determined there was evidence of man-kind thriving in the areas untouched by the glaciers. Evolutionists are also at a loss to explain how rocks from this era also show signs of a worldwide subtropical climate. Assigning millions-of-years only seems to exacerbate the situation where ascribing one thousand years, only three thousand five hundred, seems to explain the evidence.

In order for an ice age to even begin, the oceans would have to be warm near the mid-high latitudes. The land needed to be cold especially during the hotter summer months. As the warm water evaporated, the air currents carry the cold damp air over the continents. The clouds would then cause the precipitation to fall as snow rather than as rain. Since the cold summers would not allow the snow to melt, ice would rapidly accumulate. The warm ocean would be a direct result of hot subterranean water that was a result of the *"fountains of the great deep"* (Gen. 7:11; 8:2 KJV) bursting forth. Before the flood there was no rain, no volcanic eruptions, no snow, but a wonderful world that had been prepared for man and animals to be *"very good"* (Gen. 1:31). The water necessary for life would be provided by waters above the expanse. This relates back to what I said earlier about Noah building his boat in the middle of a desert. While the earth's crust was being traumatised by the waters bursting forth, the conditions necessary for the break-up of the super continent would have occurred. The flood's after-effects would allow for the ice age. Water evaporation would cause the greenhouse effect to diminish and the polar caps would grow. This is what caused the ice formations and the land bridges to appear. Land bridges formed by the resulting ice would allow the animals to disperse around the world.

Since water was also falling from the 'canopy' above the earth, the warming effect that maintained the pleasant conditions on earth would subside. This would cause the poles to become much colder. After the rain had ceased, plants and life would start to return to the pre-flood condition. The delicate balance would start to resume. The activity of life would return the mixture of oxygen and carbon dioxide back to normal. This, accompanying the return of water in the 'canopy' above the earth, would increase the greenhouse effect. This is similar to what we are experiencing today, only humans are said to be causing excessive CO_2 emissions that are warming the planet to temperatures higher than it was designed to accommodate. It would also be reasonable to assume that volcanic action at the end of the flood and for some time afterwards would increase the greenhouse effect.

The actual ice age event is described in the Bible (Job 37:9-10; 38:22-23; 38:29-30). Job may have seen the ice age coming to a conclusion. The slow freezing and unfreezing proposed by evolutionists makes this difficult to fathom. A massive flood followed by an extended ice age is the only explanation that makes sense.

More evidence for a warm climate at the northern parts of the earth was shown when a fossilised camel was found in Northern Canada. Palaeontologist Dr. Natalie Rybczynski, from the Canadian Museum of Nature, discovered thirty leg bone fragments on Ellesmere Island in 2006, 2008 & 2010. As a Canadian I can tell you it can get quite cold for months at a time here. The scientists involved took collagen from the bones for comparison analysis. Apparently this collagen was able to remain intact for the estimated three million years since the fossil was laid down. Dr. Rybczynski said this could show an evolutionary pattern that happened due to residing in a polar environment for millions-of-years, as the most likely explanation.[245] A simpler explanation would be that the earth was not cold but a tropical climate before the flood and the ice age after the flood required the camels to grow longer fur to combat the colder conditions.

The global flood was a cataclysm that has not be seen since. The results of such a massive catastrophe are evident if a person looks at the evidence with an open mind. Below are just a few more geological examples that point to the plausibility of a global flood:

Geological:
- Fish River Canyon in Namibia: Area around river consists of a flat plain, parched with an absence of vegetation. Interestingly the gorge flows in a downward path; what one would expect if it was cut into the sedimentary rock in a very short period of time. This dictates that the canyon's erosion began when the water level was much higher and the resulting erosion from the rapid flow caused a downwards movement as opposed to a sideways one.[246]

---

[245] http://www.redorbit.com/news/science/1112797217/giant-camel-fossils-discovered-canada-030513/ accessed 2013/09/30
[246] Creation Magazine Vol. 36 #2 2014

- Piece of wood in Sydney quarry dated by ^{14}C to thousands-of-years, while the Sandstone cover dated at two hundred million years.
- Mt. Saint Helens 1980- eight metres finely layered sediment deposited in one hour
- Burlingame Canyon (N.W. U.S.A.) looks like eroded over thousands-of-years, but torrential rainfall caused it in few days.
- Flour mill in US sack of flour petrified in few weeks after mill flooded by mineralized water.
- Dec 2004 Indonesia tsunami. Towns destroyed in few minutes.
- June 2013 Alberta Canada. Two hundred millimetres of rain in three days displayed erosion equivalent to several centuries. Hillsides carved out up to two and one half metres deep.
- In Missoula, western Montana USA, after the end of the Ice Age, reported to be about four thousand years ago, an ice dam broke, allowing the lake to virtually empty in a period of a few days. Water moving at approximately one hundred k.p.h. and one hundred eighty metres in depth washed through modern-day Spokane. When the water reached Portland OR. It is estimated to have been about one hundred twenty metres deep. The water eroded two hundred km^3 of soil and rock-like basalt.
- Sites in Mesopotamia excavated in the early 1900's display many layers of alluvium. This is sediment deposited by flowing water. Also found by digging at these sites was obvious evidence of human habitation above and below the layers.
- Sir Leonard Wolley found clean water-laid silt that varied from 3.4-3.7 metres in depth near Tell al-Muqayyer (Ancient *Ur*). It was dated to around 3500 B.C.
- Tell al-'Oheimir yielded some exciting finds. Stephen Langdon and Charles Watelin found four alluvial deposits with the top layer being about thirty cm. thick. Discovered in 1928-29 it is dated to 3300 B.C.
- Tell Fara provided evidence in the form of an alluvial deposit sixty-one cm. in height found in 1930-31 dated to around 3,000 B.C.
- Tell Quyunjik (Nineveh) once was the Assyrian Empire headquarters. Here, a mud and riverine sand strata was discovered in 1931-32 that measured almost two metres. What is most interesting is that these were found over sixteen metres below a mound surface.

- Julius Jordan reported a find of sterile stratum one and one half metre in depth at Warka Erech (Gen.10:10, Ez.4:9). He dated it to the early 2,000's B.C.
- Dar i Khazineh shows evidence of an ancient village. It is situated near the Karun River in Iran. The village appears to have been inhabited for a long time before the apparent flooding.[247]
- Andre Parrot during his search in 1930-31 came upon a 'sterile layer'. He determined it was from around 2,000 B.C. While not completely clear it has been suggested he found a flood layer.[248]

Archaeological:
- Freshwater molluscs submerged on Black Sea floor.
- Saltwater marine life, freshwater amphibian and land creature (spiders, scorpions, millipedes, insects and reptiles) fossils found in same location by researchers from Museum of Natural History in Paris.
- *Mawsonite spriggi* (jellyfish) found in Ediacara fossil reserve in South Australia buried in sandstone.
- Five hundred gigantic fossilized oysters discovered four thousand metres above sea level in Huancavelica province four hundred km., south east of Lima Peru.
- At the Grand Canyon, Redwall Limestone, commonly contains fossil *Brachiopods* (a clam-like organism), Corals, *Bryozoans* (lace corals), *Crinoids* (sea lilies), *Bivalves* (types of clams), *Gastropods* (marine snails), *Trilobites, Cephalopods*, and even fish teeth.[249]
- Fossil ammonites (coiled marine *Cephalopods*) are found in limestone beds in the Himalayas of Nepal over eight thousand metres above sea level.[250]
- Fossil-bearing marine lime-stones form the summit pyramid of Everest.
- *Ctenacanthus* and other *Chondrichthyan Spines* and *Denticles* found on top of the Rocky Mountains

---

[247] Bailey, Lloyd. *Noah.* p. 30
[248] Ibid p. 31
[249] . S. Beus, "Redwall Limestone and Surprise Canyon Formation," in *Grand Canyon Geology*, 2nd ed., Oxford University Press, 2003, p. 115–135
[250] J. P. Davidson, et al. *"The Rise and Fall of Mountain Ranges,"* in *Exploring Earth: An Introduction to Physical Geology* Upper Saddle River, New Jersey: Prentice Hall, 1997, pp. 242–247

- Fossils of whales and other marine animals in mountain sediments in the Andes
- Large quantities of marine fossils found in Ural Mountains of Russia.
- Marine life in mountains of Papua New Guinea one thousand two hundred metres above sea level.

The biggest argument presented by the long-agers is that this is the result of plate tectonics, and they would be right. The only problem is that they say it took millions-of-years, whereas creationists would say it was the result of Noah's flood. So we can agree it was plate tectonics that caused this anomaly. The problem with millions-of-years is that although the fossils would have to be buried, they would be subjected to millions-of-years of erosion. So, we are to believe that almost every major mountain top was once the sea bed and over the millions-of-years it took to rise up to their current elevation; the water above the sea bed and the water that would fall in the form of rain or precipitation, along with the water that would rush over the area, did not wash away the sand covering the fossils and in doing so damage the fossils? This coupled with all the other evidence presented, just happened? Looking at the mountains, the effects of years of erosion is evident. How did these fossils become buried in the sea bed? Why were they not scavenged by the other aquatic life? They appear in near perfect form, yet fossilised. How do deniers explain large stone blocks that seem to have been carried from a source quite distant and just left there?[251] And they accuse believers of implausibility. One convert who studied all the evidence from a naturalistic worldview said: *"When I was an unbeliever I did not see any of the evidence for a flood. Everything could explain within the millions-of-year timeframe. Now I believe I see the evidence everywhere".* Rose-coloured glasses indeed.

Lastly, archaeological finds can be quite revealing. At Tell al Muqayyar, vaults were discovered with skeletal remains of oxen teams still harnessed to wagons that contained household furniture. The tomb of the 'Lady Shubad' contained twenty skeletons of noblemen with nearby vaults displaying up to seventy. It was easily determined the remains were of noble-hood because of the baroque ornaments in which they were attired. It was determined by the depth of the remains that the catastrophe that caused the scene was approximately 2800 B.C.

---

[251] Denton, Michael. *Theory in Crisis*. p.22

As shafts were sunk into the ground, fragments of bowls, pots and jars appeared that were eerily similar to those found in the graves of kings. Approaching the bottom of the shaft, charred remains appeared. Also found was pure clay. This layer was several yards higher than the river. The surrounding clay could have only been deposited by large volumes of water. Digging deeper, the clay layer continued until astonishingly it just ceased. Here was clay that miraculously began and ended, with no intermixing in the soil directly above or below. But even more perplexing was that below the clay, not pure fresh soil but rubble, garbage and more pots were discovered. Human habitation was evident above and below the clay echelon. Above the clay line the pottery appeared to be made on a potter's wheel, but below they appeared to be hand fashioned.

To confirm the finds, another shaft was dug about three hundred metres away. The exact same results occurred. Then to further confirm the results a shaft was sunk on a natural hill. The clay layer was absent but the pottery result was identical.[252] The conclusion to all of this excavating was that a catastrophic flood such as the one described in Genesis, although described as a fairy-tale, is actually a part of history.[253]

In November of 2013, a report was released about an amazing dinosaur find. In Alberta Canada's Dinosaur Provincial Park, a nearly complete fossilized *Chasmosaurus-belli* infant dinosaur was discovered. The remains were found near a hillside. This particular fossil had no observable injuries to its body. No scavengers had even attempted to strip the carcass. The size of the skeletal remains show it was most likely only three years old. It had been found in layers of sediment suggesting it had been covered by massive amounts of water. It appears the creature was trying to escape a torrent of water but was overcome. It died there and was covered with sediments until the recent find unearthed it.[254] The researchers' explanation could also suggest it was covered during the flood. Creationists have always said it was Noah's flood that produced the world-wide fossil record. The animals were quickly buried by the copious amount of water, explaining why fossils remain intact with no scavenging marks. Here is a prime example of what would have happened during the flood. If people would only get this millions-of-years out of their

---

[252] Keller. W. *History*. p. 47-50
[253] Ibid. p. 51
[254] http://ca.news.yahoo.com/blogs/geekquinox/rare-baby-dinosaur-fossil-discovered-alberta-224033744.html accessed 2013/26/11

mind-set and look at the evidence it would become obvious to them. Next we shall examine archaeological proof for the Bible.

Chapter 6
Archaeological Evidence for the Bible?

If the Bible is true, there should be loads of evidence for the stories recorded. While archaeology cannot prove that the Bible is the Word of God, it can verify it is historically accurate. Statements to the contrary do not change the fact that archaeology does confirm the Bible. There is ample evidence for this affirmation, unless it is dismissed as forgery. This seems to be a reoccurring theme; any evidence for the Bible must be a fraud or a complete forgery. It cannot possibly be factual. As Professor Dawkins likes to say to Christians who invoke God, *"that's convenient"*. We shall start at the beginning and continue from there.

Detractors like to claim that the Bible has taken many of its stories from pagan sources and made them their own. The creation story of Genesis was supposedly taken from the Babylonians. A discovery of seventeen thousand clay tablets in modern Syria has debunked this statement. These clay fragments were made over six hundred years before the Babylonian tale. These speak of a lone omnipotent creator assembling the heavens, stars, planets and the earth. These completely destroy the theory that the monotheistic God evolved from polytheism.

The Tower of Babel story (Gen. 11:1-9) has generated some controversy. Is there any proof for what the Bible tells us about this time? Linguistics is a study of the connexion of different languages and their respective syntaxes. Similarities between Sanskrit and European languages were first noted in the early sixteenth century,[255] leading to the theory that a common language was the beginning of these respective

---

[255] Mascaro, Juan. *Bhagavad Gita* Introduction-Translation

languages. While the inhabitants were building the Tower of Babel, God confounded the languages (Gen. 11:9). This is when the inhabitants of what would become Babylon, dispersed over all the earth (Gen. 11:8). It has been suggested this is where the word 'babble' originated. It was famed linguist Alfredo Trombetti who became known for his hypothesis of the doctrine of monogenesis, first proposed in the book *"L'unità d'origine Del linguaggio",* published in 1905. This means that if all the world's languages are traced back through time to their origin, a common ancestral language will be found. Although slightly controversial, this idea is beginning to gain more acceptance as time progresses. This theory supports the Biblical story of Babel.

Sixty miles south of Bagdad between the Tigris and Euphrates rivers, Professor Robert Koldewey was able to unearth a maze of trenches, pits and heaps of rubble which show ancient Biblical Babylon. The remnants display buildings constructed of brick made from mud. Like their Egyptian neighbours, pyramid shaped buildings were constructed. Only in Babylon, they were called ziggurats and were made to honour a certain god. The one honouring their god, Marduk, was razed after being destroyed, on several occasions, until it was the highest tower in Babylon. This monument most likely was completed by King Nebuchadnezzar II (c.605-562 B.C.). An inscription left from his rule states the building was made from *"baked brick enamelled in brilliant blue."*

During the excavation of the city, as the 'Hanging Gardens' were being discovered, so was *Etemenanki* (the Tower of Babel). In Nebuchadnezzar's impressive palace, as well as the Ishtar-Gate, were found copious inscriptions. This tower in Babylon was neglected by the conqueror Xerxes, after his conquest of Babylon around 478 B.C. One of the tablets that were discovered inside the temple recalls the length, width and height of the tower. The actual construction method verifies the Biblical account.

This type of construction has been verified by archaeological digs. Asphalt bricks were used as the foundation, most likely due to being constructed in the vicinity of the local rivers that could cause flooding and destroy the building if not properly water-proofed. The inscription discovered refers to the building as being seven stages; seven squares rising above each other, with the terrace having a different measurement. What archaeologists found was a building ninety-one metres square and approximately ninety-two metres in height. Although the first tower has long been dilapidated to the point of no longer being in existence, the archaeological verification of its construction is undeniable. The Bible is completely accurate in the description of the construction and its location.

The next major narration depicts the life and time of Abraham (Abram); the father of the Jews. Abraham came from Mesopotamia. This has been confirmed by archaeological findings tracing the movements of the people from this region.[256] In 1923, at Tell al Muqayyar, clay cylinders were discovered with cuneiform writing contained on surface. After excavating the surrounding area, a whole city was discovered. Shown to be a few thousand years old, the city of Ur had been found. The ancient city displayed large spacious houses unmatched by any other Mesopotamian city that has been unearthed. The residents of Ur of the Chaldeans were wealthy and liked to flaunt their residences. These residents were polar opposites of the ones found in 600 B.C. by Professor Koldewey, which were mud-brick constructions and one story in height, containing three or four rooms with an open piazza. The ones found from the time of Abraham were two stories in height and had thirteen or fourteen different rooms. Ur was a stark contrast from Nebuchadnezzar's Babylon.

Within the constraints of the houses were hymnals and mathematical tablets that displayed plain arithmetic calculations, to more complex operations with formulas allowing square and cube roots to be computed; a task most college students cannot perform without the aid of electronic devices. It was in Ur that Noah's son, Shem and his descendants would populate the area of Mesopotamia (Gen. 11:27-32). During years of digging, the palace of the king of Mari was found. Dated to the third millennium B.C. it covered an area four hectares in size. Inside the palace were found twenty-three thousand six hundred documents. It was on these tablets names like Peleg, Serug, Nahor, Terah and Haran were found. The clay tablets confirm the genealogy of Abram as recorded in the Bible (Gen. 11:16-26). The tablets from Mari verify the existence of the cities of Haran and Nahor, which by all accounts were well established cities around 2000 B.C. Abram knew of these cities as he sent his servant to Mesopotamia; the city of Nahor (Gen. 24:10) to find a wife for his son Isaac. Abraham has been confirmed by archaeological findings tracing the movements of the people from this region.

In the 1920's extraordinary shards were discovered at Thebes and Saqqara along the Nile river. Contained upon them were inscriptions such as: *"Death strike you at every wicked word and thought, every plot, angry quarrel and plan"*. During the time of the shard, it was common-

---

[256] McDowell, *Evidence*

place to write the name of the person, his/her family and even the domicile of a cursed person. Names found were: Jerusalem, Askelon, Tyre, Hazor, Bethshemesh, Aphek, Achshaph, and even Shechem. Since these vases have been dated to eighteenth and nineteenth century B.C., it is obvious they existed, as mentioned in the Bible. Shechem ruins constructed in the Cyclops-wall fashion were discovered during 1913-1914 by German professor Ernst Sellin. Since that time, remains of Bethel, Mizpah, Gerar, Lachish, Gezer, Gath, Askelon and Jericho have been verified. The construction of these towns showed a heavily fortified city that would easily withstand attack. If necessary the Canaanite population could retire to the palace at Mari, for refuge. Shechem, Bethel, Hebron and Jerusalem were situated in the highlands. In the Plain of Jezreel a more luxurious and rich vegetative landscape would be encountered. Abram decided to obscure his entry by traveling through the hills in the south. This allowed him to enter, unbeknownst to the inhabitants, while providing abundant pastureland for his and Lot's herds.

In 1890, Percy A. Newberry investigated old tombs near Cairo. During his expedition he was able to find three vaults and two rows of pillars sticking out of the ground. The walls contained colourful scenes showing the common-day life of local aristocrats. He was astonished to find pictorials of figures that appeared to be non-Egyptians, as they were wearing clothing that did not match the locals and they appeared to be of lighter-tone skin. The scene seemed to show these foreigners being introduced to nobleman. Hieroglyphics on a document held by one of the observers called the newcomers, sand-dwellers or Semites. Their leader was called Abishai and he had with him thirty-six travel companions. One of the men in the caravan was carrying an eight-stringed lyre; common to the Israelites. As this drawing has been attributed to approximately 1900 B.C., is seems reasonable, this scene depicts Abraham's travel to Canaan and then to Egypt.

After he and Lot returned, they went their separate ways due to infighting between the herdsmen (Gen. 13:7). Lot chose to go to the region near Sodom and Gomorrah (Gen 13:10-11). There is little evidence to show what happened from this time until the destruction of the twin cities due to their decadence (Gen. 19:1-29). There have been many naysayers that question the destruction, but evidence has been found supporting the Biblical story.

Sodom and Gomorrah were near Siddim. Excavations near Babedh Dhra near the south shore of the Dead Sea have shown evidence of massive destruction by fire. As much of the area is covered by ash several feet thick, it appears that this could be the location of the infamous cities. Nearby, asphalt, petroleum and natural gas reserves have been discovered. Along the Jordan Valley, geologists see a crack in the earth's crust. They have been able to determine that the vale of Siddim plunged into the abyss along the Dead Sea south shore shortly after 2000 B.C. According to Jack Finegan the destruction of Sodom and Gomorrah took place around 1900 B.C. These cities now lie submerged under water at the southern section of the Dead Sea.[257] This is extremely unfortunate as the chances of finding any more archaeological evidence is remote.

At the south shore of the Dead Sea (Negeb), there is a range of hills approximately forty-six metres high and sixteen km. from south to north. The vast majority of the rock is pure salt. Known as Jebel Usdum by local Arabs, the erosion of millennia have caused an eerie shape of almost statuesque forms. Anything left in the open is quickly encrusted by a layer of salt- Lot's wife? (Gen. 19:26).

During the 1970's the Ebla archive was found in northern Syria. These archives were invaluable, in that the inscriptions were about the Patriarchs. These clay tablets dated to about 2000 B.C. verify that Abraham, Isaac, Jacob and others were actual historical figures. These tablets were also able to silence the critics that said Canaan did not exist at the time, although Genesis clearly used this as the name of the land God was giving to Abraham and his descendants. Ancient customs reflected in the stories of the Patriarchs have also been found in clay tablets from Nuzi and Mari. Any claims that Abraham is not a true historical figure, seems to be obtuse. Enough evidence has been found that contradicts such a position. Next we must explore the Egyptian captivity and the Exodus out of bondage into the Promised Land.

It has been suggested if the Jews were in fact enslaved in Egypt for over four hundred years, there should be some evidence. On its face this is a reasonable hypothesis. Historians will attest that Egypt was almost obsessive when it came to recording their history. The annals trace each Pharaoh by name all the way to 3000 B.C. Perplexingly this all changed around 1730 B.C. and continued until 1580 B.C. When the Hyksos invaded Egypt and violently overthrew the Pharaoh's reign, things changed. History shows that Middle Kingdom of the Pharaohs was the end of the Egyptian dynasty.

---

[257] Keller. *History*. p. 95

Egyptian historian Manetho recounted the end came during the time of Tutimaeus, with minimal resistance. Salitis was named the new ruler in Memphis. The arrival of Joseph's family coincided with this time period. Manetho termed them king-shepherds (hyksos), where 'hyk' means king and 'sos' means shepherd. The Hyksos ruled from the delta region, which was situated in the vicinity of Goshen, the area assigned to the Hebrew slaves. Since these infiltrations coincided, both groups would be equally despised.[258]

The man to whom Joseph was indentured was named Potiphar (Gen. 37:36). Joseph was able to rise to the position of viceroy (Gen. 41:42); exactly as shown by artistic interpretations drawn on palace murals. Joseph rode in the second chariot of the Pharaoh (v.43), a custom brought to Egypt by the Hyksos. Manetho also wrote about Ham, Noah's son, being the father of Aegyptus (Mestraim). It was Aegyptus who would be one of the first to move to the area known as Egypt at the dispersal. Although the Bible says one of Ham's sons was Mizraim, this was not the name recognised by Hebrews as Egyptian. Manetho confirms that the 'dispersion of the tribes' happened five years after Peleg was born. Genesis 10:25 says Eber had two sons, Peleg, being one and during his time, the earth was divided. Egyptologist Patrick Clarke verifies that the Egyptians did call themselves Kham (Cham or Ham).[259] Joseph's name is borne out near the Nile River. The town Medinet-el-Faiyum has a waterway called Bahr Yusuf or Joseph's Canal. Joseph or Yusuf was not an Egyptian designation. The Bible depicts Joseph as an astute bureaucrat (Gen. 41:53-54). Historically there is no doubt that famine, drought and irregular harvests were not completely uncommon to the Nile region. An inscription on a large rock of the Ptolemies refers to a seven year famine near the beginning of the third millennium. There is also strong evidence of granaries in the Old Kingdom. About the famine, King Zoser wrote about his grave concern about the failure of the Nile River to flood for a period of seven years, the net result was a shortage of food.

The land surrounding the Nile River floods on an annual basis. It is this flooding that made life possible in Egypt. To the east and west are stretches of vast deserts; but alongside the Nile lies black alluvial soil, providing rich land for cultivating crops. Due to the unfriendly surrounding desert, ninety-five percent of Egyptians live on five percent of the land.[260]

---

[258] Walton, J. *Genesis.* p. 687
[259] Carl Wieland. Creation Ministries Magazine. *Ancient Egypt confirms: Genesis is History.* Vol. 35 No. 4. 2013. p. 66.
[260] Matthews et. al. *Humanities.* p.12

The failure to flood, as told about by King *Zoser*, would be a disaster to the people. Only an imaginative and proficient leader could prevent mass starvation and loss of life.

Other evidence for the famine comes from the tomb of Ameni in Beni-Hassan. He lived during the time of Sesostris I during the 12th Dynasty. An inscription says:

> "No one was unhappy in my days, not even in the years of famine, for I had tilled all the fields in the name of Mah, up to its Southern and Northern frontiers. Thus I prolonged the life of its inhabitants"

With Joseph being second in command, Ameni would have been a subordinate. The fact he tried to take credit, is human nature. An Egyptian Pharaoh would never allow a sand-dweller to rise to such a prestigious position (Gen. 46:34). It is during Hyksos' reign that Semitic names are found, with references to their position of authority with considerable numbers of Semites living in the area and being mentioned as serving with the Egyptian government hierarchy.[261] Herodotus confirms the name Jacob-Her is found on many scarabs from the Hyksos' rule. The Bible does not record the four hundred thirty years of captivity, only the ten plagues and the Exodus. But contrary to what Mr. Stenger suggests[262] there is actually a great deal of evidence of Israelite presence near Egypt before the thirteenth century B.C.

We have already seen that Joseph and family lived during the time of the Hyksos, in Egypt. The Pharaoh at the time of the Exodus was most likely Rameses II, and he would have known nothing of Joseph (Ex. 1:8-11). The Egyptians would not have recognized anyone with ties to the Hyksos. But the evidence is quite clear about his existence.

Percy A. Newberry discovered paintings at Beni-Hasan, which originated from 1900 B.C. A painting, found in a tomb that lay west of Thebes displays Rekhmire, a public representative of the government, watching over the making of bricks necessary for all the construction occurring at the time. What is most notable about the paintings is it shows dark-skinned overseers maintaining watch over lighter-skinned men who were wearing only linen aprons. The fair-skinned labourers could not possibly be native Egyptians. The manner, in which the people are depicted, also shows the work is forced labour and not voluntary. The depictions of the tomb walls are eerily reminiscent of the Bible passage

---

[261] Walton, J. *Genesis.* p. 674
[262] Stenger. *Hypothesis* p. 185

where the Egyptians made the Israelites live in servitude making bricks and mortar (Ex. 1:13-14). What is most interesting is an inscription at this time refers to the 'PR' hauling stones and bricks for Pi-Ramses-Meri-Amun. In Hieroglyphics, the Egyptians used 'PR' to describe Semites.

After varying opinions and much disagreement, archaeologists finally agreed on the actual cities that housed the slaves. At Wadi Tumilat, evidence of Pithom (tell er-Retaba) and Succoth (Tell er-Maskhuta) was found. In addition to the granaries already described, writings about storehouses were also found. The slave labour for the building craze of Ramses appears to be the descendants of Joseph as they lived where the granaries were constructed.

The site for Pithom was found in 1900 and in 1930 Pi-Ramses-Meri-Amun (Avaris) was finally proven to have existed. Professor Montet, excavating from 1929-1932, happened upon statues, columns, sphinxes and building remnants that had the Ramses II crest. This proved beyond any doubt it was Pi-Ramses-Meri-Amun, or the Biblical city of Ramses.[263]

The Egyptians must have realised a well-fed slave is a hard-working slave. While in the desert the Israelites would complain to Moses about the abundance of food they had in Egypt (Ex. 16:3, Num.11:4-5, 18). Was this just belly-aching, or were their dietary needs met? In a school letter written on papyrus to teacher Amen-em-Opet, student Pai-Bes wrote about the life experienced by the slaves in Egypt. Food was plentiful, the lakes/streams full of fish, birds are everywhere, and the fields yield bounties of fruits and vegetables. He extolled the joy felt by everyone. It is clear there were slaves in Egyptian households.[264] Sir Alan Gardiner recalls that records show an increased abundance of Asiatic slaves,[265] and it appears that they were the descendants of Joseph.

Jewish historian Josephus tells us that the Egyptians were barbaric to the Israelites and devised ways of inflicting as much pain as possible. Sir Flinders Petrie described a town build from mud bricks. The pottery found in this town was without doubt from a people not native to Egypt. Another expert is Rosalie David, who was in charge of Egyptology at Manchester Museum. In her book *"The Pyramid Builders of Ancient Egypt"* she talks about the Brooklyn Papyrus. On this relic, a woman, called Senebtisi, exerts her legal right to the ownership of ninety-five servants. In looking at the names, twenty-nine could be identified as Egyptians and another forty-eight were, in Egyptian terminology, "Asiat-

---

[263] Keller. *History*. p. 120
[264] Encyclopedia Britannica (1964). Vol. 8 p. 35
[265] Ashton et al. *Argument* p. 263

ic". Though the exact birth place could not be guaranteed, the "Asiatic" were most likely of Semitic origin according to Ms. David.

The barbarism in the treatment of Jewish babies can also be seen in finds at Kahun. Beneath the floors of houses were found boxes with infants, sometimes three to a box. The babies were determined to be less than a few months at the time of death. This was not an Egyptian custom. Even babies born to Egyptians parents were mummified and buried in the manner of adults. These children obviously belonged to another culture. Why would so many babies be found buried in this manner? True, infant mortality rates were high at this point in history, but finding multiple bodies in a single box seems to suggest something more sinister (Ex. 1:15-16). This would easily explain all the children hidden under the floors of the houses.

It was the plagues that convinced Pharaoh to release the people. The Leiden Museum in Holland has on display a papyrus that seems to refer to the plagues. The Ten Plagues would account for the disastrous picture described. Though not conclusive, it is highly suggestive. I doubt the Egyptians would concede in recording they were soundly trounced by the God of the Hebrews. Admitting this to the world would be inviting invaders to come and conquer them.

Archaeologically, there is also evidence of a mass evacuation of Kahun. During the time of Khasekemre-Neferhotep I, Kahun was a thriving community. After the completion of building in the vicinity, it would be expected people might leave for another town to do more construction. This is a completely reasonable and plausible scenario. But what is the explanation for the town becoming deserted and most of the inhabitant's tools and worldly possessions being left behind from not only the shops but also the houses? Could it be that the people just got up and left without any advanced notice or planning and left with only what they could easily carry? (Ex. 12:39)

What about the actual journey to the Promised Land? What evidence is there for that? Jacob's descendants arrived in Egypt (Gen. 46:27), including Joseph and his two sons. It has been estimated that about two million people left Egypt for the Promised Land. Some have questioned this number saying it is not reasonable. The Bible tells us they were in Egypt for four hundred thirty years. Approximately seventy people began the sojourn. To have two million after four hundred thirty years we would need a yearly population increase of about 2.4 percent. Is this plausible? Think back to the chapter on evolution. From 1900-1950 the rate of increase was 1.09 percent and 3.1 percent from 1950-2000.

That is an average of 2.1 percent. While in Egypt the Jews multiplied quickly (Ex. 1:7). Given the life expectancy three to four thousand years ago, 2.4 percent for that time is not exorbitant, and at the very least not an exaggeration. People at the time were also quite proficient at procreation. Let's look at the sons of Jacob: Reuben-four sons, Simeon-six sons, Levi-three sons, Judah-five sons, Issachar- four sons, Zebulun- three sons, Gad- seven sons, Asher-four sons, Joseph- two sons, Benjamin-ten sons, Dan-one son, and Naphtali- four sons. That's fifty-three grandsons born to Jacob plus the unmentioned number of daughters/granddaughters. If that continued for four hundred thirty years there would be many Israelites in Egypt. These numbers are not hyperbole. It is estimated that Ramses II, son of Seti, had well over one hundred children[266] and could have had as many as ninety-six sons and sixty daughters.[267]

Professor William Foxwell Albright confirms that the record of the start of the journey to the Promised Land is correct in every detail.[268] The best description of the actual journey takes place in Numbers 33. To travel with children, and the animals that would be present, allowed for a maximum trek of twenty km. per day. The goal would be to travel in as hospitable an environment as possible. It would be imperative water would be found at the end of each day or they were able to bring enough with them to make it to the next watering hole. When following the path to the Promised Land, they did not venture far from pastureland or the many oases along the route (v.27). The first oasis is called Elim in the Bible; modern-day Wadi Gharandel. So this part of the record can be shown to be completely accurate as, confirmed by Professor Albright.

Some have openly criticized manna and quails from Heaven as pure myth. This is misquoted, as we are told it was a wind that brought the quails to them (Num. 11:31a). This can still be seen today. According to the Hebrew calendar the Exodus began in the month Abib, equivalent to March-April in the Gregorian calendar. This is when many birds migrate from Africa to Europe through the Eastern Mediterranean. Quails, with other types of birds, fly across the Red Sea. Josephus recorded Bedouins were able to catch them by hand.[269] This was due to the fact that after their journey from Africa the birds would need rest along the

---

[266] http://www.touregypt.net/featurestories/ramesses2intro.htm accessed 2013/26/04
[267] Aidan Dodson & Dyan Hilton, *The Complete Royal Families of Ancient Egypt,* Thames & Hudson 2004 p.166
[268] Cited in Ashton et al. *Argument* p. 121
[269] *Antiquities*, III, I,5

shores of the sea. Due to the hot arid conditions, the birds would remain dormant during the day and take to flight when the sun went down, The Israelites would then be able to catch them in their nets (Ex. 16:13).

Manna is still exported from the Sinai region. It is found recorded in nearly all botanical indexes of the Middle East.[270] In 1843 Breitenbach, Dean of Mainz, wrote the "*Bread of Heaven*" is still gathered to be sold to the pilgrims. According to Breitenbach, the 'bread' falls around sunrise. It looks like the morning mist and adheres like beads to the grass, stones and twigs. It is quite soft and moist with a honey-like taste (Ex. 16:31). It was Friedrich Simon Bodenheimer and Oskar Theodor, of the Hebrew University, Jerusalem, that produced photographs validating these previous statements. The Bedouins also confirm that, in the good years, they would be able to collect 1.8 kg of manna. This would be more than enough to satisfy anyone (Ex. 16:16). Manna is still produced by the Tamarisks in the Sinai right up to the Dead Sea along the Wadi el Arabah.

After leaving Elim, they came to the Wilderness of Sin (Num. 33:12), a plateau that can be sweltering during the day. The encampment happened at Dophkah. In 1904, an expedition, headed by Flinders Petrie, discovered a temple near the side of a cliff. Found here was the undeniable evidence of burnt offerings. To the utter amazement of the participants, 'Rameses II' appeared, carved into the sides of the temple wall. Further investigation revealed stone fragments with unusual characteristics. Though similar to Egyptian hieroglyphics, there was a stark difference. The number of different characters was too few to be from the Egyptians.

People familiar with the area were able to determine these were reminiscent of the writing style of Canaanites from around 1500 B.C. and not exactly like hieroglyphics and cuneiform. The so-called illiterate Jews had their own writing style. But no-one was able to decipher the text until Sir Alan Gardiner was able to make sense of some of the pictorials. It was the shepherd's crook that was instrumental in his untangling the messages. Then, in 1948 all of the tablets were decrypted by experts from the University of Los Angeles. There was absolutely no doubt they were from around 1500 B.C. and Canaanite writings. What is most amazing is that our alphabet was derived from these drawings.

The progression from pictorials to corresponding letters or words is well documented. When the letter or word that represents what the pic-

---

[270] Keller, *History*. p. 129

torial dictates is shown, it is not that hard to decipher. It shows the progression, and helps prove that the Israelites did have written word at the time, confirming Moses was able to pen the Pentateuch, contrary to skeptics trying to call into question the Biblical record.

After leaving Dophkah they stopped at Alush; then to Redhidim where Amalek came to fight with them (Ex. 17:8). The current-day name for Redhidim is Feiran; a miniature paradise with shade provided by palm trees. It was here that Moses stroke the rock that gushed forth water for the Israelites (Ex. 17:6). This causes many a skeptic to taunt believers of such an improbable event. Major C.S. Jarvis confirms that he has seen for himself such an event. While digging for water, Sergeant Bash Shawish mistakenly struck a limestone rock. Before his fateful action, they had noted a slow trickle of water flowing from the limestone rock face. The rock split open and a gush of water come forth, giving veracity to the story of Moses' actions.

Israel then moves on to Sinai where Moses receives the Ten Commandments. The Ark of the Covenant made out of acacia wood, which was native to the Sinai and still abundantly used, was constructed. From here they move on to Kadesh which is two hundred forty km. from Sinai. This area is to the west of the Gulf of Aqabah. The descriptions of the lands in the Bible mate perfectly with the topographical information provided in Scripture.

In 1887, three hundred seventy-seven clay tablets were found at Tell el-Amarna in the form of cuneiform letters. The letters from the time of Amenophis III included writings, in Akkadian, from Palestine, Phoenicia and Southern Syria. Some of the letters were written in Canaanite dialect, speaking of Suwardata who was Prince of Hebron. His name along with the name Indaruta, are both of Indo-Aryan descent. Biryawaza of Damascus, Biridiya of Megiddo, Widia of Askelon, and Birashshena of Shechem are also of this lineage. Interestingly, Indaruta, who was prince of Achsaph, is also found in the Vedas and other Sanskrit writings. These people are called Horites in the Bible. An Egyptian papyrus from the fifteenth century B.C. confirms that Canaan was called Khuru, showing the Hurri (Horites) was dispersed throughout the land.

Unfortunately the next thirty-eight years are vacant in the pages of the Bible. The Bible records a considerable amount of time spent in the Negev. This allowed access to abundant water at Kadesh. The Israelites did wander around Midian and the Sinai. But, unlike what most people think this area would not readily be called a desert; more like a wilderness. It was at this time Moses sent out the twelve spies on a reconnaissance mission. Dr. Rudolph Cohen, after twenty-five years of painstaking excavation, was able to find Middle Bronze Age I pottery tracing the route of the journey to the Promised Land. He retorted to criticism of his findings that the similarities between the route of the Exodus and the Middle Bronze I migration where so close to being succinct that to call it coincidence would be an overstatement.[271]

Nelson Glueck was able to determine, through archaeological findings, the areas where they camped were populated by semi-nomadic tribes around the thirteenth century. But there is not an abundance of evidence of a large group of people abiding here for almost forty years. Would it be unreasonable to expect some evidence of habitations? That is a valid query. They did not know from one day to the next what to expect. They would, without doubt, be sure to carry everything with them, in case it was needed again. This would include personal belongings, necessary items for campfires such as wood etc. The next stop may not be able to provide the necessities to cook food. They would also be sure to leave nothing behind as everything was necessary for survival. It is not outside the bounds of logic that very little would be left to provide artefacts of a previous occupation. Natural meteorological occurrences could easily obscure anything forgotten.

Once a year, tens-of-thousands of participants gather in Nevada's Black Rock Desert to create Black Rock City. The participants are dedicated to community, art, self-expression, and self-reliance. They stay in the desert for one week. One of the main requirements of participating in the retreat is to leave no trace whatsoever.[272] Leaving no trace means that nothing is left behind and the area is left in an even better state prior to the incursion.[273] The Israelites were also told to be careful in their treatment of the land (Deut. 23:13). Is it not unreasonable to assume that they did the same thing as these modern-day adventurers?

After wandering through the wilderness for forty years as a punishment for their lack of faith, they were finally ready to enter into Canaan. The idea was to enter from the east, first overtaking the Jordan area. To conquer the land they would have to battle the kingdom of Bashan, Amorites, Moabites, and Edomites. The first to feel the wrath of the invaders would be the Edomites, the first kingdom between the Jordan and the Upper Transjordan. The Edomites, distrustful of nomads, had

---

[271] Cited in Ashton et. al. *Argument* p. 270
[272] http://www.burningman.com/ accessed 2014/05/03
[273] http://www.burningman.com/whatisburningman/about_burningman/principles.html#.Uxi-B4WGfNE accessed 2014/05/03

refused the Israelites passage through their territory when Moses asked (Num. 20:14-21). This caused them to go northwards, with stops at Oboth and Punon for water. They migrated along the Sered River circling around Moab. They finally reached the land of the Amorites (Num. 21:13). Denied permission to use the King's Highway, the Israelites had enough. They soundly defeated King Sihon (21:21-32). Travelling by Bashan they defeated King Og (21:33-35).

Structures known as the Great Stone Graves were constructed in an oval formation providing evidence of the Biblical account. In 1918 a dolmen was found near Amman, by Gustav Dalman. Amman now exists where Rabbath-Ammon once stood. The physical dimensions of the dolmen correspond to the description of Deut. 3:11. The dolmen's resemblance of this description is eerily similar. After much investigation it was made apparent that these dolmens are common-place in Palestine.

It is at this point that King Og, in desperation, decides to use black magic; a complete disaster, to prevent his defeat and calls upon Balaam (Num. 22-24). The Hebrews had defeated everything that stood in their path to the Promised Land. It was time to enter.

The book of Joshua recalls the conquest of the Promised Land. Before they were to enter into the land, Joshua sent two men to spy out what was before them. While in Jericho they were protected from the king by Rahab, who hid them from the inhabitants; in exchange they promised she and her family would be spared, when the Israelites overthrew Jericho (Josh. 2:1-24).

As with the parting of the Red Sea, this has been ridiculed by non-believers. But it is fact, during the dry season the water at Jericho is only about nine metres wide. If a dam was placed near this narrow spot the flow is easily blocked providing an easy pathway across the river. Arab records from the time show there was a blockage that stopped flow in 1267 A.D. This phenomenon has been repeated after a local earthquake in 1927, 1924 and 1906. It is not a stretch to believe this could have happened at the time of the invasion.

North of Jericho lays the ruins of the city Tell es-Sultan where traces can be found of a civilization dating to the Bronze Age. From 1907-1909 excavation by Professor Ernst Sellin and Professor Karl Watzinger of this area caused dramatic results. What was found describes the Biblical city of Jericho. It had two parallel walls approximately 3-3.7 metres apart, with the inner wall being 3.7 metres thick. The outer wall was built with strong foundations and was just under two metres thick and about eight to nine metres high, made of brick. [274]

In 1930 Professor John Garstang confirmed that the space between the two described walls had a plethora of rubble. Evidence of a massive fire was abundantly clear. The houses lining the walls had been burned to the ground with the roofs lying flat. The dating of the destruction varies from expert to expert, but has been set at either 1400 B.C., or between 1250-1200 B.C. Some say this is the result of the battle with the Israelites. Some do not accept that theory. But what is agreed upon is that the walls of Jericho were at one time standing as protection from invading forces and a massive cataclysm caused them to collapse.

When the ancient city of Jericho was being excavated from 1930-1936 it was found that the city outer walls fell outward, and the inner walls fell inward, burying the buildings adjacent to the wall. There was also evidence of great crevices in the bricks. This destruction would allow attackers to simply scale them and advance into the defeated city.

Many will remember the Sunday school rhyme about the walls of Jericho that *"came tumbling down"*. The Hebrews were able to take the city straightway as told in the Bible (Josh. 6:20). While this evidence is compelling, sometimes all that is available is customs at the time of writing. Since it has been so long, it is reasonable to not find actual physical evidence. Other criteria must be used to determine factuality of a statement. Professor Garstang hypothesized it was the result of an earthquake. Since Jericho is in an earthquake zone, on the surface, that would seem reasonable. But if it was an earthquake, why did the outer walls fall outward and the inner walls inward, especially with a 3-3.7 metre foot gap between them? Walls do not usually behave this way in an earthquake. Having the walls lie completely flat and not pile up sure make it easy to just walk right into the city.

What is most interesting, is when excavating the northern section of the site, there was a portion of the wall that remained somewhat intact. The wall at this small section was approximately two and one half metres high. A few small houses remained standing built against the section of bricks. Interesting, the entire city was demolished, yet houses constructed together remain upright. Could one of these houses be where Rahab and her family took sanctuary as the annihilation took place around them?(Josh. 6:17-25) The evidence shows erroneous statements have

---

[274] Keller. *History*. p. 159

Jericho being destroyed in 2400 BCE, almost a millennium before Joshua arrived.[275]

The route taken after Jericho, to subdue the land, has been shown from archaeological studies. Evidence of city-by-city invasion and destruction can be seen. It appears that Joshua initially avoided the strongholds of Jerusalem and Gezer. The Israelites were not warriors and realised it would take time to overthrow all of the cities. The city of Debir lies about 19 km. from Hebron. This city was a mainstay in the Negeb, constructed with an enclosing wall to dissuade invaders. At Tell Beit Mirsim in 1926, W.F. Albright and M.G. Kyle, were able to show that it had been decimated (Josh. 10:38) by an intense fire, the resulting ashes containing shards pointing to destruction in the thirteenth century. Above the ashes they were able to determine a new Israeli settlement had sprung up.

Not far away lays Lachish. Measured, in the 1930's, to be almost ten hectares, it also was defended by a resilient wall. Evidence shows that it too met destruction from an invading force. A bowl from the fourth year of Merneptah confirms a date of 1230 B.C. (Josh. 10:32). A hymn from 1229 B.C. immortalizing his campaigns says:

"Canaan is despoiled and all its evil with it. Askelon is taken captive, Gezer is conquered, and Yanoam is blotted out. The people of Israel is desolate, it has no offspring: Palestine has become a widow for Egypt".

It should be near impossible for anyone to deny, from this Egyptian evidence, Israel had settled into the land of Canaan around 1229 B.C.

Kathleen Kenyon has re-examined the evidence found at Jericho. In her book *"Archaeology in the Holy Land",* she describes how the evidence points to a new people taking over, after the destruction of Jericho. She was able to trace this anomaly to virtually every other city within Palestine. She described the new people as a nomadic tribe only interested in the rural lifestyle, to the point where they took over the land and eliminated all traces of a civilization from the Early Bronze Age.[276]

In 1956 James Pritchard found similar evidence at Gibeon. It appears that a new group of people, with new customs including types of burial and pottery types, migrated into the territory. Although he tried to use this evidence against the invasion, it was his misinterpretation of the

---

[275] Stenger. *Hypothesis.* p. 186-187
[276] K.M. Kenyon. *Archaeology in the Holy Land.* Thomas Nelson. Nashville TN. p. 134

timing that actually confirmed Scripture. Mr. Pritchard has put the Biblical invasion during the Late Bronze Period. But, as shown, the invasion actually occurred during the early-mid Bronze Age. He had proven the Biblical account of the Gibeon overthrow without even realizing his find. The evidence is clear. Joshua was an actual person and there was an invading force into Canaan in the thirteenth century B.C.

The time in the Promised Land was not easy. The book of Judges recalls those early years where the Israelites had to fight off invaders. Debir, Bethshemesh, and Bethel show where they began to build lives for themselves after rebuilding the towns they had vanquished. Excavations in the area show huts and borders constructed over the upper-class palaces of the earlier time. These modest homes were nothing like the forebearers and the belongings inside show the meek existence of the owners. Walls, designed to protect the inhabitants had been rebuilt, but to nowhere near the design strength. They just did not have the time required, and do to so would require slave labour. Obviously, after just leaving bondage in Egypt, this would be something they would abhor. They followed their desires and enjoyed the freedom this new land provided.

New areas became inhabited. They employed methods of survival, must likely learned during the wandering, and employed methods of construction not seen in Canaan until this time. It would be the local tyrants trying to overpower them that would allow for their military ability and might to grow. Invasions by Moabites, Ammonites & Aramaeans causing destruction has been verified at Bethel; happening four separate times between 1200 & 1000 B.C.

Leaders came as a reprieve for the Israelites. Othniel, Ehud, Deborah, Gideon, Jephthah and Samson all arrived at the exact moment they were needed to lead the Jews. Regarded as fables by some people, research in the area has confirmed the stories are factual. A discovery in Jezreel, namely Megiddo and Taanach, show around 1150 B.C., Megiddo was destroyed. Clay pots found show that it was rebuilt around 1100 B.C. and the artefacts were the same as those used by Israelites. These relics have also been found near Samaria and Judea. Evidence points to the onslaught of Megiddo to be around 1125 B.C.

During the time of Gideon, Midianites invaded using a new method of attack (Jdg. 6:5). This would be the first time camels were used in this manner. During the Bronze Age, camels were not a common commodity, even for the Egyptians, whose texts remain silent on the subject. It was in the eleventh century cuneiform texts that the camel appears and the frequency of reference increases. The time of Gideon coincides with this date.

The invading Philistines are the next group dealt with at length by the Bible. They captured Askelon, Ashdod, Ekron, Gaza and Gath (1 Sam. 6:17). After battling the Hebrews, they captured the Ark and took it from Ebenezer to Ashdod (6:1) where they placed in the temple to their god Dagon. The temple was plagued with problems (v.3-5) and plagues of tumours stymied the people (v.6). They decided that the Ark must return to the Israelites (v. 7-12) returning it to Kirjath Jearim (7:1).

This arrival of a foreign people also coincided with a new pottery. This pottery was easily recognisable and found only in the cities mentioned above. This new form, abundant from 1400 B.C.-1200 B.C., was quite similar to those found in Mycenae. When Mycenae was destroyed, the Greek imports ceased. The pottery of the Philistines was strikingly similar. It has been hypothesized that the Philistines came through Mycenae on their journey to Canaan. The Bible says God brought Israel out of Egypt, but He also brought the Philistines up out of Caphtor and the Syrians from Kir (Am.9:7). Caphtor was modern-day Crete. One of the striking facts is that the mugs of the Philistines used a filter to prevent the barley husks used to manufacture beer, from becoming lodged in the throat of the drinker. The story of Samson refers to the heavy drinkers the Philistines must have been.

Although they appeared to like their fermented drinks, the Philistines also were quite adept at the use of iron; extremely valuable at this time. They must likely honed this skill when they encountered the Hittites. There was not a single blacksmith in Israel (1 Sam. 13:19).

During the time of Samson the Philistines were concentrating on their goal to conquer Canaan. Excavation of a site near Seilum uncovered evidence showing the temple that housed the Ark was obliterated around 1050 B.C. Further digging also found similar evidence in Tell Beit Mirsim, Debir and Beth-Zur. To gather all the tribes together, Saul was ordained as king (1 Sam. 10:1). Saul gathered together a fighting force that would battle the Philistines for control of the land. His warfare tactics are still used today, three thousand years after his death.

During WWI Major Vivian Gilbert was scouring his Bible for a reference hidden in the recesses of his mind. He remembered how Jonathan was able to strike a fatal blow to a garrison of Philistines at a place where two sharp rocks called Bozez and Seneh laid. Jonathan and his armour-bearer were able to totally confuse the Philistines to the point where they thought they were being overrun by Saul's troops (1 Sam.

14:14-16). Major Gilbert devised his plan of attack. He sent a small company of men through the pass where they scaled the cliffs and set up their positions. In the morning the Turks reacted the exact same way. Thinking they were surrounded, they bolted. All of them were either killed or captured. Upon reflection Major Gilbert wrote that after millennia, British troops were able to mimic the tactics of Saul and Jonathan. Unfortunately for Saul, this was only winning the battle and not the war. He was eventually defeated, killed alongside his sons.

It was in 1933 that Professor Albright discovered Saul's bastion near Tell el-Ful (Gibeah). It lay in ruins and was confirmed by clay shards strewn about. Dated around 1020-1000 B.C., seventy-two km. north of this find, lays Tell el-Husn (Beth-Shan). Around the same time as the find at Gibeah, archaeologists from the University of Pennsylvania found foundational walls of two temple buildings. Artefacts found within show these temples were dedicated to Astarte and Dagon. Here inscribed is the reward Saul received for his impudence in fighting against the Philistines. They confirm the Bible's description of their actions (1 Sam. 31:10).

Egyptian artefacts record the term Shasu of Yahweh. The word Shasu refers to Semi-nomads or wandering people. These references were recorded during the rule of Thutmosis III, Amenhotep II, Thutmosis IV, Amnehotep III, Akhenaton, Seti I, Ramses II, Merneptah and Ramses III. These Semitic herders lived in Lebanon, Syria, Canaan, the Transjordan and the Sinai. Shasu does not directly apply to Israelites as it also included Edomites, Ammonites, Moabites, Amalekites, Midianites, Kenites, and Hapiru. It should be apparent that these are the people the Bible says were conquered by the Hebrew armies. Interestingly, a reference dated to around 1250 B.C. was found identifying a group of giant people living in the Canaan region. It is highly plausible these are the people spoken of in the bad report given to Moses after the scouts explored the Promised Land (Num.13).

Inscriptions were found on the temple walls at Soleb, in modern-day Sudan, two hundred sixteen km. south of Wadi-Halfa, and Amarah-West, also in the Sudan. The Soleb inscription dates to around 1400 B.C. and the Amarah-West to the thirteenth century. Although some questions do arise over the meaning of these writings, what is not disputed is the name of the Jewish God, Yahweh, is written ot the stone. This is just more proof that the Egyptians knew about their God. Before the Exodus, Pharaoh denies knowing Yahweh (Ex. 5:2). Through The Plagues, Pharaoh comes to know Yahweh, as a deity, as he asks Moses and Aaron to pray for Him to remove the plague of the frogs (Ex. 8:8). Since the term

Shasu refers to the people of the Promised Land, it should be clear that the Israelites did live in this land at the time, but it was their distinction of worshipping Yahweh that set them apart.[277]

The next person with which the Bible deals with is King David. We first hear about David when God instructs Samuel to anoint him as king after Saul fails miserably to live up to God's expectations. It is after his defeat of the Philistine Goliath, his story starts to gain momentum. David is a source of much debate. Some say his kingdom never existed, even going as far as to say David is just as mythological as Abraham, Moses and Jesus.[278] Untrue; the vast majority of archaeologists in Israel have no doubt David was a historical person and not myth. I have already dealt with Abraham and Moses showing their historicity is without reasonable doubt. Jesus will be dealt with in the next chapter. So let's look at his encounter with Goliath. It must be pure myth according to the naysayers.

Archaeologists have recently been finding artefacts that support Biblical writings about David. Found in the last twenty years at a site not far from Galilee, was a piece of pottery, with the name of Goliath on it; dated to 950 B.C.[279] This would make this piece of clay's origins about the time the Bible describes the ultimate confrontation. Although many deny the possibility of a man nine feet tall, the current, still living, tallest man, is Leonid Stadnik at eight feet five inches.[280] Robert Pershing Wadlow was born, educated and buried in Alton, Illinois. His height of 8'11.1" qualifies him as the tallest person in recorded history.[281] At the time of his death he weighed four hundred ninety pounds.[282] With this in mind, the story of Goliath is completely believable.

David was known, in the Bible, as a poet and musical virtuoso. Wall paintings found at Beni-Hasan show musical instruments, namely the eight-stringed lyre (Ps.6; Ps.12). The New Kingdom of Egypt (1580-1085 B.C.) inscriptions have been found that recall the instruments of the Canaanites. After he was installed as king, he moved the throne to Jerusalem after defeating the Jebusites (2 Sam. 5:6). The Philistines attacked him in an effort to regain the city where they were soundly defeated and

---

[277] http://www.assistnews.net/Stories/2010/s10010053.htm accessed 2014/27/02
[278] Stenger. *Hypothesis*. p. 187
[279] http://www.nbcnews.com/id/9997587/ns/technology_and_science-science/t/scientists-find-goliath-inscribed-pottery/ accessed 2014/27/02
[280] Guinness Book of Records
[281] Ibid
[282] http://www.altonweb.com/history/wadlow/ accessed 2011/03/06

driven back to Geba as far as Gezer (5:17-25). David brought the Ark of the Covenant from the house of Abinadab, to the city of David with joyfulness (6:1-12). It was not a direct route; there were some stops along the way. After bringing the ark home, God made His covenant with David (7:1-17).

David then went on a rampage. He conquered Moab (8:1), the forces of Hadadezer (v.3), the Aramaeans (Syrians) (v.5) and the Edomites (v.14). Conquering Edom allowed David access to the iron he so desperately needed. This also allowed him a passageway to the Red Sea, on to South Arabia, East Africa and then eastward toward the Assyrians. Cuneiform texts from Tigris around 1,000 B.C. mention a threat to their land from the west. This threat came from the Aramaeans. But David decided to pre-empt this attack. He thrashed King Hadadezer, giving him presence along the Euphrates (1 Chron. 18:3). Assyrian texts from the time confirm an attack on the Aramaeans.

Modern diggings show the widening of his kingdom. Cities on the Plain of Jezreel were burned; Beth-Shan was decimated. Shattered temples, deep layers of ashes near destroyed walls, ritual objects and Philistine pottery were recovered. Above the destruction there is no evidence of inhabitation for centuries afterward. Foundations in Jerusalem show it was David who oversaw the construction. On the east side lays Ain Sitti Maryam, called Gihon in Biblical times. This is the main water supply for the city. In 1867 Captain Warren located an anomaly near the location where the water flows out of the rock. Further investigation would bring forth an intriguing find.

After climbing a narrow shaft he came upon a domed chamber. Inside were old glass bottles and jars. A small opening in the rock led to the centre of the city near the Foundation of the Virgin (Ain Sitti Maryam). Interestingly, in 1910 it was the same as it was in second millennium B.C. The rock had been altered as to provide an escape for inhabitants of Jerusalem. David used this to enter Jerusalem surreptitiously (2 Sam. 5:8). This may not seem like much, but if the original Hebrew is read the word *'sinnor'*, translated to shaft, can also mean channel. How was this recorded in Scripture if it was unknown?

The person that recorded everything at this time was the scribe. His job was of utmost importance. The happenings had to be accurately recorded in order to preserve the king's accomplishments. During David's rein the method of recording events changed from cuneiform writing, on clay tablets, to papyrus. The style of writing also changed to the now-known alphabet. Papyrus disintegrates quickly with the humid cli-

mate of the area. It is easy to understand why records of centuries earlier, recorded on clay objects, survived, while very little from this era did. The Egyptian artefacts longevity can also be attributed to the dry climate in the desert area. There are also other reasons why evidence is sometimes not forthcoming. It is termed 'fragmentary nature of evidence':
- Only a fraction of writing actually survives
- Only a fraction of available archaeological sites have been examined
- Only a small percentage of sites have been excavated
- A fraction of each site is actually examined[283]

In Hirbet Qeiyafa, Israel, the discovery of a three thousand year old pottery shard in July of this year (2014) may indicate that he was the ruler of a large kingdom. The shard dated via ^{14}C as being from 1,000-975 B.C., was found near remnants of a fortified settlement. This seems to indicate some kind of kingdom existed at this time. Deciphering the text will most likely take months. The words that have already been verified are judge, slave and king. There is much more needed before this find can be used to completely validate the Biblical account of King David's exploits and rule over a vast kingdom.

Just recently it has been proclaimed that the remains of the Palace of David have been discovered. While there is some controversy over this, and there probably always will be, it is an interesting discovery. I suspect if a papyrus was found, recording of the entire life of David confirming everything written about him in Samuel, it would be disregarded. In 1993 a stone, with an inscription about the House of David, dating back to before 750 B.C. was found near Galilee; reportedly the first record of King David outside the pages of the Bible. Now this is not evidence of a large kingdom, but it seems to show David did actually exist. The most likely response would, undoubtedly, be fake or fraud.

Evidence of his palace, given the magnificence of its construction as described in the Bible, would be a good starting point. After seven years of excavation archaeologists from the Hebrew University of Jerusalem claim to have found the temple of David. The remains are at Khirbet Qeiyafa and consist of a rather large compound built to withstand invading forces. Yossi Garfinkel suggested that it may have been used by David himself. He was of the opinion Khirbet Qeiyafa could be one of the best examples found showing a fortified city in existence at the time of King David. Artefacts at the site included items that would be expected if

---
[283] Ron Rhodes. *Archaeology & the Bible*.

from the late first millennium. Also leading to the belief it was Hebrew, was the absence of swine bones. Although this is not definitive proof, the absence of pork products is highly suggestive.

Dating of buildings in the area, including another proposed site found by Eilat Mazar in 2005, date to tenth century B.C. Critics claim that it could have been other people living in the area at the time. More and more new findings are showing this to be *"a collapsed theory (while) we have fresh data"* according to Professor Garfinkel. While a monument of who actually constructed many of these elaborate sites would be quite beneficial, that does not preclude saying it may have been King David who supervised the construction.[284]

Then, why is there so little evidence for David's kingdom? This is a difficult question to answer. Is it possible that the art of recording on the new form of papyrus was in its infancy and not perfected? Is it possible it was destroyed somehow? The answer to both these questions can, reasonably, be inferred, as yes. New inventions and advancements always take time to either be perfected or at least make viable. It should also be reasonable, to any person who wishes to be even slightly objective; when the Babylonians invaded Judah everything was completely destroyed. Jerusalem was obliterated by Nebuchadnezzar in 586 B.C. Many of the writings and records of the time were destroyed. This is probably why the Chronicler rewrote the history from Adam all the way up to the return of the Jews, after the decree of Cyrus. It had to be rewritten; much had been destroyed. Later historians have affirmed that much of the writings from the first century A.D. have been lost or destroyed. If manuscripts from two thousand years ago could have suffered loss, it is completely plausible manuscripts from 1000 B.C. may have suffered the same fate.

If almost by divine influence this changed in 1993 in Tel Dan. An inscription on an Aramaic stele fragment bearing the name of King David was discovered. Found during the day, with many people in the immediate vicinity, its finding could be fully verified. Around the area was ninth century B.C. pottery. The writing was also unmistakably ninth century Aramaic script. It appears to have been written by King Hazael of Aram (Syria). It was inscribed in victorious celebration of the defeat of Israel and Judah around 842 B.C. It refers to the king of Judah as being *"the house of David"*. Was this a blaspheming of the king and his general

---

[284] http://www.cbc.ca/news/world/israeli-archeologists-say-they-ve-found-king-david-s-palace-ruins-1.1390782 accessed 2013/11/11

who had handed the Aramaeans a dramatic defeat about two hundred years before (2 Sam. 8:3-10)? The defeat at the hands of the Aramaeans would be a definite blow to the Israelites ego. The Aramaeans remembered David and this inscription would be a slap in the face to his descendants. They would not remember a chieftain who, to them, would be not worth the bother. The inscription also is in the characteristic writings of Aramaeans of this time period.[285] All efforts to call into question the validity of the inscription have been scuttled. The Moabite stone has also been recently re-examined, showing David's complete thrashing of his kingdom years earlier (8:2).

Artefacts from David's time are most likely lost forever, unless the Muslims allow a thorough search below the temple mount where evidence could possibly exist. But they refuse. Why this is their position, is an intriguing question. Of what are they afraid?

What about Solomon? His kingdom was even wealthier than his father David. The abundance of his kingdom has been termed fairy tales by many people. Surely there is some record of his reign. Some historians have said the Biblical references to Solomon's wealth were greatly exaggerated, to the point, where some denied that Solomon ever actually lived. It would also be extremely easy to exaggerate the truth. Did the writers of the Bible practice hyperbole and embellish Solomon's exploits? Recovered records from the past show that wealth in antiquity was concentrated with the king and Solomon's prosperity was entirely feasible.

In 1937 Dr. Nelson Glueck led an expedition through Negeb to Wadi el-Arabah. Here they found a steep rock-face consisting of yellow feldspar, silvery-white mica, reddish-black iron ore and malachite ($Cu_2CO_3OH_2$). At the site of iron ore, they also discover passageways drilled into the rock that shows mining operations of long ago. Trudging on, they come to Tell el-Kheleifeh. Almost immediately the researchers find copper fish-hooks in the rubble. Further digging reveals tiles and parts of demolished walls. Along with these are rock piles of slag, surrounded by green-tinted sandstone. All of these findings are almost adjacent to the Red Sea, explained in 1 Kings 9:26-27. Outside the Bible, writings of the Phoenician priest Sanchuniathon confirm the shipyard construction operations.

Further investigation revealed foundations for constructing buildings, dating to before 1000 B.C. It would be in 1940; buildings construct-

---

[285] G. Rendsburg *"On writing BYTDWD in the Aramaic Inscription from Tel Dan"* Israel Exploration Journal. Vol. 45 no. 1 1995 p. 22-25

ed in the undeniable method of the first Iron Age were discovered. What perplexed many of the diggers were the vast quantities of copper remnants found. But they soon had the answer to their quandary. They were able to determine that one of the buildings could have only been used as a furnace for smelting copper. It was eerily similar to modern-day Bessemer-system construction. What is even more astonishing is that even though it is confirmed to be a copper furnace, smelting experts of today are unable to explain how the copper was refined; especially the fourteen ft^3 smelting pots strewn about.

Tell el-Kheleifeh was confirmed to be Ezion-Geber, beside Eloth, after more finds. Solomon built many ships at this seaport (1 Kings 9:26), as it was in the centre of the flourishing copper industry. No other empire has even come close to matching its magnificence (1 Kings 7:15-45). Dr. Glueck was able, via these finds, to show Ezion-Geber could rightfully be compared to modern-day Pittsburgh for the copper-smelting capabilities.

More research conducted by Flinders Petrie led to the discovery of iron-smelting operations at Wadi Ghazze. Although smaller, it was similar in design and construction to the copper-smelters at Tell el-Kheleifeh. The exhaustive determination of archaeologists proves Biblical accounts that were ridiculed as preposterous.

King Solomon was also revered for his massive stables. Discovered in 1935, at Tell el-Mutesellim, stone pilings, in the shape of a square and aligned in rows, point to remains of a mighty stable. As the digging continued they found these stables were grouped together in the vicinity of a piazza. Designed to allow horses to be easily housed, a coarsely paved, three metre wide passageway was centrally located through each stable complex. The rough nature of the walkway could be used to prevent injury if the surface was wet and slippery. The presence of troughs and an obvious method of providing water to the stalls further demonstrate the true nature of the buildings.

After surveying the area, it was determined that there were stalls for four hundred fifty horses and one hundred fifty chariots. But, this was not the only place such luxurious stables have been found. Other locations include a massive find at Megiddo, along with finds at Tell el-Hesi, Hazor, Taanach, and Jerusalem. After these archaeological finds, the words of the Bible seem much more plausible.

Confirming the prosperity of Solomon's kingdom was undertaken by the television show 'Nova', which aired on November 23, 2010 and National Geographic on October 28, 2008. A fascinating watch, the validity of the claims of the wealth of King Solomon were explored. In the show

Eric Cline of the George Washington University stated there is absolutely no proof of Solomon outside the Bible.[286] This is just another example of the reoccurring theme for skeptics. They just cannot bring themselves to accept the Bible, no matter how many times it is shown to be accurate. But, as with almost all archaeological finds, the Bible is proven again and again. This time, remains of a massive smelting operation in Jordan had been unearthed.

Archaeologist Tom Levy had been doing excavation work to further explore the advancement of the kingdom of Edom near Petra. As Mr. Levy's search continued, he was led to the valley of the Dead Sea Rift near Wadi Feynan (Khirbet en Nahas). The findings by Mr. Levy confirmed that this area was at one time a Jewish stronghold. He also found no evidence of pig bones, although every other Palestinian find does have pig bone remnants. It will be the timing of the smelting operation that will give credence to the historical authenticity of Solomon.

At this site, solidified slag, the by-product of metal smelting, was discovered. Digging in the area produced unequivocal evidence of natural copper ore. After ten years of research it was determined that a copper smelting operation had existed for hundreds-of-years. Interestingly Khirbet en Nahas translates to *"the ruins of copper"*[287] in English. This operation was not on a small village or tribal chieftain scale. The area consisted of walls for a factory, an administrative building, a tower, a temple and was ten hectares in size. An area this size would require almost one thousand men working around the clock to keep the blasting furnaces churning out copper. The fifteen plus shafts that could be over thirty metres deep, dated to about three thousand years ago. These difficult conditions suggested that the workers were most likely forced labourers. They would have to be inside the shafts and mine galleries for months at a time. The slag that was found indicates that while this particular operation was in effect, it produced in the vicinity of four thousand five hundred tonnes. That is a massive amount of copper. This would not be the work of a chieftain; it must have been an ancient kingdom in charge. As the mines were in the vicinity of Edom whose kingdom was it?

Samples were taken and sent to a lab at the University of Oxford. The results were almost mindboggling. The artefacts dated to the tenth and eleventh century B.C. This puts them between 900 and 1100. Remember, I have already said no swine bones were found anywhere in the

---

[286] http://www.pbs.org/wgbh/nova/ancient/quest-solomons-mines.html accessed 2013/06/12
[287] Ibid

immediate vicinity. Islam, that forbids the intake of pork, did not exist until fifteen centuries later. It would not be Arabs; who were descended from Ishmael and Esau. This was during the time of King David and King Solomon. Although not definitive proof the details seem to provide credence to the Biblical account.[288]

This though, is not the final piece of evidence. At Khirbet Qeiyafa, geometrically shaped pottery was discovered. It was sent to Santa Barbara Ca. for analysis. Using photo spectroscopy, Canaanite writing using Hebrew words was seen. The Bible tells us the kingdom fell shortly after Solomon's death (2 Chron. 12:2-3). Interesting, it appears that the smelting operation also ceased around the time of Shishak's attack. Shishak would not waste his time attacking a tribal chieftain.

From about 2000 B.C. to 400 B.C. the chronological order of the kingship is infallible. This is also true of the kingship that existed in other countries. The mathematical possibility of pure circumstance accounting for this record is 1 in 7.5×10^{23}.

The most dramatic discovery to authenticate the Bible, as being historically accurate, is the Dead Sea Scrolls. During late winter in 1947, a Bedouin boy was looking for a lost sheep about eight miles from Jericho. On the floor in a cave he found scrolls made of leather that had been preserved by sealed jars. Scholars reviewing the scrolls placed the origin to 68-100 A.D. When parts of the scrolls were examined it was determined that only seventeen letters were open to interpretation from the fifty-third chapter of Isaiah (Describes the coming Messiah). This proved to be quite a find and has been considered the oldest manuscripts at the time. The fact that translations of the Bible had been accurate century after century is astonishing. It is only reasonable to assume that great care was taken in the transcribing to ensure authenticity. It is almost as if those given this task knew disbelief was coming.

The most intriguing aspect of everything that has been found in archaeology is that to date there has not been a single archaeological find that shows the Bible to be in error in any way.[289] This can only lead an open-minded person to come to the logical realization, the original manuscripts were inerrant.[290] Dr. Nelson Glueck served as president of Hebrew Union College from 1947 until his death, and his pioneering work in biblical archaeology resulted in the discovery of fifteen hundred an-

---

[288] Walton, John. *Genesis*. p. 47
[289] Morris, *Modern Science*
[290] Kroll, Woodrow. *Authority of God*. Back to the Bible Radio Broadcast. UCB Canada May 11, 2010

cient sites. Dr. Glueck agrees that no find has ever contradicted the Bible's historical accuracy.[291]

This is further commented upon by one of the best known archaeologists William F. Albright, when he said that *"there can be no doubt that archaeology has confirmed the substantial historicity of Old Testament tradition"*. Many other scholars including Millar Burrows of Yale and Sir Frederic Kenyon, director of the British Museum, agree with these statements.

During the time of antiquities it was a normal event when persons would have their likeness imparted to either stones or other artefacts. This may have included a signet ring that was used by the king or ruler to be imprinted on the seal of his orders to the people. The following are examples of such instances where a recorded image has been found of a Biblical person.

- Shishak, the Egyptian king who plundered the Temple during the reign of Rehoboam (1 Kings 14:25-26).
- Jehu, king of Israel, who took power in a bloody coup; the only surviving likeness of a king of Israel or Judah (2 Kings 9:1-10:36).
- Hazael, king of Aram, enemy of Israel (1 Kings 19:15, 17; 2 Kings 8:7-15, 28-29; 9:14-15; 10:32-33; 12:17-18;1 3:3,22,24,25; Am.1:4).
- Tiglath-Pilser III, king of Assyria, who invaded Israel (2 Kings 18:19, 29; 16:7,10; 1 Chron. 5:6,26; 2 Chron. 28:20).
- Sargon II, king of Assyria, who defeated Ashdod and completed the siege of Samaria and took Israelites into captivity (Is. 20:1).
- Sennacherib, king of Assyria, who attacked Judah but was unable to capture Jerusalem (2 Kings 18:13-19:37).
- Tirhakah, king of Egypt, who opposed Sennacherib (2 Kings 19:9).
- Esarhaddon, king of Assyria, who succeeded his father Sennacherib (2 Kings 19:37).
- Merodach-baladan, king of Babylon, whose messengers Hezekiah showed the royal treasury, much to the indignation of Isaiah (2 Kings 20:12-19).
- Xerxes I, king of Persia, who made Esther his queen (Esther; Ez. 4:6).

---

[291] Glueck, Nelson. *Rivers in the Desert; History of the Negev.* Jewish Publications Society of America. Philadelphia. 1969

- Darius I, king of Persia, who allowed the returning exiles to rebuild the Temple in Jerusalem (Ez. 4:24; 6:15; Hag.1:1, 15).
- Augustus, Roman emperor, 27 B.C.-A.D. 14, when Jesus was born (Luke 2:1).
- Tiberius, Roman emperor, A.D. 14-37, during Jesus' adulthood and crucifixion (Mat. 22:17,21; Mark 12:14-17; Luke 3:1; 20:22-25; 23:2; John 19:12,15).
- Claudius, Roman emperor, A.D. 41-54, who ordered the Jews to leave Rome (Acts 11:28; 17:7; 18:2).
- Herod Agrippa I, ruler of Judea, A.D. 37-44, who persecuted the early church (Acts 12:1-23; 23:35).
- Aretas IV, king of the Nabateans, 9 B.C.-A.D. 40, whose governor in Damascus attempted to arrest Paul (2 Cor. 11:32).
- Nero (referred to as Caesar in the New Testament), Roman emperor, A.D. 54-68, to whom Paul appealed (Acts 25:11,12,21; 26:32; 28:19; Phil. 4:22). [292]

What are some of the other finds that confirm Biblical records of events?
- The Hittites, a people that the Jews were told by God to conquer so they could occupy the Promised Land, were once thought to be a Biblical legend and of no historical value. A complete reversal on this idea occurred when their capital and records were discovered at Bogazkoy, Turkey.
- It was once claimed there was no Assyrian king named Sargon (Is. 20:1) because this name was not known in any other record. Imagine the crow-eating that must have happened when Sargon's palace was discovered in Khorsabad, Iraq. The mentioning of his capture of Ashdod was recorded on the palace walls. It would have been interesting to see the skeptical historian's faces when fragments of a stela, memorializing the victory, were found at Ashdod itself.
- Another king who was in doubt was Belshazzar, king of Babylon (Dan. 5). The last king of Babylon was Nabonidus according to recorded history. Tablets were found showing that Belshazzar was Nabonidus' son who served as coregent in Babylon. Thus, Belshazzar could offer to make Daniel *"third ruler in the kingdom"* (Dan. 5:16 KJV) for reading the handwriting on the wall; the highest available position. Here we see the 'eye-witness' nature

---
[292] Ibid

of the Biblical record, as is so often brought out by the discoveries of archaeology.[293]

- In 1990's clay tablets from Hazor confirm King Jabin of Hazor; mentioned at Mari as Ibni-Addu. 'Jabin' a dynasty name, like Caesar, has been found in eighteenth century Mesopotamia, and fifteenth century Egyptian writings. Pottery found at Hazor show destruction by fire (Deut. 7:5) around thirteenth to fourteenth century B.C. Only the Israelites could have accomplished this; fellow Canaanites would not destroy idols of their own gods and Egyptians would not ruin statues of their Pharaohs.
- In Yemen archaeological discoveries confirm the existence of the Queen of Sheba. An alliance was necessary with Israel for her to export to the rest of the world.
- Paintings on walls of tombs in Beni-Hasan show a coat with a red and blue pattern. Could this be Joseph's coat? (Gen. 37:3)
- The Murex snail provided the necessary dyes for the colour purple used for royalty. Large quantities of snail shells have been found at Tyre and Sidon. Esarhaddon, king of Assyria, in an inscription, refers to bleached linen. Stone basins have been found and confirmed to be dyeing containers.
- Flowers, shrubs and blossoms still present in Palestine have been shown to be the source for "*myrrh, aloes and cassia*" (Ps. 45:8)
- Josephus recalls balsam existed in Palestine since the time of Solomon. In 70 A.D. Titus Vespasian assigned a guard to protect balsam plantations in Jericho.
- Botanists have been able to locate all spices listed in the pages of the Bible. Archaeologists have found bowls to hold the spices, in ruins.
- The stronghold at Mizpah was identified between 1927 and 1935
- King Ahab and the stories about him have been deemed historical fact.
- Moabite writings of King Mesha have been found.
- The cruelness of the Assyrians has been confirmed.
- Assyrian texts confirm the Bible's description of the invasion of the Northern Kingdom
- The destruction of Nineveh has been confirmed

---

[293] http://www.christiananswers.net/q-abr/abr-a008.html accessed 2013/21/12

- The military might of the Philistines is confirmed through paintings at an Egyptian temple dated 1175-1150 B.C.
- Ashdod (Josh.13:3; 1 Sam. 6:17) has been found. At the site is an open area where most likely a temple stood
- Mari documents confirm the Amorites
- Susa, in modern Iran has been excavated. This was the city of Esther, wife of Xerxes

New Testament:
- The name Caiaphas is inscribed on an ossuary found in November 1990 in the Peace Forest
- Seven thousand five hundred inscriptions have been found about Herod-the-Great
- A stone found at Caesarea Maritima with name of Pontius Pilate
- At a theatre in Corinth Greece; an inscription to Erastus
- In a public building in Delphi, fragments of a letter dated 52 A.D. from Claudius to Gallio. He was called 'Gallio proconsul of Asia'. (Acts 18:12)
- Thirty-five inscriptions with term, politarchs (Acts 17:6)
- Archaeological excavations at Capernaum have found a synagogue and maybe Peter's house
- Pool of Bethesda found near Church of Saint Anne N.E. quarter of Jerusalem
- Pool of Siloam found in 1897 in Jerusalem measuring sixty-nine metres long with stairwell of three steps going down into the pool.
- Sixty stones at the mouths of tombs found throughout Israel and Jordan
- First century inscription to Lecture hall of Tyrannus in Ephesus has been found
- Inscriptions on several stone fragments dated from 25-50 A.D. found at Corinth verifying Tribunal structure
- Jacob's well where Jesus spoke to the Samaritan woman (John 4:1-42) was discovered near Mount Gerizim
- Ruins of the winter palace, where Jesus met Zacchaeus (Luke 19:2-10), used by Herod-the-Great, excavated at Jericho
- Tomb of Lazarus discovered in Bethany
- Limestone ossuary of James with inscription: "James the son of Joseph, brother of Jesus"

- 'Straight street' found in Damascus (Acts 9:11)
- Temple of Artemis found in Ephesus
- Twenty five thousand seat theatre found in Ephesus where uproar happened with Paul's teaching (Acts 19:23-41)
- Antioch excavations show city's ethnicity was robust (Acts 11 & 14)
- Shrines to pagan gods/goddesses found in Philippi. Paul wrote stern warnings about the practice.
- All seven churches mentioned in Revelation 2-3 have been discovered.
- Eighty-four different statements from Acts 13-28 have been verified as factual
- A scene depicted at the Arch of Titus confirms the looting of the Temple in 70 A.D.
- Inscription from Jerusalem says: *"No foreigner may enter within the barrier which surrounds the temple and enclosure. Anyone caught doing so will be personally responsible for his ensuing death"*. A riot broke out when Paul attempted to take a Gentile into the Temple (Acts 21:28-29)
- Chester Beatty papyrus #45 dates to third century A.D. contains the four Gospels and Acts 4-17. Papyrus #46 dates to 200 A.D. and has ten Pauline epistles and book of Hebrews. Papyrus #47 dates to third century and has Revelation 9:10-17:2
- Bodner papyrus #47 dates to 200 A.D. has the Gospel of John. Papyrus #75 comes from third century and has Luke and John.
- Found in 1979, two amulets were found at Ketef Hinnom. Dated to around 600 B.C. they contain paleo-Hebrew writings of a priestly blessing (Num. 6:24-26). It appears this is the oldest Biblical passage to survive antiquities. The text states that Yahweh is stronger than evil, is a rebuker of evil and it has been hypothesized they could have been used as omens.[294]
- At Khirbet Qeiyafa a structure about one thousand metres^2 has been discovered that appears to correspond to King David's palace.[295]
- The findings at Khirbet Qeiyafa, a fortified hilltop city about thirty km. southwest of Jerusalem may indicate David ruled a kingdom within a great political organization.[296]

---

[294] http://www.livescience.com/40046-holy-land-archaeological-finds.html accessed 2013/19/11
[295] Ibid

- *"This is unequivocal evidence of a kingdom's existence (Davidic), which knew to establish administrative centers at strategic points,"* read a statement from archaeologists Yossi Garfinkel of the Hebrew University and Saar Ganor of the Israel Antiquities Authority (IAA).[297]

There can be little doubt. Archaeology has confirmed much of the Bible. Further discoveries can only remove more doubt from the unbeliever's minds, unless of course all of these finds are fakes or forgeries.

---

[296] Ibid
[297] http://www.livescience.com/38318-king-david-palace-found-israel.html accessed 2013/19/11

Chapter 7
The Jesus Mythology?

With science, archaeology, and history showing the Bible is accurate and true, what doubt can be left? There is still the matter of Jesus' divinity. Unbelievers have lots to say about Jesus. He did not do any of the things attributed him. He most certainly did not rise from the dead. The Christian Messiah never existed, but is a huge hoax perpetrated on a naïve, gullible people. The entire story of Jesus is based on paganism. The virgin birth is an extraneous later addition to the story and should not be taken literally.[298] The myth of Horus proves that the story of Jesus is based on paganism.

Another rebuttal says Jesus himself is a fabricated myth. There is absolutely no historical evidence that He ever existed. There is no non-Christian record of any such person before the second century.[299] During the time of Jesus there was a strong denial of His existence.[300] His story came to become only known several centuries after His purported death.[301] There are many artefacts destroyed by literalist Christians at the time of Celsus, a second century pagan philosopher. Adding to the list of problems is that many church leaders at the time disputed the Gospels' account. Modern historians such as Kuhn and Gerald Massey state that He died at a ripe old age and was not crucified. If a person was to take all Jewish literature from the first century, there would not be any reference that can be authenticated referring to the man who called Himself the King of the Jews. Surely since Jesus lived at the time of Caesar Augustus and Tiberius there would be some historical record. During this time, secular writers either knew nothing of the man Jesus or they did not

---

[298] Freke & Gandy. *Jesus Mysteries*.
[299] Doherty, Earl. *Jesus Puzzle*
[300] Harpur, Tom. *Pagan Christ*
[301] Ibid

write about Him. It seems only reasonable that He never existed or someone would have mentioned Him. The so-called prophesies of the Old Testament about Jesus are not verified in any place outside the Bible.[302] Mr. Stenger also says that the stories of Jesus were written to fit the ideas of the Jewish Messiah[303]; no independent evidence of fulfilled prophecy has ever been found[304]; there is no independent evidence showing Jesus was born in Bethlehem[305]; and there is no evidence of the trial and crucifixion of Jesus.[306]

Saying Jesus never existed is gaining popularity. The problem is, not one reputable historian has ever made such a claim. When talking about the birth of Jesus some have expressed doubt about the story, even going as far as saying that the taking of a census did not occur. Without a census, Joseph would have no reason, to leave Nazareth, to go to Bethlehem. Archaeological discoveries have shown, beyond any doubt, Romans did in fact cause a census to be actuated every fourteen years. Augustus was the originator of this undertaking and mandated it be taken not only for Roman citizens, but also Egypt, Syria and Palestine. It was at Antioch, a fragment with Roman inscription written upon it showed that Quirinius was given a military assignment in Syria coinciding within the fourteen year span between censuses. One took place in 6 A.D. Roman documents confirm that Cyrenius was the governor. He was sent to be the first Procurator of Judea, 6 A.D. (Luke 2:1-3). This is also important because the Bible says Jesus was born during the time of Herod. Herod died in 4 B.C. Therefore, Jesus must have been born before 4 B.C. This was authenticated by Flavius Josephus. The final piece of evidence verifying a census was a piece of papyrus found in Egypt detailing the means of conducting the census.

The star followed by the wise men is a bone of contention. December 17, 1603 Johannes Kepler observed the conjunction of Saturn and Jupiter in the night sky. After ruminating about the celestial event that night, he remembered a passage he had read by Rabbi Abarbanel. It said that the Messiah would come with the conjunction of Jupiter and Saturn within the constellation of Pisces. Kepler reworked his calculations over-and-over again. This exact phenomenon had also occurred around 6-7 B.C. Astrological tables confirm it was 6 B.C. Kepler then de-

---

[302] Stenger, V. *Hypothesis*. p. 177
[303] Ibid p. 179
[304] Ibid p. 183
[305] Ibid p. 178
[306] Ibid p. 180

cided to date the birth of Jesus at 6 B.C. and the conception at 7 B.C. But, it was not until 1925; P. Schnabel was able to decrypt Neo-Babylonian cuneiform, confirming that Jupiter and Saturn experienced a conjunction in the year 7 B.C. The spectacle was recorded for a period of five months. Mathematical calculations show that the planets aligned three times and were most visible in the Mediterranean area.

When planets are in close proximity to each other they can take on the appearance of a singularity and to an unknowledgeable person they may look like a large shining star.

The conjunction began around February, 7 B.C. At this time Jupiter moved out of Aquarius and moved toward Saturn in Pisces. Since the sun was also in Pisces its brightness outshone the other two. Around April 12 both planets were in close enough proximity to only show an eight degree difference in longitude. May 29 the bright 'star' was completely visible for two hours near day-break. They were so close to each other; the twenty-first degrees of Pisces, there was a difference of only zero degrees longitude and .98° latitude. Another conjunction would happen on October 3 in the eighteenth degree of Pisces. Interestingly October 3 was also the Jewish Day of Atonement. The final conjunction happened on December 4 in the sixteenth degree of Pisces. It would be near the end of January 6 B.C., Jupiter would move into Aries. The only time this has happened in all of recorded history, according to astronomers using computer diagnostics, was in April, 7 B.C. What is most fascinating is that for a period of one week everything aligned so perfectly that, in the sky, the star stood still (Mat. 2:9). Although it would be miraculous for these things to occur at this exact moment in time, science once again verifies things taught by the Bible.

The wise men told Herod they saw the star in the east (Mat. 2:2). The NLT says "...*We saw his star as it rose*". This seems to be a more accurate translation from the Greek. The original Greek text says "*En te anatole*". This wording is singular and not plural as would be represented by the word anatolai. The singular suggests that they saw the star's early rising or what could be termed the heliacal rising.[307]

When discussing the birth of Jesus, nonsensical claims are easily disproved. Firstly, Jesus was not born on December 25, as most of these so-called scholars claim. Christmas is celebrated on December 25; thanks to an edict by Pope Julius in 345 A.D.[308] Justinian made it a legal

---

[307] Keller. *History*. p. 332
[308] Harpur, Tom. *Pagan Christ*

holiday in 354 A.D. This date represented three days after the winter solstice.

The first month of the year would be the month Abib (Deut. 16:1). The angel of the Lord appeared to Mary in the sixth month telling her that she would be with child from the Holy Spirit (Luke 1:26-38). Although the Bible specifically relates the timing to her cousin's pregnancy, it would not be unreasonable to also assume that it was also the sixth month of the year. Why mention it otherwise, since the timing related to Elizabeth's pregnancy is not relevant to the announcement? The sixth month of the Jewish calendar is Elul, which corresponds with the months of August-September on the Gregorian calendar.[309,310] The reason the months do not align perfectly is that the Jewish calendar began upon the Exodus out of Egypt. The night of the Passover was to be the beginning of the Jewish year (Ex. 12:2). This did not happen on what we commonly call the first day of the year; January 1. Since it takes approximately nine months for a human child to be born from conception to delivery, this would mean that Jesus would be born in the Jewish month of Iyar, or for us in April-May, the same time as the 'conjunction' shown above. The Bible makes it clear that Jesus would not be born in December.

Meteorologists have been able to confirm at the time of Jesus' birth the average temperature in December was 3° C, and in January 2°C. The average rainfall in December is 2.4 cm and in January 3.2 cm. Around December 25 frost is a common daily event and shepherds would definitely not be residing outside with their flocks (Luke 2:8). Additionally, the Talmud states flocks are put out to pasture in March and then brought out of the elements at the end of October or the start of November.

John-the-Baptist and Jesus were related through their mothers, as shown. Now some have suggested that John-the-Baptist was a fictional character. But Josephus spoke of him when he said the John-the-Baptist was a righteous man who humbled himself before God and baptised people for remission of sin. Being terrified of his influence Herod confined him to the dungeon in Machaerus and eventually had him beheaded. Machaerus was on the east side of the Dead Sea. Although excavations have not yet been undertaken, it is quite obvious from the ruins that is was once a castle with a dungeon.

---

[309] http://www.jewishvirtuallibrary.org/jsource/Judaism/calendar.html accessed 2013/12/11
[310] http://www.jewfaq.org/calendar.htm accessed 2013/12/11

All four Gospels recall His trial, sentence and crucifixion. After painstaking research, the events are without doubt, reliable accounts. Excavations have determined where the trial took place and through research the events, during the trial, can also be verified. The name Annas shows up in the Gospel of John (John 18:12-14).

What about the crucifixion? Jews at the time were not allowed to execute someone on their own. They needed the Roman procurator to confirm sentence. Jesus was condemned when He said he was the "*Son of God*"; a blasphemous statement. He was sent to Pontius Pilate. Josephus and Philo of Alexandria both describe his brutality. Philo called Pilate a cruel man with no empathy in his heart. His reign in Judea was filled with bribery, thievery, oppressive behaviour and executions without the benefit of a fair trial.

He hated the Jews and made that feeling well-known throughout his time in Judea. At first Pilate found Jesus innocent of all charges (Luke 23:4). Since Jesus was despised by many Jews, Pilate saw an opportunity to rub his power in their faces. But, at the unruly crowd's insistence, he capitulated. He did not wish to get Rome involved in the dispute. Jesus was sentenced to be crucified; a horrendous method of execution. Cicero called it a cruel and fearsome method of killing a man while Josephus reiterated it was "*the most pitiable of all forms of death*".

He was sent to be crucified a short distance away. Recent medical experiments have confirmed how death occurred. When a person is nailed to a cross the blood sinks below the torso. It takes six to twelve minutes for the blood pressure to drop to half normal and the pulse rate doubles. The heart receives insufficient blood and the person passes-out from lack of blood to the brain. To alleviate their suffering the one nailed to the cross would push up on a stand just below his feet to allow blood flow again. To put an end to it all, the executioner would break their legs below the knee with sharp blows from a club. Death ensued quite quickly after this due to asphyxiation. Since the Sabbath was fast approaching and it was Passover week, it was necessary to bury Jesus immediately. He was taken down and placed in a new empty tomb owned by Joseph of Arimathaea.

One of the most noted writers at the time was Flavius Josephus. He was a Jew who became a Pharisee before he turned twenty and wrote extensively about Jesus. He called Jesus a wise man that was able to perform wonderful works, in direct reference to the miracles He performed, that many people, even those who think they are historians or history protégés, like to call myths. Josephus spoke of the integrity, conduct and virtuosity of this man named Jesus. He also spoke of the crucifixion at the hands of Pilate. Whether or not Josephus actually called Him 'the Christ' is debatable on both sides of the forum. Josephus also mentions Jesus when he spoke of the death of James, Jesus' brother (Mat. 13:55).

The four Gospels were written so that the words, deeds and teachings of Jesus would live on. If the things Jesus did and the things he accomplished were not preserved, then the three years of His ministry would have been completely in vain. The minor dissimilarities in the Gospels do not change the body of work. The few variations can easily be explained, although skeptics, unbelievers and detractors use these in an attempt to discredit the writings of the Apostles.

One of the lessons in every law school in the country involves eye-witness testimony. The experiments vary, but inevitably the result is the same. A scripted event occurs. The witnesses, i.e. students, are asked for their recollections after the event. Almost unquestionably the accounts are different. The varying accounts reported can be subtle or they can be extreme. While the overall content of the testimony will be reliable, the details may not. This shows an event did happen although the details can be dissimilar. This does not mean that the event did not happen without any doubt, as used by many to discredit the Bible.

As I write this, the JFK assassination is being remembered. This is an excellent example of eye-witness variants. People who were in Dealey Plaza have given many different versions of the events. The testimonies provided happened within hours or a few days of the event. Reportedly:

- There were four to six shots.
- One shot came from the grassy knoll.
- One shot came from the highway overpass.
- A shot came from the left rear of President Kennedy.
- Ten witnesses who were questioned by the Dallas Sheriff's office, some testifying to the Warren Commission, said they smelled gun smoke on the street. Significantly, that day the wind was blowing at fifteen knots toward the school book depository and into Oswald's face. Therefore, gunpowder smoke from six floors up could not have been smelled at ground level.

These are some vastly differing stories about what happened November 22, 1963. The testimonies given were to police that same day and to the

Warren Commission which completed its task by November 1964. An event cannot be discounted just because the testimonies as to some of the details are not completely succinct.

The best Biblical example of varying reports is what happened after the Resurrection. There are some minor variations, not the major discrepancies espoused by unbelievers, but the important aspects are similar. These recollections were recorded not hours or months, but decades after the event. The writers of Mark and Luke were not eyewitnesses, relying on what was told to them by people who knew the Apostles at the time of the Resurrection. If it was actually them, then the slight variations might be explained by the number of years transpired between the Resurrection and the penning of their Gospel. The accounts in Matthew and John are quite similar.

Here, I am sure, nay-sayers will quote that Scripture is inerrant (2 Tim. 3:16). This is true of course. But it does not mean that God dictated what was to be written. Reading the different books of the Bible, the authors' personality and writing characteristics shine through just as any other written work. To be absolutely certain about what was written would require the original manuscripts, which unfortunately no longer exist. Also in the last two thousand years, it is more than plausible copying errors or mistranslations have crept into Scripture. The written work was 'inspired', so the message of what was written is what important, not every single word.

Women were also not highly regarded in the ANE. As each Gospel recalls it was Mary who first interacted with Jesus; this is highly significant. This would not be how a story would be normally told. It should have been the Disciples that first encountered Jesus, with the women in tow. Since it was Mary Magdalene, it can be reasonably inferred there is truth to the story. By-the-way Magdalene was not a prostitute. This nonsense was started by Pope Gregory-the-Great in a sermon in 591 A.D. Thankfully the Catholic Church corrected this in 1969, albeit quite late. Open-minded individuals should have no problem believing the entire account, and understanding the small variants.

Let's compare the modern-day event I have referenced. Everyone agrees the JFK event was November 22, 1963; it happened around 12:30 PM CST; he died that day; there were several gunshots fired. There is no doubt between any witnesses as to these statements. There are though, varying descriptions of the events. As for the Resurrection, every recounting in the Bible agrees: Jesus rose from the dead; it was on Sunday, the first day of the week; it was just after sunrise and it was

Mary Magdalene that first saw and spoke with Him. Since some accounts appear to vary, does this means it did not happen? If so, does that mean the report on the assassination of JFK cannot be trusted? That would be a completely asinine statement. Hence it is reasonable to say Jesus did arise regardless of the current inconsistencies.

But they are just that, current versions. If the retellings were exactly the same, I am certain the response would be conspiracy or collusion on behalf of the writers. The infallibility of Scripture rests in the original manuscripts. It is impossible to know where and when copying errors or mistranslations crept into the recounting of the fateful weekend. Remember my cake analogy? It now appears the skeptics also want some chocolate syrup for that scoop of ice cream.

Detractors also say that since the accounts of Jesus were written decades after His death and most of the authors were not eye-witnesses, it cannot be believed. Human memory is not one hundred percent reliable decades after an event. Yes, the main body of the recollection will be accurate but the minutiae may not be completely precise. It does not mean the events did not take place. Mark, who many speculate wrote his Gospel first around 70 A.D., received his information from Peter. Now that is, obviously, an excellent source. Luke received much of his from Paul. No-one would argue Paul's information was first-hand eyewitness testimony. There is little agreement on Matthew and John. Evangelicals say they were Jesus' Disciples, while others question that. The bottom line is, just because the Gospels were written years after Jesus that does not mean they are unreliable or the events recounted did not transpire. Does it really matter? Let's look at some historical facts. Below are a number of manuscripts and the time of writing for important historical figures.

NT Greek- Five thousand manuscripts
Tacitus- Twenty manuscripts
Plato- Seven
Demosphanese- Two hundred
Pliny- Seven
Herodotus- Eight

Bible- One hundred twenty to one hundred fifty years after actual events (the originals are sadly gone, lost or hidden)
Alexander the Great- Two hundred years
Tacitus- One thousand years

Plato- One thousand two hundred years
Herodotus- One thousand three hundred years
Demosphanese- One thousand three hundred years

So if we dismiss the writings about Jesus, written within one generation, we most also dismiss the writings about all of the above. Does anyone truly believe that would be a sagacious thing to do? Yes, most of the NT was written by people who never saw or physically interacted with Jesus. But, what history cannot say this? The history of the Assyrians, Babylonians, Egyptians, Greeks, Medo-Persians and Romans is ancient history and no-one doubts the records. Why is everything about Jesus called fictitious?

The early church was founded in Jerusalem. If, as skeptics try to claim, it was all false and an overstatement of the actual events in the life of Jesus, how can any person believe the church would have flourished. While we know the writings of Jesus were close to His actual time on the earth, OT manuscripts can also be dated to the time the events unfolded. Thirty-nine sources from antiquity verify the writings about Jesus[311] (This might be a bit ambitious as some of the references can be slightly ambiguous). To quell any doubts the reference must be direct and clear.

Trying to pick and choose what is real and what is false is foolhardy. If the historical parts are true then it is reasonable to believe the stories relating to His divinity are real. If Jesus was not real why did so many people start to follow Him after His death and the Resurrection? The people saw what the Romans did to Jesus. To follow Him would most certainly invite the same fate. The only valid reason is in the factual truth of what Jesus said about Himself and how the Disciples would spread to the world about Him.

Christianity is the only religion based on an actual person, rather than a philosophical nature, which reports its founder, arose from the dead. Muhammed died on June 8, 632 A.D. In the Mahaparinibbana Sutta, Buddha's death is recorded. Krishna is also gone. Since Jesus had to rise from the dead in order for the religion to flourish, it must be recorded that He did indeed come back to life. If it can be proven that Jesus did rise from the dead, then credence will be afforded to everything he said and attributed to Him before the crucifixion.[312]

There are many meritless theories as to how the body vanished. Firstly, eyewitness account must be verified for any historical event to

---

[311] Strobel, *Case for Creator*
[312] McDowell, *Evidence*

take hold. People must have seen an empty tomb in order for the Disciples to claim that their Lord had risen. The historical fact that the body of Jesus disappeared from the tomb owned by Joseph of Arimathaea, means that an explanation is mandatory. All that would be necessary to totally discredit the claims of a risen Saviour would be for someone to visit the tomb and see the body still there. But the tomb was empty, as testified to by many observers. Any such claims would be met with immediate ridicule.[313] When people truly study the facts, without reservation, they come to the conclusion the idea of the Resurrection being a fairy tale will dissipate as evidence is assimilated.[314]

Another superfluous statement is that Jesus never really died. The Romans had been using crucifixion as a mode of execution for many years. They were masters at the discipline. Hebrew law only allowed forty lashes when administering punishment, whereas Roman law had no such limitation, allowing those scourged to be at the mercy of the person administering the punishment. A person being subjected to such a harsh beating would be bleeding profusely and in extreme pain, needing immediate medical attention. After a severe lashing Jesus was required to carry His own crucifixion-cross to the place of His execution. When at Golgotha Jesus was then fastened to the cross by driving nails through His hands and feet. More excruciating pain and bleeding would be the result.

He would hang on the cross, for hours, in this unbearable pain. In conformation of death a soldier sticks a spear in the side of the accused. If he reacted, his legs would be broken. Jesus did not react but instead blood and water came gushing from the wound, signifying He was indeed dead (John 19:33-34). Little did the Roman centurion know he was fulfilling previous prophecy that said not one of His bones will be broken (Ps. 34:20) as they look on the one they have pierced (Zech. 2:10) with the spear.

Maybe He did not die but was only unconscious. This statement is beyond ludicrous. Here was a human being that had been beaten, abused, left to go without food and water for an extended period of time and with a spear injury in His side. He would then be placed in a tomb after being wrapped in a burial shroud. He was left there without any help, attention, medical treatment, food or water for another three days. The idea that anyone could survive such an ordeal, alone, is beyond preposterous.

---

[313] Smith, Wilbur. *Therefore Stand*
[314] Morrison, *Moved the Stone*

Pilate would also want to be sure that He was dead, so His followers could not claim He rose from the dead. Before the body of Jesus was released it would be certain that He was in fact dead. The centurion knew death when he saw it and would not risk summary execution for himself if he was in error, since death was the customary edict for any soldier found guilty of dereliction of duty. Jesus was dead without any doubt whatsoever.

In order for the body to disappear, the Disciples would have to remove it, the Pharisees decided. To ensure that the Disciples would not just come, steal the body and then claim Jesus came back from the dead, a large stone was ordered to be placed at the tomb opening. With Roman guards present, the tomb would be sealed. This would be done to prevent theft. Any person tampering with the stone would break the Roman seal and thus be subjected to death. Roman guards were also posted. Pilate wanted to ensure that the dead Jesus would stay where He was entombed.

The term posting a guard meant more than one and would normally include from ten to thirty but could be up to one hundred Roman soldiers. Also, only a complete and utter fool would post just one guard, since he alone could easily be overpowered by the remaining followers. It is certain there were enough guards to prevent any shenanigans from occurring.

Roman law was severe; there is no way the guards would allow anything to happen to the body. Roman soldiers were extremely disciplined in their duty. Are we to believe the guards let Jesus either escape or His body be taken and receive no punishment (Mat. 28:14)? If they did receive the death penalty this would be well known. No-one would believe a risen Saviour under these circumstances. I have heard an analogy used that if anyone went to the grave of a famous person and found his body to be missing they would assume it had been stolen and he had not arisen from the dead. This is a perceptive argument. The only problem is; this body is not being guarded twenty-four hours per day by numerous guards. If a body was being guarded constantly and it disappeared, how would skeptics explain that? With all these precautions, the Disciples, if they had intended to steal the body, would be faced with insurmountable odds against success.

After Mary relayed the news to the Disciples, some of the guards went into the city to see the chief priests and tell them what had happened. A conspiracy was hatched. The priests gave a large sum of money to the guards and told them to say that the Disciples had come and stolen the body while they were asleep (Mat. 28:11-13). The priests assured the guards that they would speak to the governor on their behalf to make sure they would not be held accountable or be given any judicious punishment (Mat. 28:14-15). This plan seems so ridiculous. How could they think anyone would even entertain such a notion? The guards would have to answer yes to all of the following questions.

1. The Disciples were so quiet that no guard awoke when they arrived at the tomb?
2. Not one person was awakened by the sound of this huge stone being rolled away from the tomb entrance?
3. All of the guards were asleep at the same time and did not sleep in watches?
4. The Disciples removed the body and carried it away without disturbing one single guard?
5. When reported to the authorities no reprimand or punishment was given to any of the guards?

To anyone with any common sense, this plan seems so ludicrous it is actually laughable. Since no punishment was given, it is most sensible that forces beyond what any human could sustain were exerting their influence. As a direct result there are only two distinct possibilities. Either human or divine interference caused the tomb to be evacuated. Since human interaction is quite outlandish, the obvious conclusion is that Jesus had actually been raised from the dead as He had promised He would.

    In 1878 a stone containing a decree from Emperor Claudius was discovered. It mandated that graves must not be disturbed. The bodies must remain entombed. Death was the punishment for violating the law. What is most intriguing is that prior to 50 A.D., grave-robbing was a misdemeanor. It has been suggested Claudius made this decree after Jews insisted, in 49 A.D.; the body of Jesus had been taken from the tomb by His followers.

    To also claim that the Disciples would actually steal the body makes little sense. They had followed this man around for three years listening to all He said. They truly believed Jesus was the Christ (Luke 9:20) until His crucifixion. At that point they lost their faith, not understanding when Jesus told them He would be three days in the earth (Mat. 12:40). They did not understand when He said He would destroy the temple and build it back up in three days (John 2:19). They hid from the authorities. They thought they had been duped. The person they followed was just a mere man and was dead. They had wasted the last three years of their lives. Who would worship a dead Messiah?

The disciple's faith was restored when Jesus appeared to them (Luke 24:36-49); but Jesus would have to be seen by many other people in order for all to believe. The Apostles' word alone would not suffice, as people would think they were just saying it to verify their belief in Jesus. Detractors will say that Jesus never appeared as recorded; it was either a vision or a hallucination. The idea up to five hundred at one time would have the exact same vision or hallucination is ridiculous. In order for this to occur the entire multitude would have to be suffering from the same delusion. The chances of a multitude of people having the same experiences are beyond remote. If this explanation was to be applied to any normal event in mankind's history, the resulting laughter would be deafening. Hallucinations are also usually something a person wishes to see. If they truly believed and wanted to see Him they would have gone to places normally frequented by Jesus when He was alive. They did not; Jesus appeared to them and many others simultaneously in places He normally would not have been. It is just not feasible that this many people would hallucinate the same vision, at the same time, in the same location.

During the years following the ascension of Jesus and the time of the Apostles, Christianity would continue to multiply. After 284 A.D. Christianity was made the official state religion. Quite remarkable the teachings the Romans tried to quash would become the beacon for their way of life. It would be the formation of the Byzantine Empire that replaced the eastern leg of the Roman Empire that would help Christianity become the dominant force that it did.

The Horus similarities have caused many to dispute Christ's authenticity. How can the similarities be explained? Jesus was to be born to a virgin (Is. 7:14), the same as Horus. Horus was born due to the union of a god and a mortal woman. Mary was impregnated by the Holy Spirit (Luke 2:33-34) an entity without physical form through the intervention of God, an Omnipotent being (Luke 2:35). The Horus union was a physical one. As soon as this union takes place the woman is no longer a virgin. So the birth of Horus could not have been to a virgin. She was only a virgin in the fact that she had not had carnal relations with another human. Only fabricated similarity exists here.

The act of Baptism does not ensure Salvation from person's sins as it did with Horus. While there are Christian sects that make this claim, it is not Biblical in nature. True, John-the-Baptist was using Baptism along with confession of ones sin for redemption (Mat. 3:6,11a), but he was clear, the one following him would baptize with the Holy Spirit (Mat. 3:11b). Jesus made it abundantly obvious that God would fulfill His promise and a new method of Salvation, would be born. Jesus preached over and over again that belief in Him and only Him would lead to eternal life (Rom. 6:23, Rom. 10:9, Eph. 2:8-9). Baptism would become a sacrament for the believers to symbolize the death, burial and resurrection of Christ (Col. 2:12, Rom. 6:4).

While Horus died at Easter it does not necessarily mean that Christ was killed at the same time. As with Christmas, Easter is tied to pagan astronomical and astrological roots. In modern times Easter is celebrated at different dates based on the vernal equinox, fixed on the first full moon following the spring solstice. This is because the god Ra/Horus caused the worshipping population to base all their decisions on the movement of the sun, moon and stars. Jesus was killed during the Passover in Abib. Passover has changed over time to more accurately match with the celebration of Easter, but not at the time of Jesus.

The actual similarities concerning Jesus are also not that discerning. While there are a few that may be similar, it does not mean that the story of Jesus is based on pagan myths. For those that still reject the provided evidence, there is another event that is undeniable and quite eerie. In 1898 an American named Morgan Robinson wrote a novel about the ill-fated voyage of an ocean liner. The name of Robinson's ship was the Titan. The Titan and the Titanic, which almost everyone knows of, had many similarities beyond the names.

Similarities:
Both were British built passenger liners.
Both had a capacity of approximately three thousand people
Both collided with an iceberg in the North Atlantic due to excessive speed
Both ships had too few lifeboats
Both were launched in April and their disasters happened in the same month
Both were the largest ship afloat.
The Titan was described as one of man's greatest works.
The Titanic was deemed unsinkable and a wonder of its era.
Both had three propellers and two masts

Differences:
Titan sailed from New York to Liverpool; Titanic, Southampton to New York.
It was the Titan's third voyage; Titanic's first
Titan was eight hundred feet long, weighed forty-five thousand tons; Titanic, eight hundred eighty feet long, weighed 46,328 tons
Titan had fifteen watertight compartments; Titanic, nine
Titan had forty thousand horsepower; Titanic, forty-five thousand horsepower
Titan's speed, twenty-five knots; Titanic's, twenty-four knots. [315]

The similarities are truly astounding. The differences are so minimal, they can, without much forethought, be ignored. The differences included a length variance of only ten percent, a weight variance of about three percent, and a top speed difference of only four percent. Either Robertson was truly psychic or this is one of the biggest coincidences to ever happen. Should we use the word coincidence or synchronicity? Coincidences occur when events are happenstance, although it seems that they might have been prearranged. Psychoanalyst Carl Gustav Jung coined the term, synchronicity.

Some people may choose to use the term higher power, fate or maybe even divine intervention in these instances. Either way the events are more than eerie. Are these two separate events causal and meaning, where meaning can be determined to be a complex mental process? This mental congruity must involve both the conscious and subconscious aspects of the human mind. The intriguing thing is that every connection doesn't need to have an explanation in terms of causation.[316] This is one of those unexplainable things that make up the everyday life in this complex world.

The important aspect of this fascinating tale is that we know the story of the Titanic is undeniable. Hollywood made a movie about the maiden voyage of the Titanic and made hundreds-of-millions of dollars from the movie-going public. A story written less than a mere two decades in advance does not diminish the horror of the event or mean it did not happen. The same can be said for Jesus. If people want to disbelieve the evidence put forward by Christian scholars, and believe the entire story of Jesus was based on paganism then they must also believe that the Titanic never happened. Logically the precedence has been set.

---

[315] http://cruiselinehistory.com/?p=3177 accessed 2012/11/11
[316] Ibid

Since the so-called mythological story of Jesus has a few similarities with pagan writings, then, so too the Titanic is the greatest hoax perpetrated in the last century (sheer lunacy).

Another major bone of contention among many skeptics is the prophecies related to Jesus. Even though the Bible has been shown throughout to be accurate and reliable, they say there is no evidence outside of the Bible of any of them being fulfilled. To see if this is factual, we will have to look at any and all written material from around this time. Any source outside the Bible that mentions any of the fulfilled prophecies or speaks of things Jesus did will completely invalidate these claims.

In actuality, nine secular historians who were not Christian sources and had no interest in propagating the news of Jesus and help spread the new religion, did write about Him within one hundred fifty years of His time on earth. They were:

1. Josephus, the Jewish historian
2. Tacitus, the Roman historian
3. Pliny-the-Younger, a Roman politician
4. Phlegon, a slave who gained his freedom and recorded events
5. Lucian, a Greek humourist
6. Celsus, a Roman philosopher
7. Suetonius a historian
8. Thallus another historian from the time and area
9. Mara Bar-Serapion, was a prisoner, but penned many events that happened.

Cornelius Tacitus, who has been called the most reliable writer of history after the turn of the first century A.D., was the son-in-law to Julius Agricola, governor of Britain from 80-84 A.D. In his penning of the time of Nero he spoke of Christianity, discussing the man Pontius Pilate had put to death. He also spoke of Christianity when relating the story of the burning of the temple in Jerusalem in 70 A.D. Tacitus' writings from the second century A.D. clearly mention the Disciples being put to death during the reign of Nero from 54-68 A.D.

He referred to Christians in his annals. He talked about the hatred towards Christians. He records the death of 'Christos' by Pontius Pilato during the reign of Tiberius. He detailed the methods by which Christians were executed. These included be torn apart by wild dogs, nailed to crosses or set on fire to provide illumination after the sun set.[317]

---

[317] Annals, XV. 44 written 115-117 A.D

Tacitus refers to Jesus, whom he called 'Christos'; to Pilate being his judge, jury and executioner, as well as a mass extinction of His followers by Nero. Nero was methodical and proficient in his plan to exterminate the followers of the new belief called "*The Way*" (Acts 9:2). Although many writings from the time of Jesus have been labeled as fakes, frauds or forgeries, this reference by a non-Christian secular writer are considered to be genuine.[318,319]

Pliny-the-Younger, was governor of Pontus/Bithynia from 111-113 A.D. In a letter he wrote to Emperor Trajan he wrote about the problems he was experiencing with Christians. He gave them a chance to renounce their faith. If they did so they were spared. If not they were punished. He was of the opinion that Christianity was nothing more than superstition. While Pliny does discuss people who have turned away from Jesus at the time, he is still concerned about how many are now filling once-deserted temples, and is showing hesitancy towards the persecution of men and women of all ages and classes. He specifically speaks about a person named Jesus and His followers.

Pliny willingly aided in the execution of Christians, and although he did not personally know Jesus, he was obviously full aware of those preaching and following Jesus. Although he does not use the name Jesus, his use of Christ and Christian show his knowledge of Christianity. His lifelong history of serving the Roman Empire shows that he was not the type of person to even remotely provide validation to the Messiah. He followed the Roman edict to eradicate these nuisances from the face of the earth. There is no way he would propagate the myth of someone who never lived.

Trajan's reply to a letter is also quite illuminating. He allowed punishment of those convicted of being a Christian. If a person renounced the faith he could be pardoned for repenting. Most of all, though, anonymous accusations were not to be allowed as evidence of misdoings.

Here, the emperor of the Roman Empire is confirming the existence of Christians, the followers of Jesus Christ. This is just another example of a place outside the Bible where Christ or Christians are mentioned. It also carries on the tradition of Nero; eliminating all who profess to be followers of Jesus.

---

[318] Catherine M. Murphy, *The Historical Jesus For Dummies*, Publisher For Dummies, 2007. p 76.
[319] Robert Van Voorst, *Jesus Outside the New Testament: An Introduction to the Ancient Evidence*, Wm. B. Eerdmans, 2000. p 39- 53

Thallus was a Greek-writing historian who wrote about the unusual events at the time of Jesus' death. He referred to a solar eclipse in 32 A.D. during the time of Tiberius at the sixth hour of the day [12 P.M.]. He also noted the earthquake that destroyed Nicaea and caused havoc in Bithynia.[320] The Gospel of Luke also records the eclipse (Luke 23:44-46).

The statistical chances against an eclipse and earthquake (Mat. 27:51) happening at that exact moment are enormous. Thallus had no reason to lie or further the spreading of the Gospel. There is only one reasonable explanation; it happened. This is independent confirmation of darkness at the time of the crucifixion.

Suetonious was a Roman author and attorney who wrote during the early part of the second century A.D. He writes Claudius banished Jews from Rome because of the ruckus they were causing due to the influence of a rebel-rouser named "Chrestus".[321] It does not seem like much of a stretch to realise this "Chrestus" was Christ.

Mara bar Serapion lived after Jesus. Although it cannot be determined when he was born or died it is known that he wrote a letter after 73 A.D. to his son, penned in Syrian dialect. Although his words are not conclusive they seem to talk about Jesus. He refers to a wise Jewish king being killed and the new laws he laid down. To what other king, who gave new laws to His followers, can this refer? It was only after the crucifixion of Jesus that Jerusalem was destroyed and the Israelites were dispersed all over the world (the diaspora). The previous destruction had seen them exiled to a particular country. Jerusalem and the Temple may have been destroyed because of Christ's rejection, as suggested by the Gospels (Mat. 23:37-39; Mark 13:1-2; Luke 19:42-44; 23:28-31).

Lucian of Samosata, was a Greek satirist who lived during the second century. He was quite judgmental of Christians referring to their faith as superstition. But, to his credit, he does not dwell completely on their naiveté but does acknowledge their morality. He wrote just after 165 A.D. about a man from Palestine being crucified. He mentions the Christians and that their prophet leader was killed. His followers believed he was a god and allowed him to be their lawgiver. This man of Palestine was crucified because of the new beliefs he brought. Although not saying Jesus, it should be obvious to whom he was referring.

---

[320] Ibid. *Jesus Outside.* p. 20
[321] Suetonius. *Twelve Caesars* p. 200

Celsus, a Greek philosopher, wrote a reportedly scathing attack on Christianity in 177 A.D. in *"True Doctrine"*. His writing is no longer available and the only documentation as to what was said can be found in the work *"Against Celsus"* penned by Origen around 250 A.D. Since Origen quotes Celsus it cannot be verified that everything said is one hundred percent verbatim, but it is generally accepted that his response is a fairly accurate portrayal of what was said. Celsus' main disdain for Christianity was by suggesting Jesus' father was a Roman soldier and that the miracles performed were by the way of sorcery. He questioned Jesus' morality suggesting He and His Disciples practiced thievery to get the money they needed to survive. He also was one of the first to use the now re-hashed objections to the Resurrection; namely delusion, mass hallucination and hopeful thinking. It is acceptable to say he knew of Jesus and the attributes that Christians were assigning to Him.

In his book, *"Jesus Outside the New Testament"*, Robert E. Van Voorst lists many of the referrals to Jesus by Rabbi's at that time. Some of the references could be ambiguous since they do not refer directly to Jesus. He speaks of Jesus escaping to Alexandria, Egypt. This happened to avoid the massacre set out by Herod when Jesus was born (Mat. 2:13). He also relates that Jesus practiced magic and led *"Israel astray"*.[322]

Nine non-Christian sources shown, mention Jesus. Nine secular sources speak of Tiberius Caesar. The defeat of the Zealots at Masada is proven by archaeology, but only mentioned by Josephus. It is not even mentioned by Roman historians or referenced in the Talmud. If we look at first century figures, i.e. Augustus, Tiberius, Nero etc. they are not referenced as much as Jesus by writers at the time. If we reject Jesus we must also reject these figures? What about those from ancient Greece? I guess we should rewrite the history books and change numerous college and university humanities courses to eliminate them from the curriculum.

There are many explanations as to why we do not have an abundance of writings from the time. Historians agree about fifty percent of the writings of Tacitus have been lost. Virtually all of what Thallus' penned is still available. In his works Suetonius speaks of Asclepiades of Mendes. None of this person's manuscripts can be found. It is also highly doubtful anyone not concerned with Jesus would have taken notice. He was just another religious leader from a small section of the empire; a nobody.

---

[322] b. Sanhedrin 107b; cf. b. Sotah 47a

What about the events that happened right after the crucifixion? Surely someone would have mentioned these miraculous events. After all according to Scripture the temple veil was torn from top-to-bottom; great earthquakes were felt; and bodies of dead saints came out of their graves (Mat.27:51-53).

The non-Biblical gospel of Philip says:
> "The veil was not rent at the top only. If it were so, then the entrance would have been opened only for those who are of high rank. And it was not rent at the bottom only, because then it would have pointed only to the lower ones. But it was rent from the top to the bottom"[323]

Confirming this would be confirming the preaching of the Apostles; Jesus was the Messiah, something no Jewish historian would contemplate; suffering the fate of Christians. Just look at what happened to the Apostles. Affirming the accounts of that fateful day would be a death sentence. It is these confirmations that would allow people to believe and to accept Jesus, as many did. When the Gospels were written there would be people alive who knew the truth. What I find even more telling than the minimal confirmation of these events, is the total absence of any contradictory writings. Saying it is false, a fabrication or a forgery is only trying to explain away a miraculous event meant to show the people at the time what they had done. Ignoring everything that does not conform to a person's worldview is not evidence. There is not one single record anywhere from the time that conclusively rebuts Scripture. It is like people today who deny the Holocaust. We still have people alive who know it happened first hand. Is it possible that in a few hundred years, it too will be denied?

There are also modern-day equivalents to events not being recorded. A recent conflict in the Gaza has caused over two thousand two hundred Palestinians to be killed. The UN has termed Israel's action war-crimes. French president Francois Hollande has termed it a massacre. U.S. president Barack Obama has decried the casualties. I agree it is a heart-breaking tragedy. It is saddening that this is happening, but hopefully a cease-fire will lead to a truce.

The U.S.A. has erupted into chaos with the killings of two men in Missouri and New York. CNN dedicates hour upon hour coverage. But even more distressing is over one hundred eighty thousand Syrians have been killed in their three year civil war. Where is the outrage over this?

---

[323] Gospel of Philip v. 125e

Where is the constant recording of events in the main-stream media? Is the Gaza-conflict a main item because Israel is involved?

It has also not been reported, by main-stream media, that four hundred Christians are killed every-day for their faith. ISIS has given Christians three choices- convert, leave Iraq or die! More Christians have been murdered in the twentieth century (forty-five million: over seven times more than those the German death camps) than in the previous nineteen centuries. Sudan alone has murdered two million since 1985. Christians are being persecuted in one hundred thirty-one countries (Pew Forum study). By 2012 the vast majority of Christians in Homs have been cleansed from their homes. That is Genocide! China is persecuting Christians horribly. This is sparsely reported by the media. In certain areas of Pakistan, an Islamic country, Christians are prevented from using the same lavatories as Muslims. This is reminiscent of segregation policies in the deep south of the U.S.A. not long ago. Where is the UN? Why does Obama seem tacit? President Hollande; three hundred fifty thousand Christians being killed every year, on average, is a slaughter. Where is your indignation? The cleansing of Christians in Muslim countries has been happening for decades. Saying that because there is limited record of something, especially regarding the vile, hated Christian, means it did not happen, is not a valid argument.

Many modern-day authors have used the NT to show fulfillment of OT prophecies. These assertions have been challenged by non-believers. They try to say that the NT authors wrote their books to fit OT scripture. They maintain no writing outside the canonical NT confirm any OT prophecies. This is a complete fabrication. The Islamic holy book, the Qur'an, is a historical source that validates the statements by scholars of prophecies regarding Jesus being fulfilled. The chart below shows which prophecies Muhammad confirmed as actual historical events. Additionally there are a few lost gospels that did make it past the canonizing phase to be included into the Bible. The gospels of Thomas, Peter, Judas Iscariot, Mary Magdalene and Mary are examples. While I agree their value in a theological manner is limited, they can be useful to counteract the skeptics' claims, historically. Even though written decades after the life of Jesus, it is just as valid as modern historians writing about Antiquities, the Dark Ages, the Middle-Ages or the Renaissance.

Prophecy	OT Reference	Reference Outside Bible
Jesus born of Mary	Isaiah 7:14	Surah 3:45 Mary 11:3
Virgin birth[324]	Isaiah 7:14	Surah 3:47; 19:20; 21:91; 66:12 Mary 9:1; 15:3; 19:3
Jesus a messenger to Israel	Deuteronomy 18:15-16; Isaiah 9:1-2	Surah 3:49-51
Jesus name[325]	Isaiah 7:14	Surah 3:45, Mary 11:3
Jesus born then gone to distant place (Egypt)	Hosea 11:1	Surah 19:22
Disciples faithful	Hosea 1:10; Isaiah 11:10	Surah 5:111
Ascended to Heaven	Psalms 110:1; 2:7; 68:18	Surah 3:55; 4:158
Jesus preach the Gospel	Psalms 78:2	Surah 5:46
John-the-Baptist; a prophet before Him	Malachi 3:1	Surah 3:39; 6:85
The character of John-the-Baptist	Isaiah 40:3-5	Surah 19:12-15 Thomas 46:1-2[326]
Jesus descended from David	Psalm 110:1; 2 Samuel 7:12	Mary 1:2-4:1; 14:2
Birth in Bethlehem	Micah 5:2	Mary 17:1; 21:1
Killing of innocent boys by Herod	Jeremiah 31:15	Mary 22:1
Jesus' use of parables	Psalm 78:2	Thomas 20:1-2; 21:1-10; 26:1-2; 57:1-4; 64:1-12; 65:1-8; 76:1-3; 96:1-3; 97:1-4; 98:1-3; 109:1-3[327]

---

[324] Some claim the word here means a young woman. But the Hebrew word *almah* or *parthenos* in Greek means a "maiden" i.e. unmarried, chaste

[325] Isaiah says his will be called Immanuel. This is not a proper name, but a title as shown earlier with all the names attributed to God and with the title "Christ" or Messiah as applied to Jesus. Immanuel means "God with us".

[326] Nag Hammadi Text

[327] Ibid

Prophecy	OT Reference	Reference Outside Bible
The betrayal of Judas	Psalm 41:9	"Jesus said to Judas: "You will exceed all... For you will sacrifice the man that clothes me""[328]
Disciples claim strength but are cowards	Zechariah 13:7	"Jesus said to the Disciples: "any one of you who is strong enough among human beings bring out the perfect human and stand before my face". They all said "We have the strength" But their spirits did not dare to stand". Further along Judas writes Jesus said "why have gone into hiding". [329]
Jesus divine nature	Psalm 2:7	"Judas to him "I know who you are and where you have come from. You are from the immortal realm of Barbelo. And I am not worthy to utter the name of the one who sent you""[330]
Jesus' ministry of compassion	Isaiah 61:1-2; 42:1-4	"When Jesus appeared on earth, he performed miracles and great wonders for the salvation of humanity"[331]
Judas is replaced	Psalms 109:8; 69:25	"For someone else will replace you, in order that the twelve may again come to completion"[332]

---

[328] The Gospel of Judas. Here Jesus is saying to Judas that he will hand over the Son of God to the authorities. "The man" refers to the divineness of Jesus and "clothes me" refers to the human aspect of Jesus. The betrayal must have happened and been perpetrated by an insider. This is not something a follower of Jesus would fabricate.

[329] Ibid. The disciples confirm their devotion to Jesus. It is recalled in the gospels how they all deserted Jesus when bravery was required.

[330] Ibid. Judas emphatically states that Jesus is the Son of God

[331] Ibid. Jesus main concern was humanity's salvation

[332] Ibid. Confirming that another disciple (Matthias) would replace Judas (Acts 1:15-26)

Prophecy	OT Reference	Reference Outside Bible
The preaching of the gospel	Isaiah 49:6; 54:1 Amos 9:11-12; Hosea 1:10; 2:23	Mary Magdalene 4:8, 10:14
Resurrection of Jesus	Psalms 16:8-11; 18:4-6; 116:3; 132:11; 2 Samuel 22:6-7; 7:12-13; Hosea 6:2	*The entire gospel of Mary Magdalene is predicated on the events after the Resurrection of Jesus.* [333] *"After he arose from the dead, his twelve Disciples and seven women continued to be his followers"* [334]
Jesus" death	Isaiah 53:7-8	Mary Magdalene 5:3
The Holy Spirit is given	Joel 2:28-32	Mary Magdalene 4:1-2
Incarnation	Psalm 40:6-8	Philip v.5
Death of Christ	Isaiah 53:7-9	Philip v 9b
Divine son-ship of Christ	Psalm 2:7	Philip v 12a
Virgin conception of Jesus	Isaiah 7:14	Philip v 17b
Resurrection of Jesus	Psalms 16:8-11; 18:4-6; 2 Samuel 22:6-7; 7:12-13; Hosea 6:2	Philip v 21b; 72b

To say Jesus did not exist, is a fabrication. Saying no-one outside the NT wrote about Him is duplicitous. Implying no-one spoke of His miraculous works is deceptive or ignorant. The prophecies of the OT were fulfilled by Jesus, no matter how much unbelievers contrarily protest.

Practically everyone who has studied the times agree that a historical Jesus did in fact live in the first century and any argument that states otherwise has been shown to be specious.[335] There are also eight

---

[333] King, Karen L. *Mary of Magdala.* p.4 A cursory reading shows that it was fact after his death. Since he appeared to them and spoke with them it must then be after the Resurrection.

[334] *Sophia of Jesus Christ* (NHC III) cited in King, Karen. *Magdala* p. 99

[335] B. Ehrman, 2011 *Forged: writing in the name of God* p. 285; Richard A. Burridge *Jesus Now and Then* p. 34; Robert E. Van Voorst *Jesus Outside the New Testament: An Introduction to the Ancient Evidence* Eerdmans Publishing, 2000. p. 16 *Sacrifice and Redemption*

things about the life of Jesus that are generally accepted as historical fact:
- Jesus was baptized by John-the-Baptist.
- He called Disciples.
- He had a controversy at the Temple.
- Jesus was crucified by the Romans near Jerusalem.
- Jesus was a Galilean.
- His activities were confined to Galilee and Judea.
- After His death His Disciples continued.
- All of His Disciples were persecuted. [336]

Many of the Christian celebrations do have pagan roots; this was done to get pagans, to whom the message was being preached, to accept it. But it was man that made these correlations, not the Bible and most certainly not God. Nowhere in the NT are we commanded to celebrate Christmas, as we are the death, burial and resurrection. The practices around the world surrounding Christmas are not set out in the Bible. Jesus chastised them for rendering the command of God useless with their traditions (Mat.15:6). While worshipping and remembering His birth is a good thing to do, we should celebrate the real reason for the season.

The Talmud actually records the trial, crucifixion and burial of Jesus. It appears in places someone has, through nefarious methods, tried to physically erase it from the pages. It can be seen that the text was actually erased, but to no avail. It can still be read with careful inspection.

The Biblical Jesus is not based on pagan beliefs. This argument is made from ignorance to the facts. We have verified Jesus did in fact exist, and how the Christian faith arose; now we must look at why is faith in Christ justified and necessary.

---

edited by S. W. Sykes Cambridge University Press p. 35-36 ; Graham Stanton, *The Gospels and Jesus* 1989 p. 145

[336] William R. Herzog. *Prophet and Teacher: An Introduction to the Historical* 2005 p. 1-6; Bruce Chilton and Craig A. Evans. *Authenticating the Activities of Jesus* 2002 p. 3-7

Chapter 8
Why is Christianity Necessary?

So after all of what has been presented, why do people still object to Christianity? The arguments may seem reasonable, but if examined closely, they dissipate into the abyss. Let's look at these rationalizations.

A reason for the disbelief in God's plan is that just because God does exist, that does not necessarily purport the need for a Saviour. The only need for a person to save the world would be if humans actually sinned and rebelled against God. While some people are obviously bad, that does not necessarily mean all people are sinners or evil actually exists. Disbelievers say that since the idea of 'Satan-the-Devil' is a myth that lost its relevance after the Dark Ages; there is no need for Salvation. There is not now, nor has there ever been any proof that an entity named Satan exists. He is just the imagination of people trying to explain away things in this world they cannot explain with regards to morality. The evil of terrorists or mass murderers could cause a skeptic to re-think their ideas, but using a purely philosophical viewpoint, this is only the result of trying to understand the bad things that permeate our society. It can be used as an excuse to mitigate one's actions.

As the church's influence has subsided, so has the need for Satan. If the church was to go out of existence, so would the ability of Satan to entice us to do evil. By proxy this means that he cannot exist, since his existence is solely dependent on the church's fate. It seems reasonable to assume that the Devil reached his ultimate plateau when the church did. The Middle-Ages was the time of the most explosive growth of the church.[337]

While witch burning and the inquisition flourished for part of the Middle-Ages, the ideas of demon possession have all but waned. Mod-

---
[337] Matthews & al. *Humanities*

ern science is proving to be the downfall of the church, so, the notion of Satan is diminishing. Satanists are not inherently evil. They just despise anything Christian. It is not the followers of this non-existent cherub we should fear, but it is the pious. The acts perpetrated in the name of God do more to display Satan's devices than any so called Devil. If Satan did exist, it can be rest assured that he is more than delighted with the actions of the so-called children of God. How do we countermand these ideas?

As we have seen God's existence is quite evident. Jesus did exist and is not based on myth or paganism. The Bible has been shown to be accurate scientifically, historically, archaeologically. But why do we need a Saviour? For Jesus the Messiah to be necessary, Satan must be real and in control. Let's see if Satan does exist and is the reason for Christianity.

The Bible is explicit on Satan. Satan was a cherub created by God. Satan (a.k.a. Lucifer), through his own vanity rebelled against God and as a result he and his followers were cast from Heaven (Rev.12:3-4). When Lucifer was cast from Heaven he took one-third of the angels with him in his rebellion. The Bible speaks of demons/fallen ones and their possession of humans. Only when these demons were cast out was a person able to live a normal life. Even Hollywood has joined the bandwagon of demon possession. Movies like *"The Exorcist"*, *"The Omen"* and *"Rosemary's Baby"* along with many others, dealt with either demon possession or Satan trying to alter mankind's future. These movies all did extremely well at the box-office and continue to sell through DVD individual sales.

The fascination with Satan and his followers should lead anyone to understand; most people do believe. It would not be illogical to think that demon possession has taken on a new form with modern man and that many illnesses today are not what they appear.[338] The demons possessing today, would be more cunning as to not arise suspicion. Of course this does not mean all mental illness is demon possession. Such a statement would be ludicrous. Many true occurrences of mental illness can be attributed to congenital problems, accidents, sickness or drug dependency. It has been said that Hitler and Stalin suffered from severe mental illness.[339] To think Hitler was insane only and not intrinsically evil would be more than a stretch; it would be pandering to a truly malevolent

---

[338] Meredith, *Satan*
[339] Deblanco, *Death of Satan*

persona. Unfortunately for humanity, the actions of individuals in the near future may become even more insidious as Satan's time draws to a close.

Satan is described as the ruler of the earth (Mat. 4:9; 12:26) and has convinced the world he does not exist.[340] The Devil's first lie was in the Garden of Eden when he told Eve she would not die if she ate of the fruit (Gen. 3:4).[341] Other lies he has told to convince people he is not real deal with reincarnation (Heb. 9:27) and the ability to speak with the dead.[342] Satan has been called the deceiver of all nations (Rev. 12:9).

Many people today claim to speak by God's direction. This is obviously not true if a person listens to the words and watches the deeds of the speaker. The vile hateful utterances cannot possibly come from a kind and loving God. The means, with which these deceivers operate, relies on the inability of humans to see through the cloud of mystery: Man does not recognize Satan.[343] When the world leader takes to centre stage everyone will marvel at his ability to display the god-like powers bestowed upon him (2 Cor. 11:14), by the support he receives from Satan. They will believe the lies he is God (Rev. 13:4). In order for this to occur, people will have to be duped by a very clever deceiver (Rev. 12:9). Satan's whole goal is to trick as many people as he can into following him (1 Pet. 5:8) and rejecting God and His plan for humanity.

Looking back at man's history, the idea that there is not a devil seems outlandish. How can any rational person think such a thing? During World War II many fleeing German nationals had a word for it. They called it *übel* or *Böse*. Many of the Jews who left Hitler's Germany used it to describe Joseph Goebbels. Translated the word means evil, but when used to describe Goebbels, it was used to describe the Devil-incarnate (Job 1:3). The man, who used his hatred to convince the German people Jews had to be dealt with, was only one in a long list of abhorrent behaviour. One of the usual comments from allied soldiers who liberated the prisoners from Auschwitz-Birkenau, Sobibor, Treblinka and Dachau, was that after seeing the atrocities committed, they were absolutely convinced of the existence of the Devil. The Ku Klux Klan, the war atrocities where soldier's rampage resulted in the multiple rapes of women and the genocides of recent memory in Bosnia, Serbia, Rwanda and the Congo, and the ultimate display; the Russian Gulag, to name only a few, can

---

[340] Kint, Roger ("Verbal"), *The Usual Suspects*, 1995,
[341] Batchelor, Doug. Amazing Facts. *Deadly Delusions, Are the Dead Really Dead?*
[342] Ibid
[343] Brother Jerome, *The Howling Man*. The Twilight Zone. MGM Studios 1960

only reasonably be termed the direct result of pure evil. To think this is not Satan, exerting his control, is again fooling those who do not wish to see him for who he truly is.

Satan, being deliriously happy with all he has been able to do, must have been absolutely furious[344] when Jesus rose from the dead. Although Satan is doing all he can to deceive the world, those who focus on God are able to see through the lies and deception. So how do we know that Christianity has all the answers for everything discussed?

To say that we cannot know positively if these events happened since none of us were present does not make any logical sense. No rational person would use this argument when discussing John Wilkes Booth killing Abraham Lincoln or the signing of the U.S. constitution. It is historical fact these events did occur, even though none of us were witness to the events. If the Resurrection was a hoax, why did the Apostles exude such a passion for preaching that He did, in fact, come back from the dead? How could twelve individuals pull off a ruse, as suggested?

Many people either remember the Watergate scandal that toppled Richard Nixon, or have heard of it. That break-in was masterminded, hatched and executed by a handful of men. It took less than one week for one person to divulge information, leading to the world knowing the truth. To think that the Disciples planned this fraudulent deception and carried it out on unsuspecting multitudes without one person breaking and confessing their chicanery, is just not believable. If they had perpetrated this scam, surely someone would have found out and exposed them for being liars, scam artists and charlatans.

Skeptics everywhere have said that there is no proof or validity to the Christian beliefs. This has led some to accept the utterance *"Christianity will be wiped from history within 100 years"*.[345] Interestingly, Voltaire said, shortly before his death, the Bible would be history within 50 years. As the epitome of irony, fifty years after the death of Voltaire, the Geneva Bible Society was printing Bibles in a house once owned by Voltaire and on Voltaire's own printing press. This just goes to show *"God has quite a sense of humour."*[346] Thankfully Christianity not only survives but is flourishing in countries hearing the beloved Gospel for the first time. The myth Church attendance is waning is also an unmitigated falsehood. While some churches have had to close, due to falling adher-

---

[344] Jeremiah, David Dr. *Tried, Tested and Triumphant.* Vision TV Broadcast Sunday May 16, 2010
[345] Arouet, François Marie. (21 November 1694 – 30 May 1778) Pen name-Voltaire
[346] Jeremiah, David Dr. Turning Point Ministries. Canadian Television Broadcast.
The Miracle Channel. 2014/06/04

ents, many are witnessing an insurgence. My church has been experiencing an upswing from time-to-time.

With all of this in mind the most undeniable proof is in the lives of the Disciples after Jesus' resurrection. Firstly, the Disciples were, foremost, human beings. They did not believe in Christ without miracles (John 4:48); the ultimate one of rising from the dead. Immediately after His crucifixion their doubt was forefront and their faith obliterated. When Jesus appeared to them after His death, they were renewed and rejuvenated. The Disciples followed the Great Commission given by Jesus (Mat.28:18b-20).

It has been suggested that the Disciples merely invented the stories of His miracles and many people today maintain they are pure myths. They conspired to form a new religion based on either imagination or outright lies. In reality they faced lengthy tortures and excruciating pain, yet they maintained their teachings until their deaths. All they had to do to escape the torture was to admit that the whole story of Jesus was pure fantasy. Why would they not do so if it meant avoiding such a death? Does it seem logical that they would do so for a fraud? This decision would ultimately cost them their lives; some in horrendous fashion.

- Matthew suffered martyrdom in Ethiopia from the infliction of a sword wound. He died in Nadabah.
- Mark died in Alexandria, Egypt after being dragged by horses through the streets
- Luke was hanged in Greece as a result of his voracious preaching to the Gentiles.
- John was tortured when he was boiled alive in a large oil-filled basin during the persecution in Rome. Miraculously he survived this ordeal and banished to the island of Patmos; an island prison. He was given the visions for the prophetic book of Revelation here. He would later die an old man while serving as Bishop of Edessa (Modern-day Turkey).
- Peter was crucified in Rome, Italy during the persecutions of Nero sometime around 67-68 A.D., hanging upside down on an X-shaped cross because he refused to allow his persecutors to kill him as they did Jesus. Peter felt he was not worthy to die in the same manner as his Lord.
- James was the leader of the church in Jerusalem. He was thrown down a one hundred foot drop from the south-east pinnacle of the temple. He was steadfastly adamant in his refusal to

deny his faith in Christ. To the antagonists utter amazement he survived the fall. They then beat him to death with a fuller's club.
- James-the-Great was the son of Zebedee (Mat. 4:21). After Christ's ascension into Heaven, James became a very vocal and outspoken leader of the church. His earthly reward was beheading. In utter shock and amazement his Roman guard watched as James defended his faith at his trial. On the way to his execution James had the ultimate revenge. The Roman guarding him became a Christian and knelt beside James to accept the same punishment. The two were beheaded side-by-side in Jerusalem in 44 A.D.
- Bartholomew, a.k.a. Nathaniel, went on missionary trips to Asia, mostly present-day Turkey. Andrew was crucified on an 'X-shaped' cross in Patras, Greece. He was tied to the cross after suffering an almost unbearable torture of being whipped severely by seven soldiers. As he was being led to his fate it is reported that he said "*I have long desired and expected this happy hour. The cross has been consecrated by the body of Christ hanging on it.*" During the two days it took him to die he continued to preach to his executioners.
- Thomas was killed in India with a spear.
- Jude was killed in Kara Kalisa (modern-day Iran) 72 A.D. with a quiver of arrows because he would not denounce his faith in Christ.
- Judas Iscariot's replacement, Matthias, was stoned and then beheaded for his faith.
- Andrew was crucified like Peter on an inverted 'X-shaped' cross. He was whipped repeatedly by seven soldiers and then was tied to the cross with cords to extend the length of his anguish. When being led up to his cross he also expressed his expectation to die as Jesus did.
- Barnabas preached throughout Italy and Cyprus. He was stoned to death at Salonica.
- Philip was crucified in Hieropolis, Syria.
- James Alpheus was thrown down from the temple by the scribes and Pharisees, after which he was stoned. To ensure he was dead, his brains were dashed out with a fuller's club. As he was being killed he cried out "*I beseech Thee, LORD God our Father, forgive them; for they know not what they do*"

- Simon the Zealot was crucified in Britannia, Europe.
- The most incredible of all was Paul. Paul (called Saul before his conversion) had been a staunch enemy of Jesus and was instrumental in killing His followers. The fact that Paul only personally knew Jesus from the encounter on the road to Damascus and Jesus gave Paul comfort through all of his trials and tribulations; it is astonishing that he would die for his faith. Paul was tortured and beheaded by Nero in Rome in 67 A.D.

Why were all of these men killed for their faith? Scripture plainly explains that. Jesus said His followers would be killed for their faith (Mat. 10:22).

Historically, the deaths of the Apostles are true and verifiable. There is only one conclusion that can be made. They had either personally seen Jesus and knew the truth, or the events in their lives following their conversion were so inspired that they were convinced beyond one iota of doubt; Jesus was the Messiah, the Son of God, and the Saviour of the world.

Another way of seeing the power of the Holy Spirit working through the acceptance of Jesus is to look at the lives of people living in the more recent past. One of the most noted is John Newton, who was born in London July 24, 1725. He was the son of the commander of a merchant ship, sailing in the Mediterranean Sea. When he was eleven years old, he made his first voyage to sea with his father. In 1744 Newton was drafted into service on a man-of-war, the H. M. S. Harwich. The intolerable conditions on the ship caused him to desert. He would be captured, publicly flogged and demoted from midshipman to common seaman. At his own request he transferred to service on a slave ship, finding his prey on the coast of Sierra Leone. He then became the servant of a slave trader who brutally abused him. This would lead John Newton to become captain of his own ship, which plied the slave trade. Even though in his childhood his mother tried to provide him with religious training, the events of his life had long since caused him to give up any religious convictions. During a voyage home, while encountering a violent storm, he thought the ship would surely sink. As with most people thinking they are about to die he exclaimed, *"Lord, have mercy upon us."* The ship was saved and while musing about the event in his cabin he began to believe that God had addressed him through the storm and grace began to work on him. He continued to be a slave trader for the next decade. This would change as God spoke to him and showed him the error of his ways.

It took a decade but his desire to serve the One that saved him caused the writing of hymns glorifying God. The, arguably, best-known is Amazing Grace. (This is the original version and not the common rendition)

Amazing grace! (how sweet the sound)
That sav'd a wretch like me!
I once was lost, but now am found,
Was blind, but now I see.
"Twas grace that taught my heart to fear,
And grace my fears reliev'd;
How precious did that grace appear,
The hour I first believ'd!
Thro' many dangers, toils and snares,
I have already come;
'Tis grace has brought me safe thus far,
And grace will lead me home.
The Lord has promised good to me,
His word my hope secures;
He will my shield and portion be,
As long as life endures.
Yes, when this flesh and heart shall fail,
And mortal life shall cease;
I shall possess, within the veil,
A life of joy and peace.
The earth shall soon dissolve like snow,
The sun forbear to shine;
But God, who call'd me here below,
Will be forever mine.

The fact a slave trader could be so dramatically changed by a religious experience, gives all who will be open-minded assurance that God does exist and His power is immeasurable.

What is the answer to the anguish of this world? God sent His beloved Son into the world to save the world (John 3:16) and not condemn the world (John 3:17). This shows the amount of love God has for the inhabitants of the earth (1 John 3:16). We can rest assure that the Bible is accurate in depicting God and the Saviour, Jesus Christ. Just ask any believing Christian. They will tell you about the transformation that happened when they committed their lives.

There is a song by Greater Vision Quartet that has the words "*I did not know I was carrying a heavy load until the load I was carrying was gone*". If you wish to get first-hand accounts of how lives are changed, speak to any graduate of Teen Challenge Farm. They will beguile you with how they were at the depths of despair either through drug addiction or violent tendencies, and a saving knowledge of Jesus completely changed their lives. Of course this is purely faith, but then so is the Big Bang and evolution.

The evidence presented should cause some questioning, in any open-minded neutral observer. The Big Bang and evolution is not pure science as espoused by many people, but is in reality a worldview, as is Christianity. It cannot be proven. Christians will freely and openly stipulate to this. How can we know for sure which is true? This is not a complicated answer. Just look at the lives of the Disciples after the ascension. They knew Jesus' claims. They saw Him every day. They saw what He did and heard His message. They watched Him be crucified. They went into fearful hiding after His burial. Three days later they went everywhere preaching the Gospel. They faced ridicule, threats of violence and even death. They were given the chance to live, if they recanted their teachings. They chose to continue preaching the news of the risen Jesus.

Now I am sure there will be many who will still deny all the evidence presented. Why you may ask? Stuart Chase put it best when he said:

"For those who believe, no proof is necessary. For those who don't believe, no proof is possible."

The old, tired, easy rebuttal by skeptics that everything confirming Scripture must be a forgery has lost any credibility a long time ago; not that it had any. It should be discernible to anyone with a modicum of objectivity; Scripture is factual. What proof is undeniable? People do not, enthusiastically, cheerfully and voluntarily die for something they know is false. I defy anyone to say otherwise. The only logical answer is: what the martyred Apostles were preaching was the unadulterated, unmitigated and undeniable truth

Bibliography

Primary Sources

Holy Bible, New International Version. Zondervan Corporation. Grand Rapids Michigan. 1990

Holy Bible, New Living Translation. Tyndale House Publishers Inc. Carol Stream IL. 2005

Holy Bible, English Standard Study Bible. Crossway Bibles. Wheaton IL. 2008

Holy Bible, New King James Version, Thomas Nelson, Nashville TN. 1990

Qur'an. Translated by Abdullah Yusuf Ali. Goodword Books. New Delhi. India 2007.

The Torah. The Five Books of Moses. New JPS Translation of the Holy Scriptures.

Secondary Sources

Antonov, Vladimir. *The Gospel of Philip.* Translated into English by Anton Teplyy and Mikhail Nikolenko 2008.

Armstrong, Karen. *A History of God, the 4,000 Year Quest of Judaism, Christianity and Islam.* Ballantine Books. New York. 1993

Ashton, John & Westacott, Michael. *The Big Argument: Does God Exist?* Master Books. Green Forest. AR. 2009

Atlantic Productions. *The Greeks: Crucible of Civilization.* PBS 2000.

Bailey, Lloyd R., *Noah. The Person and the Story in History and Tradition.* University of South Carolina Press. Columbia SC. 1989

Bana Research Group. Nov 2003

Barns, Richard. *The Dawkins Proof for the Existence of God 2nd Ed.* 2010

Batten, Don. Catchpoole, David. Sarfati, Jonathan. Wieland, Carl. *The Creation Answers Book.* Creation Book Publishers. 2009

Bell, Rob. *Love Wins.* Harper One. New York NY. 2011

Bernario, Herbert W. *An Introduction to Tacitus.* University of Georgia Press. Athens GA. 1975

Bettenson, Henry. *Documents of the Christian Church.* 2nd Ed. Oxford University Press. London, New York. 1967

Blanchard, John. *Evolution-Fact or Fiction.* Evangelical Press. Darlington UK. 2012

Bruce, F. F. *The Spreading Flame: The Rise and Progress of Christianity.* Wm. B Eerdmans Publishing. Grand Rapids Michigan. 1954

Bruce, F. F. *Paul. Apostle of the Heart Set Free.* Wm. B Eerdmans Publishing. Grand Rapids Michigan. 1977

Bruce, F.F. *The New Testament Documents: Are They Reliable?* Wm. B Eerdmans Publishing. Grand Rapids Michigan. 2003

Campbell, Joseph. *The Power of Myth.* Doubleday Publishing. Toronto ON. 1988

Chandler. Russell. *Understanding the New Age.* Word Publishing. Milton Keynes UK. 1990

Chopra, Deepak. *Life After Death.* Harmony Books. New York NY. 2006

Colson, Charles w. Pearcey, Nancy. *How Now Shall We Live?* Tyndale. Carol Stream IL. 1999

Copleston, F.S. *Christ or Mohammed?* Nuprint, Harpenden, Herts. 1989.

Cremo, Michael A. and Thompson, Richard L. *The Hidden History of the Human Race.* Govardhan Hill Publishing. Badger CA. 1994

Currie, Philip J. and Koppelhus, Eva B. *101 Questions About Dinosaurs.* Dover Publications. Mineola, N.Y. 1996

Dawkins, Richard. *The God Delusion.* Houghton Mifflin Harcourt. Boston. MA. 2006

DeBlanco, Andrew. *The Death of Satan. How Americans Have Lost the Sense of the Devil.* Farrar, Straus, & Giroux. New York NY. 1995.

Denton, Michael. *Evolution: A Theory in Crisis.* Adler & Adler. Bethesda MD. 1986

Doherty, Earl. *The Jesus Puzzle.* Canadian Humanist Publications. 2nd Ed. 2000

Douglas-Klotz, Neil. *The Hidden Gospel, Decoding the Spiritual Message of the Aramaic Jesus.* Quest Books. Wheaton IL. 1999

Eddy, Paul Rhodes & Boyd, Gregory A. *The Jesus Legend. A Case for the Historical Reliability of the Synoptic Jesus Tradition.* Baker Academic. Grand Rapids MI. 2007

Ehrman, Bart D. *Did Jesus Exist? The Historical Argument for Jesus of Nazareth.* Harper Collins Publishers. New York. NY. 2012

Elwell, Walter A. and Yarbrough, Robert W. *Encountering the New Testament.* 2nd Ed. Baker Academic. Grand Rapids MI. 2005

Free, Joseph. *Archaeology and the Bible.* Wheaton: Scripture Press Publications. 1969

Freke Timothy and Gandy Peter. *The Jesus Mysteries. Was the Original Jesus a Pagan God?* Harmony Books. New York N.Y. 1999

Gallup, George Jr. and Lindsay, Michael. *Surveying the Religious Landscape: Trends in U.S. Beliefs,* 1999.

Garland, Robert. *Greece and Rome: An Integrated History of the Ancient Mediterranean.* The Great Courses: The Teaching Company. 2008

Gardner, Martin. *The New Age Notes of a Fringe Watcher.* Promethus Books. Buffalo NY. 1988

Giancoli, Douglas C. *Physics. Principles with Applications.* Pearson Prentice Hall. Upper Saddle River. New Jersey 6th Ed. 2005

Glynn, Patrick. *God: The Evidence: The Reconciliation of Faith and Reason in a Post secular World.* Three Rivers Press. 1999

Gordon, Henry. *Channeling into the New Age.* Promethus Books. Buffalo NY. 1988

Graffe, George and Harbecke, Ulrich. *2,000 Years of Christianity.* CINE International DVD 2001

Graves, Robert (translator). *Gaius Suetonius Tranquillus. The Twelve Caesars.* Penguin Books. New York, NY. 1979

Gregory, Dr. David & Saunders Shari, *Western Culture I: Before the Reformation,* Athabasca University. 2005

Grudem, Wayne. *Systematic Theology.* Zondervaan. Grand Rapids, MI. 2000.

Hafemann, Scott J. *The God of Promise and the Life of Faith.* Crossway. Wheaton IL. 2001

Hall, H.W. *Authorities for the Text of the Chief Classical Writers.* Clarendon Press. Oxford 1913

Halley, Henry H. *Halley's Bible Handbook.* Zonderkidz Bibles; New edition (Oct 17 1988)

Harpur, Tom. *The Pagan Christ.* Thomas Allen Publishers. Toronto Canada. 2004

Hawking, Stephen. *A Brief History of Time.* Bantam Books. Toronto On. 1995

Hawking, Stephen. *The Theory of Everything.* New Millenium Press. Beverly Hills. CA. 2002

Hill, Andrew E. and Walton, John H. *A Survey of the Old Testament 3rd Ed.* Zondervan. Grand Rapids MI. 2009

Hill, Andrew E. *Baker's Handbook of Bible Lists*, New Edition. Grand Rapids MI. 2006

Huse, Scott M. *The Collapse of Evolution.* Baker Book House. Grand Rapids MI. 1983

Isaacs, Darek. *Dragons or Dinosaurs. Creation or Evolution?* Bridge-Logos. Alachua FL. 2010

Jastrow, Robert. *God and the Astronomers.* WW Norton. 3rd Ed. London W1T 3QT, England 2000

Jeffrey, Grant R. The *Mysterious Bible Codes.* Word Publishing. Nashville TN. 1998

Jeremiah, David Dr. *Answers to Questions About Heaven.* Turning Point Publication. 2013

Jewish Publication Society. *The Torah. The Five Books of Moses. The New JPS Translation of the Holy Scriptures According to the Traditional Hebrew Text.* Philadelphia PA. 1999

Johnson, Phillip E. *Darwin on Trial.* IVP Books. Downers Grove MI. 1993

Kasser, Rodolphe. Meyer, Marvin. Wurst Gregor. *The Gospel of Judas.* National Geographic. Washington DC. 2006.

Keller, Werner. *The Bible as History: Archaeology Confirms the Book of Books.* William Morrow and Company. New York. N.Y. 1964

King, Karen L. *The Gospel of Mary of Magdala. Jesus and the First Woman Apostle.* Polebridge Press. Santa Rosa CA. 2003

Kovacs, Joe. *Shocked by the Bible. The Most Astonishing Facts You've Never Been Told.* Thomas Nelson. Nashville Tennessee 1996

Kenyon, Sir Frederick G. *The Bible and Archaeology.* Harper Press. New York and London. 1940.

Krosney, Herbert. *The Lost Gospel. The Quest for the Gospel of Judas Iscariot.* Natural Geographic. DC. 2006

Lecky, W.E.H., *History of European Morals from Augustus to Charlemagne.* University Press of the Pacific. 2002

Lewis, C.S. *Miracles.* Macmillan Publishers. New York 1947

Lewis, C.S. *Surprised by Joy.* Harcourt, Brace Publishing. New York. 1956

Lilse, Jason. *Taking Back Astronomy.* Master Books. Green Forest AR. 2011

Lockyer Sr., Herbert with Bruce, F.F. and Harrison, R.K. *Illustrated Dictionary of the Bible.* Thomas Nelson Publishers, Nashville, Tn. 1986.

MacArthur, John. *The MacArthur Bible Commentary.* Thomas Nelson. Nashville TN. 2005

MacArthur, John. *The MacArthur Topical Bible.* Thomas Nelson. Nashville TN. 2010

Mack, Burton, L. *Who Wrote the New Testament? The Making of the Christian Myth.* Harper Collins. San Francisco. 1995

Maher, Bill. *Religulous. The Truth is Near.* Thousand Word, Sony Pictures. DVD. 2008

Mathewes-Green, Frederica. *The Lost Gospel of Mary. The Mother of Jesus in Three Ancient Texts.* Paraclette Press. Brewster MA. 2007.

Matthews, Roy T and Platt, F. DeWitt. *The Western Humanities. Volume I: Beginnings through the Renaissance.* Michigan State University: McGraw Hill, 2003

MacLaine, Shirley. *It's All in the Playing.* Bantam Books. Toronto ON. 1987

McDowell, Josh. *Evidence that Demands a Verdict.* Campus Crusade for Christ. Arrowhead Springs, San Bernadino CA. 1972

McDowell, Josh. *More Evidence that Demands a Verdict.* Campus Crusade for Christ. Arrowhead Springs, San Bernadino CA. 1975

McGrath, Alister and McGrath, Joanna Collicutt. *The Dawkins Delusion?.* IVP Books. Downers Grove. IL. 2007

McQuarrie, Christopher. *The Usual Suspects.* Gramercy Pictures, Polygram Filmed Entertainment. 1995

Meyer, Marvin. *The Gospel of Thomas. The Hidden Sayings of Jesus.* HarperOne. New York, NY. 1992

Miller, Ron and Bernstein, Laura. *Healing the Jewish-Christian Rift. Growing Beyond our Wounded History.* Skylight Paths. Woodstock Vermont. 2006

Montgomery, John Warwick. *History and Christianity.* Bethany House Publishers, Minneapolis, Minnesota. 1971.

Moo, Douglas J. *Romans. The NIV Application Commentary.* Zondervan Grand Rapids MI. 2000.

Morris, Henry M. *The Bible and Modern Science.* Moody Press. Chicago IL. 1956

Morris, Henry M. *Men of Science. Men of God.* Master Books. Green Forest AR. 2005

Morrison, Frank. *Who Moved the Stone?* Faber & Faber. London 1944

Nash, Ronald H. *Worldviews in Conflict.* Zondervan Publishing House. Grand Rapids. MI. 1992

Nelson, Vance. *Untold Secrets of Planet Earth. Dire Dragons.* Untold Secrets of Planet Earth Publishing. Red Deer AB. Canada. 2012

Nelson's Complete Book of Maps and Charts, Old and New Testaments. Thomas Nelson Publishers. Nashville TN. 1996

Pagels, Elaine. *Beyond Belief. The Secret Gospel of Thomas.* Random House. New York. NY. 2003.

Pate, C. Marvin. *The End of the Age has Come.* Zondervan. Grand Rapid MI.1995

Peckham, Colin. *The Authority of the Bible.* Christian Focus Publications. Scotland Great Britain. 2001

Peru, Paul William. *Outline of Psychiatric Case-Study.* Paul B Hoeger Inc. New York 1939

Pliny, *Letters and Panegyricus. Letters, Books VIII-X.* Translated by Betty Radice. Harvard University Press. Cambridge. MS. 1969

Ramsay, Sir William M. *The Bearing of Recent Discovery on the Trustworthiness of the New Testament.* Baker Publishing. Grand Rapids. Michigan. 1953.

Reeves, Thomas C. *The Empty Church: The Suicide of Liberal Christianity.* Free Press. 1996

Robertson, A.T. *Introduction to the Textual Criticism of the New Testament.* Broadman Press. Nashville Tennessee. 1925

Robertson, Morgan. *The Wreck of the Titan or Futility.* Simon & Schuster. London UK 1998

Rowe, David E. and Schulmann, Robert. *Einstein On Politics- His Private Thoughts & Public Stands on Nationalism, Zionism, War, Peace and the Bomb.* Princeton University Press. Princeton N.J. 2007

Ryken, Leland. Wilhoit, James C, Longman Tremper III. *Dictionary of Biblical Imagery.* IVP Academic. Downers Grove IL. 1998

Sarfati, Jonathan. *The Greatest Hoax on Earth?* Creation Book Publishers. Atlanta GA. 2010

Sandmel, Samuel. *Judaism and Christian Beginnings.* Oxford University Press. New York. 1978

Satinover, Jeffrey M.D., *Cracking the Bible Code.* William Morrow and Company. New York, NY. 1997

Sire, James W. *The Universe Next Door (5th Ed.).* IVP Academic. Downers Grove. IL. 2004

Smith, Wilbur. *Therefore Stand: Christian Apologetics.* Baker Book House. Grand Rapids MI. 1965

Spong, John Selby Bishop. *Resurrection. Myth or Reality. A Bishop's Search for the Origins of Christianity.* Harper Collins. San Francisco. 1994

Stenger, Victor J. *God-The Failed Hypothesis.* Prometheus Books. Amherst N.Y. 2008.

Strobel, Lee. *The case for a Creator.* Zondervan Publishing. Grand Rapids Mi. 2004

Stroll, Avrum and Popkin, Richard H. *Made Simple Books.* Double Day Publishers. Garden City N.Y. 1956

Templeton, Charles. *Farewell to God.* McClelland & Stewart. Toronto On. 1999

Thomas-Nelson. *Nelson's Complete Book of Bible Maps & Charts.* Thomas Nelson Publishers. Vancouver, Canada. 1996

Van Voorst, Robert E. *Jesus Outside the New Testament.* William B. Eerdmans Publishing. Grand Rapids MI. 2000

Walker, Taz. Ph.D. *The Genesis Flood. Fact or Fiction?* CMI (Australia). 2010

Walker, Williston. *A History of the Christian Church.* 3rd Ed. Charles Scribner's Sons. New York. 1970

Walton, John H., *Genesis, The NIV Application Commentary.* Zondervan. Grand Rapids MI. 2001

Warren, Rick. *The Purpose Driven Life.* Zondervan Publishing. Grand Rapids MI. 2002

Wasserstein, Abraham. *Flavius Josephus. Selections of His Works.* Viking Press. New York, N.Y. 1974

Weber, Eugen. *The Western Tradition.* WGBH Boston and the Metropolitan Museum of Art. The Annenberg/CPB Project: New York City. Art Cohen: Senior Producer. 1989

Wilson, Ian. *The Bible is History.* Regenery Publishing. Washington D.C. 1999

Winfrey, Oprah. *The Uncommon Wisdom of...* Birch Lane Press. (Manda Group) Toronto. ON. 1997

www.ingramcontent.com/pod-product-compliance
Lightning Source LLC
Chambersburg PA
CBHW071606080526
44588CB00010B/1043